Crossroads Choices

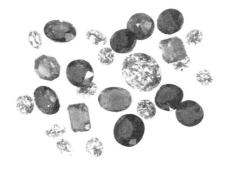

"There is gold, and a multitude of rubies:
but the lips of knowledge are a precious jewel."

(Proverbs 20:15)

The Crossroads Series
The Sequel to *Love's Choice*

Copyright 2015
by Yvonne Coats

CREDITS

COVER DESIGN
Jeannie Walker

TEXT FORMATTING
Linda Stubblefield

AUTHOR'S PHOTO
Angel Joy Photography

Scriptures used in this volume
are taken from the King James Bible.

Excerpts taken from
The Sacredness of a Christian Wedding
by JoBeth Hooker and
Candace Hooker Schaap
www.hookpublications.com

Printed and Bound in the United States

VOLUME THREE
CROSSROADS
SERIES

Crossroads
Choices

YVONNE E. COATS

Other books in the Crossroads Series by Yvonne E. Coats

A Time to Choose
(Book One)

Reared in a loving Christian home in Washington state, Bethany Prescott accepts employment as a nanny in the aristocratic home of the Davenport family after graduating from high school. Bethany soon realizes how difficult her job will be when she meets Michael, her young charge.

Seeking solace in the Davenports' church, Grace Baptist Church, Bethany joins the youth group. Her sweet loveliness and unguarded naivete quickly capture the attention of handsome Scott Lancaster. Will he be the man of her dreams?

Bethany cannot possibly foresee the impact her choices will make on the lives of those she is growing to love. An unexpected meeting with John Holman further complicates the decisions Bethany must make.

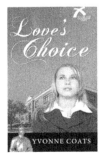

Love's Choice
(Book Two)

Yesterday Bethany Prescott was a nanny in an aristocratic home, enjoying luxuries and guiding a young boy who had been reared by permissive grandparents and absentee parents. Today she is a Bible college student learning to build relationships with other college students. New trials soon invade her life—a roommate with a dark, life-threatening secret; the continued attentions of charming Scott Lancaster; jealousy; disappointment…

Dedication

This book is dedicated with love to my precious gifts from God:

My two daughters:
Debbie Brown and Christine Wolfe

My six grandchildren:
David, Rachel, and Jonathan Brown
Kaitlin, Raquel, and Justine Wolfe

Acknowledgments

I have sent up many prayers to my Heavenly Father for inspiration and guidance in writing this Christian romance fiction story. I know He hears and answers. My hope is that His wisdom and love will be reflected in this work and that it will inspire young women to live a Christ-honoring life.

Words are not adequate to express my gratitude to my dear friend, Jillana Mann, who spent hours editing and proofreading my manuscript. My thanks also to Linda Stubblefield who did the finishing work.

I also must remember all the friends and relatives who have prayed for me as I have worked on this book. They are too numerous to name individually, but I am grateful to each one of you.

Table of Contents

CHAPTER ONE | Wedding Plans 11

CHAPTER TWO | Finishing College 30

CHAPTER THREE | Final Wedding Preparations 41

CHAPTER FOUR | The Wedding Day 58

CHAPTER FIVE | The Honeymoon 71

CHAPTER SIX | Beginning Married Life 80

CHAPTER SEVEN | Adjustments to Married Life 107

CHAPTER EIGHT | Celebrating the Holidays 123

CHAPTER NINE | Blessings From the Lord 133

CHAPTER TEN | Starting Life in Their RV Home 169

CHAPTER ELEVEN | Beginning As an Evangelist 177

CHAPTER TWELVE | On Their Own 200

CHAPTER THIRTEEN | Growing Through Trials 212

CHAPTER FOURTEEN | Joy Comes in the Morning 237

EPILOGUE 264

ABOUT THE AUTHOR 274

— CHAPTER ONE —

Wedding Plans

"...when the desire cometh, it is a tree of life."
(Proverbs 13:12)

Bethany Prescott awoke to soft light brightening the pastel walls and flower-decorated comforter in the guest room of her future in-laws' home. She rose and put on her robe. Then she crossed the room and opened the white curtains to feel the full effect of the California sun. She wanted to enjoy it before returning to her home in rainy Tacoma, Washington, in a few days.

Bethany went back to sit on the bed as she remembered with joy the events of the previous evening. John Holman had proposed and presented her with a gorgeous diamond and ruby engagement ring. She raised her left hand so the ring could catch the facets of light. Seeing the ring sparkle thrilled her, but what it represented was the true blessing—a future as John's wife and help meet. This decision to marry was an important crossroads for them, and she did not take it lightly.

John had not intended to present her with the ring at a medieval banquet in front of a crowd of people. He had meant to propose in private. But the whole crowd had been delighted when he did, and Bethany most of all. It certainly would be a memory to cherish and relate to their children!

Before getting ready for the day, Bethany whispered a prayer of thanksgiving and a request that God would guide them in their future life together. It was Sunday, and she would be going to church with John and his family. She had two more days to relax and get to know them better before heading back to Tacoma. Bethany had a feeling that once she returned home, the remainder of her Christmas break from Crossroads Baptist Bible College would be a very busy time. There was a wedding to be planned!

John was spending the nights with his grandparents while Bethany was in town. He was waiting for her at church when she arrived with his family. They attended the college and career Sunday school class together and then sat with his parents during the morning service. Afterward, his grandparents joined them at the Holmans' home for dinner. His grandmother was very happy about the marriage plans and gave Bethany a warm hug. She demanded details from Bethany about the previous evening's events.

John objected. "Grandma, I already told you all about it."

"That was from a man's perspective. I want to hear it from Bethany."

His grandfather remarked, "Give it up, John. You can't hope to understand."

Everyone laughed while Bethany and John's grandmother sat together on a somewhat secluded loveseat in a corner of the room. Bethany shared all of the details from the previous night. John's grandmother exclaimed, "I knew he left out a lot!" She and Bethany giggled together like two girls at the look of consternation on John's face. Then they went to the kitchen to see if they could help.

Monday and Tuesday Bethany divided her time between John and the female members of his family. Ruth and Naomi, his sisters, were especially delighted about the coming wedding, peppering Bethany with questions as to what kind of dress she would wear, what her colors would be, how many bridesmaids she would have, what kind of flowers, and everything else they could think of. John's mother, who was almost as excited, kept trying to run interference. "Give Bethany some space; she needs more time before she makes those decisions." Bethany promised to keep them informed of her plans.

Hearing all of this discussion caused John some concern. "Honey, are you going to be able to get things planned by August when you still have another semester of school to finish? I don't want you to get all stressed out."

"Don't worry, John. I've been thinking about it for a while, and my mom and I have tossed a few wedding ideas around. Just in case, you understand," she added, laughing. "I wasn't assuming anything."

"Right," he answered with a grin.

"That's the dimple I love," she whispered.

"Would you quit? And don't say it's cute!"

"I won't say it, but it is," she answered mischievously.

"Shush! I don't want to get my sisters started."

"Oh, now I know what I can threaten you with."

"Have a heart, Bethany."

Naomi moved closer. "What are you two whispering about?"

"Nothing, nothing important."

"Then why are you blushing, big brother?"

John winced and blushed deeper. Naomi and Bethany enjoyed a laugh at his expense.

John returned to the discussion. "How extravagant are you planning to make it? You don't have to spend a lot of money and time on my account. I would just as soon it be kept simple."

"I will keep it somewhat simple, but I want to include the traditions and sacred symbols. Is it all right with you if we have a reception at our church? Lots of brides use the combination gym/fellowship hall. And I don't want a lot of food—maybe only a few finger foods. Does that sound okay?"

"It sounds great to me."

"Let me ask your mom, also."

Mrs. Holman was in enthusiastic agreement. "I am so glad we think alike about a lot of things," said Bethany.

Mrs. Holman gave her a hug. "Me too, sweetie."

Bethany had mixed feelings on Tuesday as she prepared to fly home. Now that the engagement was official, it seemed harder to be separated from John for even a few days. But she was excited about sharing the details of John's unusual and impressive proposal and showing her engagement ring to her family. She knew her younger sister Betsy would be almost as excited as Bethany herself. Since New Year's Eve was the next day and falling on Wednesday, she would also soon be able to share her happiness with the people she had grown up with at Trinity Baptist Church of Tacoma.

In the morning she rose early to shower, fix her hair, and carefully apply her makeup. Then she rushed to start packing so she could have every possible moment with John before they had to leave for the airport.

John arrived for breakfast and afterward helped his mother and sisters clean up while Bethany finished her packing. She threw clothes into her suitcase, knowing they would have to be washed anyway when she arrived home. She set the luggage by the door of the downstairs guest room for John to carry up for her later, and then hurried back upstairs. John's mother and siblings gave her and John as much privacy as possible at one end of the living room where they pulled up chairs close together and shared memories and dreams of their future together. They laughed together at the memory of how they had met, when little Michael Briscoe had run away from Bethany, his nanny, on an icy day. John had captured him for her, and they had struck up a conversation. That chance meeting had led to her going to his church, and the rest was history.

Bethany shared that she was excited about traveling with John for his evangelistic ministry, even though she knew there would be difficulties and times of separation. Before they knew it, the morning was gone, and they were being called to lunch.

As soon as lunch was over, it was time to drive to the airport. John went downstairs and came back with Bethany's suitcases. She watched at the window as he went out and loaded her luggage in the car, fitting her main suitcase in the trunk first and arranging the rest of her belongings on top.

Mrs. Holman asked, "Bethany, did you get everything? Maybe you better check that room one more time." With a twinkle and a teasing grin she added, "You were in a bit of a rush this morning." Bethany laughed and hurried downstairs.

Soon she came rushing back, gripping the knight statuette in which John had secreted the engagement ring. "Oh, my goodness. I had him sitting on a shelf. How could I have forgotten him? I guess John didn't see him either."

"Well, we better go. They always have you get there so early, you should have time to stick it in the bag you're going to check before you board."

Naomi joked, "You better not take it in your carry on—they might think you would use it for a weapon."

They all laughed as they hurried out the door. Just as they were about to pull out of the driveway, Ruth cried out, "Bethany! Where is your coat? Won't you need it when you arrive in Washington? Did you put it in a bag?"

"Oh, no! It's still in your front room closet!" exclaimed Bethany.

John stopped the van and leaped out, calling back over his shoulder as he sprinted to the front door, "I'll get it."

Bethany moaned, "Oh, I am so sorry. What is wrong with me? I'm not usually this scatterbrained!"

Mrs. Holman soothed her, "Don't worry, sweetie. We have plenty of time. You simply have a lot on your mind, and it has been an exciting whirlwind visit for you."

John got back into the van, handed his mother the coat, and turned to look at Bethany. Teasingly he asked, "Are you sure you have everything now?"

Bethany answered, "I can't make any guarantees, but I think I do. If you find anything, you can bring it to me at school. You know, of course, that this is all your fault?"

Pretending to be offended, John asked, "How do you figure it's my fault?"

"You caused me to get all rattled with your big surprise."

As he started up the van he asked, "Would you rather I hadn't proposed?"

"I didn't say that!" Everyone laughed at her reply.

At the airport John could only stop at the curb long enough to take her luggage out of the back for her. His mother got out and gave her a hug as she handed her the coat. Even though she didn't need it, Bethany slipped it on so she didn't have to carry it and the statuette. Her bags were strapped together, so she would only have to pull one. Ruth handed her the statuette through the open van window. Bethany waved to Naomi and John's brother James and then turned to John as he gave her the handle for her bags. They had said their goodbyes at the house. They both whispered, "I love you," before John got back in the vehicle and drove away.

Bethany headed inside and went directly to a restroom, where she carefully wrapped the statuette inside some of her clothes. Then she went to the check-in counter.

In the waiting area, she pulled out a book but found she could not concentrate. Her mind alternated between memories of the eventful night at the banquet and thinking about wedding plans. She had eight months to get ready, but five of them would be spent at college. Now that she was bound for home, the time dragged by as she anticipated sharing everything with her family.

Her thoughts went back to John, and the wonderful traits of her fiancé flooded her mind. Oh, how she loved him! She thought about the blond, broad-shouldered man and almost laughed out loud as she remembered how she had dreamed at eighteen of a tall, dark, and handsome boyfriend. Now Bethany was sure that John Holman was the man God had for her, and the man she loved with all her heart.

Finally it was time to board. Bethany was happy she had a window seat; she always enjoyed seeing the Washington scenery as she flew over and approached Sea-Tac Airport. She hoped clouds would not hide beautiful Mt. Rainier today.

When Bethany reached her row of seats, she discovered another young woman was already in the seat next to hers.

"Excuse me, I have the window seat beside you."

The young woman immediately rose and stepped into the aisle. She was several inches taller than Bethany, and asked, "May I put your carry-on bag up above for you?"

"Oh, thank you very much. That would be a real blessing."

When they were both seated the two struck up a conversation.

The young woman, whose name was Lorraine, turned out to be a Bible college student from California. She was going to Seattle to visit grandparents during her Christmas break from college.

"That is great! I'm on Christmas break from Crossroads Baptist Bible College in Indiana."

"I thought you might be a Christian from the way you are dressed and when you said it would be a blessing if I helped you. What were you doing in California?"

"I was visiting my fiancé and his family for a few days."

"Ooh, that sounds exciting. I noticed your ring. May I see it more closely?"

"Of course! You are the first person outside of family that I get to show it to!"

"Really? That must mean you just received it on this trip?"

"Yes. I am so excited! You are also the first person to whom I could say 'my fiancé,' " said Bethany with a laugh.

"The ring is gorgeous. What is the wedding band like?"

"It has a semicircle of rubies to complete a circle around the diamond. Together they look like a flower. My fiancé designed it himself."

"How romantic! What does he look like?"

"Here, let me show you his picture." Bethany drew John's picture from her bag.

"Wow! Is he as nice as he is handsome?"

"Definitely. He is wonderful! He is working on his master's degree, and then he is going into evangelism. I am going to travel with him as much as possible. I am so happy and excited!"

"When are you getting married?"

"In August, even though he will have a year more of college. He is going to start on deputation right after our honeymoon as we travel back to Indiana. We both sing, so that will also be a part of our ministry. I also play the piano and accompany him or both of us."

After spending a few minutes talking about her upcoming events, Bethany turned the conversation to Lorraine, asking what her plans were and whether she had a boyfriend.

Bethany was grateful for the distraction. Time flew by as they shared their experiences and hopes for the future. Bethany told her about waiting expectantly for John to propose for months, and how it had turned out to be so meaningful. Before they had even begun dating, with a slip of the tongue, she had called him "her knight." John, who loved teasing her, had never let her forget it; it had become their sentimental token. With his family joining them as chaperones, he had taken her to a medieval banquet and presented her with a knight statuette with an engagement ring hidden inside. Then even he had been surprised when he ended up going down on one knee.

She fingered her engagement ring appreciatively and explained, "He's adding to my 'multitude of rubies.' My parents started my 'multitude' with a ruby ring for my high school graduation. They intended for it to remind me of Proverbs 20:15: '*There is gold, and a multitude of rubies: but the lips of knowledge are a precious jewel.*' "

"That is very special," commented Lorraine.

The magnificent view of Mt. Rainier rising through the clouds caught their attention then, and soon afterward the announcement came that they were approaching Sea-Tac. Bethany said, "It has been great meeting you and talking the whole way. It helped make the time fly by. Otherwise, I would have been so fidgety!"

"I enjoyed it too."

Bethany was not disappointed when she met up with her family at the airport. Betsy grabbed her left hand to see the ring at the same time she greeted her sister. "Hi, Bethany!"

Mrs. Prescott was a little more discreet and gave Bethany a hug before looking at the ring. James also gave his eldest daughter a hug before admiring the diamond and ruby ring. Brian said, "Hi, Sis. I hear you had an exciting time. Guess I might as well get it over with and look at your ring now."

Bethany gave him a playful slug on his arm and covered up her hand. "I wouldn't dream of boring you and making you look at it."

"Aw, come on, Sis. I was only teasing."

"I know," said Bethany with a grin and held out her hand.

"Wow! Some rock!"

When they had helped with her baggage and were settled into the van, Betsy asked, "Please tell us all about the night when John proposed." Bethany was happy to fill them in on all of the details of that special night.

Margaret asked, "Did you have a good time, Bethany? The Holmans seemed like really nice people when we talked to them on the phone."

"They are! They treated me wonderfully. And Mrs. Holman thinks and feels about things a lot like we do. I mean, like not going overboard with the wedding and things like that. John's sisters are so excited. They wanted to know all my plans. I promised to keep them clued in."

"We have a lot to talk over in a short amount of time. I don't want to leave everything to be done after you get home from college in May."

"I've been thinking the same thing," agreed Bethany.

Mr. Prescott asked, "What do you want to do about a dress, Bethany?"

"What do you mean?"

"Do you want to buy one?"

Confused and disappointed, Bethany answered, "Isn't Mom up to making it? Or do you not want to, Mom? I am sorry; I just always assumed…but I know it would be a lot of hard work. Maybe you don't have time?"

"I have always dreamed of making wedding gowns for both of my girls, but I don't want to assume that you want a homemade one. Maybe you would rather buy one?"

"And pass up on a talented seamstress's making me her own unique creation? Oh, no, Mommy, if you have time and are up to it, I want you to do it. Besides, if we bought one, we would have to make adjustments, or I would have to wear a jacket or something over it. You can hardly find any that aren't strapless."

Her mother smiled. "Well, I thought that would be your answer, but Daddy and I wanted to be sure. So we will plan to go to the fabric store tomorrow. Do you want to go along, Betsy?"

"Of course!"

"Now, what about bridesmaids?"

"I've been thinking about that so much. I had never planned to have a large number, but I can't decide between my special friends. Of course, I want Betsy as my maid of honor…"

Her sister interrupted with a squeal. Leaning over from her bucket seat in the van, she managed to grab Bethany and give her a big hug. "Thank you, thank you, thank you!!"

"You didn't think I'd leave you out, did you?"

"I wasn't sure, since I'm so much younger and everything."

"No way—you have been my roomie and pal all my life—until I went to college."

"Oooh, Bethany, I love you!"

Margaret smiled. "Well, at least that's settled. Now what were you saying, Bethany?"

"If you think it's okay, I thought I would also have a matron of honor—Donna, and ask Sarah, Cindy, Carrie, and Kathleen to be bridesmaids. I hate not having John's sisters, Ruth and Naomi, but I don't want it that big. I thought I would ask them to take care of the guest book and the gift table and to sing during the ceremony.

"I'm thinking about trying to find a pattern, buying the fabric, sending it to the bridesmaids, and letting them find someone to make a dress for them. Since I didn't have to pay tuition this year, I have enough savings if the fabric isn't too expensive. I figure it's going to cost them enough to fly out here. I hope they can all manage it."

Betsy asked, "What about colors?"

"I want pink and black—I think that's a pretty combination."

"That would be pretty, but the guys aren't going to want to wear pink ties and cummerbunds or vests."

"I know, Betsy, they can wear black tuxedos with black cummerbunds and have pink rosebuds for the boutonnieres."

Margaret Prescott said, "I think those ideas all sound fine. I hope we can find a fabric you like. Before we can buy it, you will have to talk to the girls and see if they want to come and can afford it. I wonder especially about Carrie."

"I know. I am praying there will be a way for her to be able to come."

Betsy asked, "Will you have enough money for the bridesmaids' dresses and your own, Bethany?"

Before Bethany could answer, her dad broke into the conversation, "She doesn't have to worry about her own. Your mom and I have already decided to foot the bill for her dress."

"Oh, Daddy, I didn't expect that. That is very sweet. Thank you!"

"You are welcome, sweetheart."

The rest of the ride home from the airport was filled with the females' conversation about wedding plans. Brian tuned it all out and had his nose stuck in a book. Mr. Prescott listened patiently and occasionally asked a question or made a suggestion.

Bethany told them her thoughts of holding the reception in the church gymnasium and serving finger foods along with the cake. "John and his mother both said it sounded fine to them."

"Oh, Bethany, don't you want to go somewhere fancier?" asked Betsy.

"No, I really want to stay at the church. It makes it easier on everyone, and it is a lot less expensive."

Betsy sighed. "Sometimes you are just too practical and not romantic enough."

"Not romantic enough for what?"

"My taste, I guess."

"Don't worry, Betsy, we have talented people in the church who will help us decorate so it looks like a fairy tale castle—how will that be?"

"I hope we can."

Margaret reassured Betsy by adding, "We will get some magazines to look through for ideas or go on the Internet. Maybe you can put your imagination to work. Through the years, I have jotted down notes and ideas I picked up at weddings I have attended. Some of them might be of help to you."

"Really, Mom? You have certainly been thinking ahead."

"I guess I am a romantic at heart too."

"Do you know where your notes are? We could look at them tonight."

"Oh, yes!" agreed Betsy enthusiastically.

"As soon as dinner is over, I will look for them while you and Bethany clean up, okay?"

"Ooh, this is going to be so much fun!"

"Just remember though, it is Bethany's wedding; and she has the final say. Okay?"

"I know, Mom."

When they arrived at home, they did as planned and had fun reading and musing over the ideas Mrs. Prescott had jotted down. Bethany liked several and thought she would probably use them. They also looked through a booklet about the spiritual symbolism of some of the traditions. They found it to be very helpful. When they retired for the night, both Betsy and Bethany had a hard time settling down to sleep.

Betsy commented, "I am so excited I don't know how I will stand it until August. How will you ever make it?"

"I have so much else to think about during this last semester of school that I am sure the time will fly by, and I won't even feel like I have enough time!"

In spite of having a hard time getting to sleep, both girls woke early, eager to get to the fabric store to look at material and patterns. They all made sure they had their time with the Lord, ate a quick breakfast, and then were at the store when the doors opened.

First, they looked at patterns for Bethany's dress and for the bridesmaids. They found a pattern with a modest neckline and options for short or long sleeves that could be used for both. Betsy's face lit up with delight. "Wow, I love this design!"

Margaret asked, "What do you think, Bethany?"

"Oh, I agree with Betsy. The dresses would be graceful and elegant. The pattern makes me think of knights and ladies of old. It will be perfect for my wedding. I had already thought about using the knight statuette in the decorations."

"How would you want the sleeves?" asked Margaret.

"I think the traditional long sleeves with the tapered point for mine and the short sleeves for the bridesmaids. What do you think, Betsy?"

"That sounds perfect, except can Mom add a train on the back of yours?"

Bethany turned to her mother and asked, "Would that be possible without too much extra work for you?"

"I am sure I could."

Betsy exclaimed, "Oh, your gown is going to be so beautiful!"

Next they looked at fabric. Betsy found a pink fabric with black polka dots. She snatched up the bolt and practically ran to where Bethany and Margaret were looking at white satin for the bridal gown.

"Look, look! Isn't this just perfect?"

"Oh, Betsy! Yes, yes! I love it."

"That would work," agreed Mrs. Prescott. "Put it in the cart, and I will find out if they can get more from another store. We are going to need a lot."

"Oh, I hope they can," said both girls simultaneously. They looked at each other and started laughing, struggling to keep quiet so as not to be discourteous and unladylike.

Mrs. Prescott also laughed softly, and commented, "I didn't think it would be so easy! Now let's concentrate on fabric for Bethany's gown."

They picked out a fabric with an attractive beading pattern already on it and then found the white tulle for Bethany's veil. Since she knew that her body was the temple of Christ, she would wear a veil over her face, symbolizing modesty. When John lifted it to kiss her for the first time, it would picture the high priest entering into the holy of holies.

They bought the pattern and fabric for Bethany's and Betsy's gowns and for Bethany's veil. The store also arranged for more of the pink fabric to be transferred and held for them. When they left the store, they were surprised at how much they had accomplished in a short amount of time. They went to a coffee shop and enjoyed drinks and a snack. While enjoying their treats, they relaxed and discussed other plans.

Mrs. Prescott asked, "What kind of flowers will you have and what other decorations?"

"I would like an arbor in the middle of the platform, so we'll be standing in front of it. It could be decorated with pink and white flowers and greenery. We could use silk flowers for those and other places, but I would like fresh flowers in big white baskets on either side of the platform. Mrs. Hadley from the church does a nice job with the flowers for the Lord's Supper table every Sunday. Maybe she would do the flowers more reasonably than a professional florist. I'll call her soon."

"The pink and white gladioluses in our yard should be blooming in early August and would work for the baskets," Margaret offered.

"Oh, that would be perfect," agreed Bethany.

"What about the gym decorations?" asked Betsy. "I'm still not convinced it can be as pretty as going somewhere else."

"I was thinking of having another decorated arbor with tulle and lights strung around it at the entrance."

"I have an idea for the tables, Bethany."

"Let's hear it, Sis."

"Use pink tablecloths with a strip of black tulle along the top edge and scatter pink rose petals on top of the tulle."

"That sounds perfect, Betsy. Thanks for sharing." Betsy's beaming face showed how happy she was that Bethany liked her idea.

When they returned home from the fabric store, they took naps so they would be rested for church and then to stay up to welcome in the new year. When Bethany rose, her mother encouraged her to call her friends while she and Betsy prepared dinner.

Remembering the time difference in states farther east, Bethany hurried to get her cell phone. First, she called Donna, who was to be her matron of honor. A year earlier, Bethany had been the maid of honor for Donna when she had married Peter Agnew. Bethany had met

Peter when they both worked for the Davenport family—Bethany as nanny for their grandson, Michael Briscoe, and Peter as chauffeur. They had both met Donna when they started attending Faith Baptist Church in Detroit.

She and Donna had become good friends. When they went to college, they had been roommates during their freshman year, along with Sarah (now Norberg) and Cindy Burgess. The four of them had developed a special bond of friendship.

When Donna heard Bethany's voice on the phone, she immediately asked, "Do you have some special news?"

"Yes! Did you know about it?"

"About what?" asked Donna.

"That John was going to propose and give me a ring?"

"Ooh, I am so happy for you! No, I was just hoping and guessed it might be that."

Bethany heard Donna calling to Peter, "It's Bethany. She and John are engaged!"

Then she asked Bethany, "What's the ring like? When are you getting married?"

Bethany described the rings' flower-like pattern, and added, "I love them. John even designed the set himself."

"That's special."

"I know. Anyway, we are getting married in August, and I want you to be matron of honor. Betsy will be maid of honor. Do you think you could?"

"I will make it happen. I'll start saving my pennies."

"You don't have to worry about the cost of a dress, except getting someone to make it. I will buy the fabric."

"Are you sure, Bethany?"

"Yes. Remember, I don't have to pay tuition this year."

"That will definitely help. I will start watching for special rates for the airfare."

"I hope Peter can come too."

"I know he will want to. I think we can swing it."

When they had hung up, Bethany called Sarah Norberg. She and her husband Paul were also still living in Indiana while he studied for his master's degree at the Crossroads Baptist Bible College. Sarah was also excited and happy for Bethany and readily agreed to be a bridesmaid. Since Sarah was working, she felt they would be able to manage the airfare. Bethany then called Cindy with the same result and finished by calling Carrie. This young woman had started out as one of Bethany's roommates her second year. Even though Carrie had been forced to drop out of college that year, Bethany had become and remained her mentor. Carrie had grown into a lovely, spiritually mature young woman.

Carrie was thrilled about the wedding and being invited to be a bridesmaid, but she was hesitant about whether she would have the necessary funds. Bethany asked, "But you would like to be in the wedding if it could be worked out?"

"Of course!"

"Let's just pray about it then, okay?"

She had one more friend to ask—Kathleen Durham, and at least she was local. She and Bethany had grown up together attending the Trinity Baptist Church of Tacoma, Washington, and the church's Christian school. Like Bethany, Kathleen was also in her last year at Crossroads Baptist Bible College.

That night at church, when Bethany spoke to her, Kathleen enthusiastically agreed. As she was looking at Bethany's ring, other people noticed and came over to admire it. Betsy also brought several of her friends to see the ring. It was an exciting evening for Bethany. While the pastor prayed in the new year, Bethany thought about the change of course her life would take before this year was over.

The next morning John called from California to find out whom she was having for bridesmaids. After she gave him the list, he suggested that he ask Peter and Paul to be groomsmen. He was a close friend with both of them, and they could escort their wives. He asked her if she thought it would be okay for his brother James to be his best man—even though he was younger.

"I think that would be perfect. He and Betsy would look nice together since they are about the same age. We aren't sure about Carrie yet; I hope we can work something out. You will need at least two other men to escort Cindy and Kathleen."

"I will be thinking about that. Let me know about Carrie as soon as you know, okay?"

"Yes. Don't forget to pray about it."

"I won't. Honey, I miss you so much. It feels like we've been apart for weeks—not just one day."

"I know. It's amazing, isn't it?"

"It's good this next semester will be busy for both of us. Hopefully, the busyness will make the time pass quickly. It is so hard to think about waiting eight more months for you to be my wife. I don't want to let my family know, but I can't wait to get back to college and be with you."

"That's so sweet, John. I feel the same way. But at least I'm keeping busy these last few days of Christmas break."

"What else have you been doing that's keeping you busy? I'm mostly sitting around and visiting. I slipped out for a walk so I could talk to you while I get some exercise and fresh air."

"We are working on wedding plans so Mom can start buying things and sewing. She is going to make my gown and Betsy's dress. And I have decided on the colors."

"What colors did you choose?"

"Pink and black."

"Pink?"

"I thought the men could wear pink ruffled…"

Bethany was interrupted by John's exclamation of horror. "Bethany! I never thought you would even think about…"

He was interrupted by her merry laughter. "Got you! Don't worry. You will all have plain white shirts. You can wear a white cummerbund with a black tuxedo, and the other men can wear all black. You will all have pink rosebud boutonnieres."

"Thank you! You little jokester, you had me worried for a second. Anything else?"

"Yes, lots, actually. We have discussed flowers and whom we will ask to do them. We went to the fabric store and found a pattern for all of the dresses. We even bought the fabric for Betsy's and mine and for my veil. Do you know what the bridal veil symbolizes?"

"I haven't really thought about it."

"I'll bring you a booklet to read. It is really special."

"You know, sweetheart, I am actually getting excited about our wedding too."

"Well, I certainly hope so!"

"Don't be offended—you aren't, are you?"

"Well…explain what you meant."

"Most of us guys are more interested in being married than in the wedding itself. That's more a female thing. But I know the ceremony is important, as well as saying your vows in front of witnesses and the Lord at the altar. I take that part very seriously. One thing that does excite me is showing off my beautiful bride to everyone."

"Thank you for the compliment. I definitely want you to read the booklet I have—it will make it all more meaningful for you, I'm sure."

"Will you bring it back with you to school?"

"Yes."

"Bethany…"

"Yes?"

"I love you."

Laughing softly, she tenderly answered, "And I love you, John."

Reluctantly, they ended the conversation. If they couldn't be together, they wanted to at least be able to hear the other's voice; at the same time, they both knew they had to think of their other loved ones. This would be their last Christmas spent with family as a single person. They had to give them some undivided attention too.

When they hung up, Bethany called Mrs. Davenport. Martha was pleased to hear the news. Bethany said, "I am really hoping all of you can come out for the wedding. In fact, I would like to have Michael be the ring bearer. Do you think he would like that?"

"Oh, he would most definitely be ecstatic about being in your wedding, Bethany."

"I hope Elaine can get away."

"With this much notice, she should be able to make the necessary arrangements."

"I will call her this evening and talk to her and Michael."

"I will pass on the news to my husband. We have been hoping for this; we are very impressed with John and feel you two are meant for each other."

"Thank you, Mrs. Davenport. You and your husband have been a great blessing to me."

"I am anxious for your spring break, so I can see your ring. You will be spending it with us again, won't you?"

"You are very kind. Yes, I believe I will be staying with you one last time."

"Probably not the last time. There may be times when you and John are traveling through that you can stay here. We would love that."

"So would we. Thank you. Goodbye for now."

In the evening, after Bethany had spoken with Elaine and Michael, George Davenport called. "Hello, Bethany, and congratulations. We are so happy for you and John."

"Thank you, sir."

"I am calling to ask if there is anything I could do financially to help. Who are you having for bridesmaids? Do any of them need help getting there, or with anything else?"

"Oh, Mr. Davenport, I couldn't…"

He interrupted her. "Now, Bethany, this is something I would love to do. Think of me as a second dad and tell me what I can do to make your wedding day perfect. Is there something you have been praying about? I sincerely feel the Lord wants me to do something."

"Well, if you put it that way, I was hoping to have Carrie as a bridesmaid. I have told you a little about her, and she can't afford to fly out here."

"I believe I can take care of that and her hotel bill. What about her dress?"

"I am buying the fabric for the girls, but she will have to get someone to make it for her."

"If she has to pay someone, I will cover that also. Is there anything else?"

"Oh, no, that is extremely generous of you. You don't know how much I appreciate it, and Carrie will also. We have been praying about it, and God is using you to answer our request."

"Well, I am happy I can; all the praise goes to Him. He gave me everything I have, and I am just giving a little portion back to Him. I am hoping our family can make a vacation trip out of this. Elaine and

Michael would enjoy seeing the Pacific Northwest. I hear we get one more visit from you as a single lady in the spring. I'll see you then."

"Yes, sir. Thanks again. Goodbye."

Bethany heaved a huge sigh of relief, and after telling her family the good news, she called Carrie. She was so grateful and excited that she would be able to be in Bethany's wedding that she started crying, and they ended their conversation. Bethany then called John to let him know that he would definitely need another groomsman to escort Carrie.

Before leaving for her last semester of college, Bethany managed to work out a few more details for the wedding. She called their friend, Mrs. Hadley, who agreed to do the flower arranging. She refused to accept any payment for her services, telling Bethany it would be her wedding gift. All they would have to pay for was the flowers. They agreed on using a combination of fresh and silk.

Bethany called one of her mother's friends about having her daughter Angie act as flower girl. She was a sweet, outgoing, well-mannered girl close to Michael's age. Mrs. Scott called on Thursday morning and assured Bethany that Angie was thrilled with the idea. She also offered to sew a dress for her daughter.

Bethany was able to leave for college, feeling they had a good start on wedding plans. She had not anticipated such a busy Christmas break, not knowing ahead of time that John was going to propose. But she was thrilled about starting wedding preparations. Becoming John's wife would soon be a reality!

— CHAPTER TWO —

Finishing College

*"Study to shew thyself approved unto God,
a workman that needeth not to be ashamed..."*
(II Timothy 2:15)

When Bethany arrived at college, she enjoyed showing her beautiful ring to each of her special friends as she met up with them. Cindy and Carrie both sought her out on the first day back. Even though Cindy was more mature than when the girls had first met, she could still be exuberant when excited. She gave Bethany a quick hug and then grabbed her hand. Carrie was still cautious about being appropriate, so after greeting Bethany she asked politely if she could see the ring. After showing it to her, Bethany said, "Let's all go have dinner together. I will tell you both about how John proposed and the plans we have made so far for the wedding."

As they walked together, Carrie said, "Oh, I can hardly wait to hear all about it! I am so excited about being a bridesmaid. It is really nice of you to ask me, Bethany."

Bethany linked arms with her as they walked. "Why wouldn't I? We have become good friends, and you have become a very lovely young lady."

Over dinner, Carrie drank in every word. Cindy was also thrilled to hear all of the details. Carrie wistfully whispered, "I hope somebody will propose to me that romantically someday."

Cindy answered, "We can't possibly guess who you might be thinking about." Carrie blushed, but joined in the giggles. She indeed was hoping things would work out between her and Doug Whittier, whom she had been dating for several years.

Later that evening, Bethany took the booklet about the sacredness of marriage with her to meet John at the college snack bar. She gave him the booklet, and they each ordered a soda. Doug spotted them and stopped by their table. "Congratulations you two! Exciting news."

While they were talking, Randy Conner came by. Both Doug and Randy admired the ring and asked John where he had bought it. Both of these young men were thinking about the next step they wanted to take in their relationships with Carrie and Cindy, respectively. However, they knew they would have to be patient, as they had schooling to complete.

Friday, John and Bethany met for lunch. John returned the booklet about the symbolism of the wedding ceremony and said, "That was really interesting and helpful. I did not know about all the symbolism. It will really make the ceremony more significant to me."

"I know. That is how I felt too."

"Now that the engagement is official and we are making plans, I am getting impatient for the wedding day to arrive. It's good I have a lot to keep me busy and my mind occupied, or I would go crazy waiting."

Bethany laughed. "I feel the same way."

When registration was completed and second semester had begun, Bethany had a full schedule of classes plus many hours of piano practice in preparation for her senior recital. Still, she managed to think about wedding plans, which she discussed often with John when they met for coffee or Friday night dates. Sometimes John's sister Ruth would join them, and she was always anxious to hear about every detail.

Bethany also talked over everything with her mother every Sunday when she called home. Bethany found that her prediction about the time flying between December and August was coming true for her.

In February, John asked her to go to the Valentine's banquet. She decided to wear the dress she had used for Sarah's wedding. When she learned that Carrie and Doug were going also, she offered to let Carrie borrow the red and white dress Bethany had worn the previous year. Carrie was very grateful. Both couples enjoyed the romantic evening.

Shortly before spring break, Martha Davenport called Bethany and told her they wanted to invite Carrie to come with Bethany for the week. "We have heard so much about Carrie, we would love to meet her in person."

"I will extend your invitation to Carrie and get back to you. It is very thoughtful of you to ask her. However, we wouldn't be able to come until Sunday afternoon this time. Carrie is going to be a bridesmaid in a wedding Saturday, and I have been invited to attend."

Martha asked, "Oh, who is getting married?"

"The woman who helped Carrie the year she had to drop out of college. Carrie is so excited about being in the wedding."

"That will be great fun for her."

Carrie was very enthusiastic when she heard about the invitation. "I will speak to my foster parents about it, to be sure they don't mind. Since the Davenports are being so generous to me, I am sure Mr. and Mrs. Briggs will think it is a good idea."

In a few days, Carrie told Bethany she would be thrilled to accept the invitation. "Should I write to the Davenports to accept and thank them, Bethany?"

"That is an excellent idea, Carrie."

Carrie showed the note to Bethany before sending it. Bethany assured her she had written a very appropriate response to the invitation.

When the time came to pack for the visit, Carrie's old insecurities returned. She was very concerned about making a good impression on the Davenports. Bethany helped her choose clothes and accessories to take and reassured her that the Davenports would see what a fine young Christian woman she had become. She knew that they would feel Carrie was worthy of the help they were giving her to be in Bethany's wedding.

Saturday Bethany helped Carrie with her preparations for being a bridesmaid for Miss Jordan. Bethany helped her fix her hair and do her makeup in the dorm room before her foster parents, Mr. and Mrs. Briggs, arrived to give them a ride to the church. Bethany went with Carrie to the bridal party dressing room for moral support and to help her with her dress and hairpiece. Then Bethany joined the Briggses in the congregation. Carrie made a beautiful bridesmaid, and once she relaxed, she was delighted with the event and her part in it.

On Sunday when the two girls headed for the train station, again Carrie was a mixture of nerves and excited anticipation. She had not traveled by train before and thoroughly enjoyed that experience. When they arrived in Detroit and switched to the chauffeur-driven limousine, she was awestruck and speechless for most of the ride.

At the house, Michael raced out the door with his usual enthusiasm to greet them. He gave Bethany a big hug and then politely shook hands with Carrie when Bethany introduced them. Bethany was surprised and delighted to learn that he and his mother Elaine were also staying with the Davenports for the week. Bethany exclaimed, "Michael, you have grown so much since I last saw you! Let's see," she mused, "you just had your ninth birthday, didn't you?"

"Yes, and I am in the fourth grade," he proudly stated. He added, "Thanks for the funny birthday card you sent me. I really liked it."

"Maybe you'll also like something I have in my suitcase," Bethany responded with a conspiratorial grin.

"You brought me something?"

"Yes, a late birthday gift. Just something small."

"Thanks! I can hardly wait to open it. You always give me neat stuff!"

The Davenports and Elaine had come out and were waiting for them on the porch. Bethany and Elaine greeted each other warmly, followed by Martha and George Davenport. They all admired her engagement ring. Elaine exclaimed, "It's gorgeous!"

Bethany introduced Carrie, and they welcomed her as they had Sarah in the past when she had accompanied Bethany. The two girls were shown to separate guest rooms to freshen up. The Davenports had eaten earlier, but the cook had saved some food for the girls to eat before leaving for the evening service. Bethany had dug the small gift out of her suitcase, and Michael sat with them in the kitchen and opened it while they ate. He was delighted with the matchbook car to add to his collection.

Bethany enjoyed seeing her friends and Pastor Butler at Faith Baptist Church once again. She was pleased to share the news of her and John's upcoming wedding and to introduce them to Carrie. Later, Bethany and Elaine discussed plans for the next four days, which included shopping as well as taking Carrie to see some of the local points of interest. They were careful to include time for Bethany to spend with Michael.

Martha would join them for a shopping spree on Wednesday. She and Elaine wanted Bethany to join them as they shopped for new dresses for Bethany's wedding. Martha had secret plans to spoil all three girls with lunch, a stop at a favorite coffee shop, and buying each of them some item of clothing or jewelry. She would watch for them to show an interest in something and then get it for them.

On Monday, the three young women took Michael with them to visit the local zoo, where they bought hot dogs and drinks for lunch. In the monkey house, Elaine bought peanuts. While Carrie and Michael were occupied with throwing them to the monkeys, Elaine and Bethany sat down on a bench and had a few minutes of private conversation. Elaine shared how the Lord had recently laid it on her heart that Michael needed to know his father. They had not heard from him since shortly after the divorce. She was also concerned about his spiritual condition. "I don't think his family went to church much, and I am pretty sure he wasn't saved. Will you pray about it? I am going to try contacting his mother in the near future."

"I will definitely add that to my prayer list, Elaine."

That evening when they went down to the dining room, Carrie took two beautifully wrapped gifts with her. Before being seated, Carrie made a little speech.

"I hope you don't mind homemade things. I don't have a lot of money, as you know, but I wanted to bring something as a hostess gift. This is for you, Mr. Davenport, and this one's for you, Mrs. Davenport."

George Davenport tore open the package and found cream-cheese candies made with a candy mold and also some fudge.

"Aha! How did you know I like chocolate?"

"Just a lucky guess. I mean, I hoped…most men…"

"These others look good too. They are almost too pretty to eat, but I think I'll manage to force myself," he said with a grin as he popped a sweet-smelling cream cheese candy in his mouth and passed the box to Michael.

"Oh, wow! You're going to share?"

"Sure."

"I think I'll check out the fudge. Is that okay, Mom?"

"Just one, for now."

George winked and said, "After dinner, we'll have more."

When Mrs. Davenport opened her gift, she found a beautiful doily of the old-fashioned variety that had been stiffened to hold its shape to look like a flower, with the different layers standing up.

Martha Davenport was obviously pleased and moved by the lovely gift. As she placed it on the table, a little gasp of delight escaped her lips.

"Oh, Carrie, did you do this?"

"Yes. My foster mother taught me last summer, and I have been practicing when I can find a little spare time. I don't know if you use this kind of thing. They really aren't in style…"

"Oh, don't you worry about that. Many of my friends admire hand-crafted arts as much as I do. Isn't it exquisite, Elaine?"

"It certainly is."

"See? And she is an interior decorator. It reminds me of my grandmother," she said in a choked voice. "She made these and decorated her home with them. They didn't have much in the way of expensive knick-knacks and such. You did a beautiful job—I think this is probably almost a lost art."

She gave Carrie a quick hug and then found a tissue to dab at her tears. She laughed as she said, "Grandma would have had a lace-trimmed hankie tucked into a pocket or something for such an occasion. This will not only remind me of a certain sweet young lady, but also of my grandmother. I just love it and appreciate it so much. Did you make the delicious-looking candy also?"

"No, Mrs. Briggs did, and they brought them to me earlier in the week. She wanted me to have something to show my appreciation for this invitation."

After dinner when she sampled one of the mint-flavored cream cheese candies, Martha Davenport said, "Please send my compliments to Mrs. Briggs. These are delicious."

George responded, "Yes, they are, and there's plenty to share. She was very generous."

At the end of the evening when the girls went upstairs for bed, Carrie motioned for Bethany to follow her into her room.

"Oh, Bethany, I was so nervous about my gifts. Do you think they really like them, or are they just being polite? Do you think they were appropriate?"

"Carrie, who wouldn't like the candy and that beautiful doily?"

"I just thought…well, you know, it's old-fashioned…"

"I don't care, and obviously Mrs. Davenport didn't. Her reaction was natural and sincere, I can assure you. Relax and enjoy yourself, Carrie. The Davenports are down-to-earth people in spite of their money. Martha wasn't always. She has changed a lot. Sometime I'll tell you about that. Goodnight, Carrie."

Bethany gave her a reassuring hug before leaving to go to the room she was using.

On Tuesday, Mrs. Davenport kept Michael while the girls went out. She took him shopping for a new outfit of clothes and then took him to lunch.

Mrs. Davenport took the girls to expensive dress shops on Wednesday. While they looked for outfits for Martha and Elaine to wear to the wedding, they saw some beautiful formals. Martha recalled a discussion she had overheard the night before, when Carrie had been telling Elaine how generous Bethany had been to loan her dresses for the Valentine's banquets. Martha told Carrie to try some on, "…just for the fun of it." Carrie went along with her suggestion and was astounded when Mrs. Davenport bought her a dress and a fancy sweater to wear over it for the next year's banquet. Despite Carrie's protestations, Martha was determined. Carrie was so moved, she began to cry and hurried to the women's restroom to get control and repair her makeup.

They were successful in finding dresses for Martha and Elaine, and Martha bought gifts of jewelry for Bethany and Elaine. Their gifts weren't as expensive as Carrie's, but neither minded that. They were almost as ecstatic for her as she was herself.

At dinner that night, Carrie thanked both Mr. and Mrs. Davenport profusely for all they were doing for her. "I am a stranger to you, and yet you do all of this for me. I want you to know how much I appreciate your generosity."

"You are entirely welcome, Carrie. We enjoy doing it, especially for people like you who are so grateful," responded George Davenport.

Mr. Davenport changed the topic of conversation to their plans for the trip out to Washington State in August. After the wedding, they would travel down to California to visit Disneyland and enjoy other sights. Michael could hardly contain his excitement. "I don't know if I can stand to wait for four months!" he exclaimed.

Bethany teased him. "You! How do you think I feel?"

Martha asked, "How are your plans coming along for the wedding?"

"Oh, very well. My family and I discussed a lot of plans for the wedding in the last two days of Christmas break and even did some shopping—for the pattern and fabric for the dresses. Mom and I talk every week. I hate for her to have to do so much, but she seems to be enjoying it. She is doing a lot of sewing too. I hope she isn't exhausted when it's all over. At least I will be there for the last two months to take some of the pressure off of her."

Mr. Davenport glanced at his watch and suddenly exclaimed, "Look at the time! We have to get ready for the midweek service." Everyone left the table and hurried to freshen up, find their Bibles and coats, and pile into the limousine.

The following day Martha Davenport rode with the two young women in the chauffeur-driven limousine to the railroad station. During the ride she told Carrie, "You must come back next year for spring break. We won't have the pleasure of entertaining Bethany, so we'd love to have you again."

Carrie looked astonished. "Oh, Mrs. Davenport, how sweet of you. I would enjoy coming. Thank you."

"We will be looking forward to your visit."

"I definitely will be also!"

When the girls had boarded the train and found their seats, they settled back with contented sighs. They had thoroughly enjoyed their time in Detroit, but both were anxious to get back to college and to the young men waiting for them there. Bethany had mixed emotions about the end of her senior year only being about two months away. She would enjoy the time of wedding preparations once she returned home, but it would mean being away from John for two and a half months. She shared her thoughts with Carrie.

"Just remember, after that short time apart, you will have the rest of your lives to spend together. I just know you two will be so happy. I hope things work out like that for Doug and me," she added, wistfully.

"I really think they will, Carrie. I am praying for you two."

"Thanks, Bethany. Did you ever get impatient?"

"Oh, my goodness. What a question! I was beginning to wonder if he was ever going to formally ask me. I definitely know exactly how you feel."

"Bethany, tell me about Mrs. Davenport. You said she has changed a lot. What happened?"

"When I first came out to work for them, they were going to a Baptist church that had grown cold and formal. I was disappointed because we never saw anyone getting saved or baptized. Mrs. Davenport turned cool and suspicious of me when I mentioned being reared in a home where my parents believed in spanking. She had never spanked Elaine, and now she wouldn't spank Michael. That caused some real problems for me because Michael knew I couldn't discipline him or make him do anything.

"From things she said, I began to suspect that Mrs. Davenport had simply joined the church with her husband, without really ever being saved. So I started praying for her. Also, Mr. Davenport rededicated his life and started taking his family to Faith Baptist, where we went with them this week. Eventually, she and the cook they had then, Michael, and Peter, who was their chauffeur, all were saved. The change in Mrs. Davenport was tremendous. Now she is an enthusiastic Christian, as well as a warm and caring person."

"Wow, Bethany! You had a wonderful influence on that family, didn't you?"

"I don't take the credit, Carrie. I was pretty backslidden myself for a while. I thought I loved a guy from the church they took me to at first, and he started making me question my standards. He worked with John, and God arranged for our paths to cross. John invited me to go to a revival at Faith, and then Mr. Davenport got interested and went. That church made a big difference in all of our lives."

"I guess that shows how important the right church can be."

"Yes! I really learned that from the experience."

The girls were thrilled to find John and Doug waiting to greet them at the train station—even though they couldn't drive them back to college. They grabbed the girls' luggage and walked with them to the meeting place for the bus to take them back to campus. John and Bethany didn't talk much. John was enjoying listening to Carrie's excited recital of everything she had seen and done in Detroit, especially her descriptions of the elegant home and the pampering of the Davenports. Before the girls boarded the bus, both couples made plans to meet on campus to catch up on the events of the past week.

Soon they were all busy again with classes, work, social life, and involvement in the ministries of the Crossroads Baptist Church. Bethany practiced diligently for her piano recital, wanting to finish her college career on a positive note. She also had papers and projects to complete for her other courses. There was no feeling of time's crawling by.

Finally the day came for Bethany's senior recital. John prayed with her before she played, which helped calm her. Several of the pieces she played were hymns that she had arranged herself in classical styles, and she was able to pour her deepest expression into those most of all. Afterward, everyone said the recital had been beautiful and meaningful. She was glad to have done well and was pleased to have one more challenge successfully completed.

Final examinations were the last hurdle, and Bethany was concentrating so hard on being prepared, that the weekend before, she did not even remember to call home to visit and discuss wedding plans. The Prescotts knew finals week was upon her and were not surprised, nor did they call her. They were also very busy—preparing to fly to Indiana for her graduation.

Once finals were over, Bethany called home. Betsy happened to answer the phone. Bethany could hardly get in a word as her sister told her all about their preparations for coming out for the graduation. Betsy shared what she was bringing to wear, asking Bethany for advice as to whether it would be appropriate. She also shared her excitement about seeing the Crossroads Baptist Church and Bible College. She was anxiously anticipating attending college there in another year.

Finally, Bethany said, "Now let me talk to Mom or Dad, please. We need to make final arrangements for John to pick you all up at the airport."

"That is really nice of him. I really like my future brother-in-law."

Bethany laughed and waited for Betsy to give the phone to one of her parents.

On graduation day Bethany thought back to five years before when she had been nervous about her high school graduation. There would be a much larger crowd watching today, but this time she didn't have to speak. That was a relief. She was thrilled that, besides her family and John in the crowd watching, special friends had driven up from Detroit for this momentous day in her life. The Davenports had come, bringing Elaine, Michael, and Mrs. Carpenter with them. It was a very special reunion day for the Prescotts and Davenports—the two men had served together in the Army many years before. The Prescotts were happy for the opportunity to meet Mrs. Carpenter, about whom Bethany had often talked.

Her friends and family watched proudly as Bethany walked across the platform in her cap and gown to receive her Bachelor of Science in Music Education degree.

After the ceremony, George Davenport insisted on treating everyone to dinner in a very nice restaurant. Michael was now a polite, very well-behaved nine-year-old, and no one had to worry about taking him to an upscale restaurant. Bethany could well remember when that was not true! It thrilled her soul to know she had played a part in the great changes that had come about in the lives of Michael, his mother, and his grandparents. God had used her during the year she spent as a nanny, in spite of the fact that she had been struggling with major decisions in her own life. She recalled how she had almost gotten sidetracked, but God had helped her to take the right path during a major crossroads in her life.

Bethany looked across the table at John and found his gaze was on her. Noting her serious expression, he mouthed, "Everything okay?"

She responded with a radiant smile and the answer, "Everything!"

CHAPTER THREE

Final Wedding Preparations

"When thou art bidden of any man to a wedding...."
(Luke 14:8)

The first morning after flying home from Indiana, the family gathered for breakfast before Mr. Prescott left for work. He commented, "It is good to have Bethany back with us, even though it is only for a few months. I know it is going to be a very busy time for you ladies. Let's all try to keep matters in proper perspective so it will be a happy time of building memories and not a stressful experience. Brian, I know you have some lawn mowing jobs lined up, but you still have your normal chores around here. Your mother and sister may occasionally need your help with some extra things also."

"Yes, sir."

After her husband had asked the blessing for the food, Margaret started the bowl of scrambled eggs around while commenting, "I doubt if any of us unpacked last night since we got home so late. I know I just fell into bed. So we all better do that this morning. Bethany, you especially will need some time to get settled back into your and Betsy's room."

Bethany answered, "Don't forget I am used to an earlier time zone. I awoke early and have all my clothes unpacked and put away. I'm afraid I woke Betsy, so she did hers and then helped me since I had so much more. I put the bedding that I had used at college in the hamper—I will get it washed and put away."

She added thoughtfully, "What is left that I need to help with for the wedding? Or are there some things around the house that you haven't been able to keep up with? I know you have been doing a lot of running around shopping for things and have spent a lot of time sewing."

Her mother considered the question. "I have lists we can check, but right off the top of my head, the thing that has been bothering me is bags and boxes of things stuck here and there without much organization. Just before the trip I bought a shelf unit to use. I want you to get all of the things for the wedding put on those shelves—reception items together and decorations for the auditorium together. I also bought some small storage bins with lids. You can use them for small items now; after we have decorated, we will put the bins in the bridal dressing room, labeled with the name of each bridesmaid. Then they will each have a place to put the shoes and jewelry and hairpieces they will wear for the wedding. As they change, they can put their belongings in their own storage bin. It will be much more orderly that way, and the girls won't be losing things."

"What a great idea, Mom!"

Margaret laughed and answered, "I wish I could take credit for it. Mrs. Wells, the church wedding coordinator, came up with the idea after several years of experience of seeing girls scurrying around trying to find things that were buried."

Bethany said, "I will get the girls' names on those bins this morning while I'm thinking about it, so we won't have that to do at the last moment."

"Good idea."

Betsy spoke up. "Shall I help her, Mom?"

"Yes, just as soon as we get the kitchen cleaned up."

Betsy moaned, and Bethany said, "I'll help with that before I start on the project. Let's see how fast we can get the kitchen work done." As they cleared the table together, Bethany asked, "Betsy, do you want to make the name labels for the bins?"

"Sure. I'll try to make them pretty. I'll use colored paper in the wedding colors and write the names in calligraphy."

"That would be great, but I didn't know you did calligraphy."

"I got a book about it and have been practicing quite a bit."

As they all worked on cleaning up the kitchen, Margaret said, "Bethany, after lunch, I need you to try on your gown. I do so hope everything fits okay."

"Are you almost done with it, Mom?"

"Yes, just a few final touches and the hem."

"Ooh, I am so anxious to see it and try it on."

"Mom, may I try on my bridesmaid's dress for Bethany?"

"Yes, but why don't we wait to do that after lunch too?"

"That's a great idea," enthused Bethany. "I am looking forward to seeing both of your dresses. Is yours finished, Mom?"

"Almost. I can try it on for you later."

"Oh, good!"

By lunchtime, Bethany and Betsy had done a lot toward getting everything gathered together on the new set of shelves, which had been set up in a corner of the laundry room. As they sat down for lunch, Mrs. Prescott asked them about their progress. Betsy teased Bethany, "We would probably have it done, but of course, Bethany had to look at everything we have bought so far, and ooh and ah over all of it!"

Bethany playfully punched her sister on the arm.

Margaret asked her daughter, "What do you think, Bethany? Is everything okay?"

"Oh, yes. All of it! I especially like the pink and black tulle for the reception. The sparkle in it especially brightens up the black. You two have done a great job. Is there much left for me to do?"

"Oh, yes. We have to make the arrangements for renting arbors and pillars, decide on the topper for the cake…"

Bethany interrupted, "What do you mean? I thought I could use the one that's been in the family for years. Didn't your grandmother have it on her cake?"

"Yes, but I didn't want you to feel like you had to use it."

"Oh, Mom, I love traditions. Of course I want to use it. Do we have it here?"

"No, we have to get it from your cousin. She was the last one to use it. I had already checked with her—just in case, and she is ready to mail it to us as soon as we let her know you want it."

"I better call Jessica about the cake topper today. We will want it in time to show it to the bakery so they can figure out how to safely put it on top. We don't want it to get broken. How many people in the family have already used it?"

Margaret ticked off on her fingers as she counted. "Grandma, my mother, her sister and brother, my sister and me, three of our cousins, plus two of your own cousins. So you will be the third in your generation. That makes you the twelfth! You do realize, of course, that it is old-fashioned?"

Bethany knew the unique porcelain bride and groom wedding cake topper was indeed old, yet lovely. She answered, "Yes, but that is what makes it so special."

"I have made inquiries about bakeries, and I think I know which one we should use."

"Thanks, Mom. It seems like you have done so much. I was telling Mrs. Davenport I hoped you weren't going to be exhausted by the time of the wedding."

"I am fine. I am really enjoying it so much. Why don't you call your cousin Jessica as soon as you finish lunch? Then we'll have our 'fashion show.' "

After they cleared away the lunch things and had the kitchen clean, Bethany called her cousin. Jessica assured Bethany that she would get the cake topper in the mail immediately. Bethany went to find the others. She was delighted to find them both in their dresses for the wedding and complimented her mother on the beautiful job she had done.

They immediately urged her to try on her bridal gown. When she had it on and stood in front of the mirror, Bethany was overcome with emotion. When she turned to give her mother a grateful hug for the time and skill she had put into the gown, she discovered her mother was also wiping away tears. Betsy came into the room, having taken off her bridesmaid's dress, and exclaimed with excitement, "Bethany, you look gorgeous. I have never seen a more beautiful bride!"

"I don't know about that, but I sure do love my dress."

With a happy smile, Mrs. Prescott said, "It fits well. I am so relieved. Next week we need to go shopping for your headpiece so I can attach the veil to it."

"Oh, yes, I am looking forward to choosing one. Do you think we could do some other shopping? I need a few items for my wardrobe, like a new robe and undergarments."

"Yes, we will make a day of it. I think Betsy could use a new outfit for the summer."

Betsy enthusiastically interjected, "Oh, that will be fun!"

After changing out of the gown and carefully hanging it up, Bethany joined Betsy in the laundry room to finish their organizing. At two o'clock Margaret Prescott called, "Come and take a little break. I have hot chocolate and cookies ready."

They had barely seated themselves when Brian bounded into the dining room. "Did I hear someone say 'cookies'?"

Margaret laughed. "I'm sorry, Brian. I thought you were outside, or I would have called you. I'll get another mug."

When she returned, Margaret asked, "By the way, what did Jessica say?"

"She will put the topper in the mail tomorrow."

"Wonderful. Now, let's look over my to-do list."

"Oh, boy. I've got to drink this fast and get out of here."

Laughing, Margaret said, "Oh, Brian, don't worry. Relax and enjoy your cocoa. Nothing on the list is for you to do."

"Are you sure? That's a nice change."

Betsy answered, "Oh, you poor, overworked boy."

"How are you girls doing with the organizing?" asked Margaret

"I think we are almost done—unless we find more bags somewhere."

Betsy assured her sister, "We have all of the bags in the laundry room, and only a few more items need to be put away."

Bethany said, "Mom, you have to see what a nice job Betsy did on the labels. Go get one to show Mom, Betsy."

Smiling with pleasure at the compliment, Betsy hurried to get one of the labels. When she came back into the kitchen, Margaret examined it and also complimented Betsy. "You really have been practicing. The names look very nice."

Margaret checked her list then and contnued, "I am very grateful that all those bags of things are nearly put away! Bethany, you should have time this afternoon to make one or two phone calls. I have a list of questions for the rental places. I want to see who has what and compare prices. You can start with that. We want to get what we need reserved fairly soon. We need to review our plans and make sure of the exact number of columns and arches we need."

That afternoon Bethany called several rental stores and asked the questions her mother had listed. They were able to decide on one that had everything they needed and at a reasonable price.

In the meantime, Betsy had finished up with the organizing. Margaret had been unpacking the suitcases she and her husband had taken on the trip and had done a few loads of laundry. By four o'clock they all agreed a nap was in order. As the three of them went up the stairs Margaret said, "It was a busy time at graduation. With jet lag added, I won't have any problem falling asleep. I am so happy with the progress we have made that I believe I can just relax for an hour. Then I'll be ready to get up and tackle dinner."

That evening at dinner James asked, "Well, did you all get your unpacking done?"

Brian was the first one to respond. "It didn't take me long. Then I got two lawns mowed and edged. The people said they liked my work and would recommend me to their friends," he added with a touch of pride.

"That's good to hear. I am proud of you, son."

Margaret spoke up. "We ladies achieved a lot too. Besides unpacking and doing laundry, we have made a start on organizing and planning for the wedding."

"I hope you aren't pushing yourselves too much."

"No, honey. We all worked together, and we all had an afternoon nap. You are the one who is probably ready to drop. You had to work a full day."

"I do believe I will head for bed early," James responded with a grin.

In bed that night, Bethany thought about how, in spite of missing John, she was happy to have this short time to spend with her family. It was good to enjoy the routines, the favorite meals, and the warmth of family time again. Her thoughts were interrupted by Betsy who had questions about college life, dating, falling in love, and every aspect of "growing up."

After seeing the campus, Betsy was even more pumped up about going there after finishing high school. Bethany spent a few minutes answering some of her sister's inquiries, and then told her they both needed to get to sleep. "Tomorrow is Saturday, and we will have to get up early for the bus ministry. How about you save some of your questions for another time?"

Bethany had anticipated having many conversations on these subjects, but she also hoped that her wedding would occupy a lot of Betsy's time and attention during the next few months.

The next day Bethany was happy to rejoin the bus ministry at her home church. The bus director put her on Betsy's route, as they needed someone else to drive Betsy and some other teen girls. First, they visited part of the route and then did door knocking to witness and try to sign up new riders.

Sunday Bethany enjoyed being in her home church. Many adults greeted her warmly, having known her throughout her growing-up years. Many had been her Sunday school and junior church teachers. Other young adults were also home from college for the summer. She enjoyed visiting with them all, young or old.

When she greeted Pastor Noble, he stopped her and asked, "Is your fiancé, forgive me, what is his name?'

"John Holman."

"Oh, yes. Will he be here a few days early for the wedding? I would like to have a premarital counseling session with you two, if possible."

"Yes, he is coming in on the Monday before the wedding."

"Oh, good. We should be able to fit that in then?"

"Yes, of course. I will set up an appointment when I know more about our schedule for that week."

On Monday and Tuesday, the Prescott women thoroughly cleaned the house, doing some extra spring-cleaning projects and catching up on some of the little details that Mrs. Prescott had been forced to postpone in recent weeks. Margaret thanked her two daughters for their willing cooperation. "I feel so much better about things now. It bothers me when I know things are not up to my usual standard. Tomorrow I can devote my time to finishing up my dress and Bethany's gown. That will be a big relief."

Bethany answered, "Cleaning is the least I can do after all the time you have put in to make my wedding a special day."

Betsy said, "It wasn't so bad. It was actually kind of fun with our working together. Besides, I learned some things I will need someday to keep my own home clean. I didn't have time to help you much during the school year with after-school sports, piano practice and lessons, homework, and bus calling on Saturday."

"Yes, I learned some things too," added Bethany.

"Well, I'm glad about that!" exclaimed their mother.

"Mom, I have been wondering about something. When are we going to do all of the decorating? We can't do it all the day before and also have rehearsal and the rehearsal dinner."

"No, no. I have spoken to the wedding coordinator and Mrs. Hadley. We are going to do the decorations for the reception in the gym on Thursday. That will only leave the church auditorium for Friday. We have several ladies lined up to help on Thursday, and Mrs. Scott will be there Friday, since Angie has to be there for rehearsal in the evening. The Holmans also invited Mr. and Mrs. Scott to go to the dinner. I thought your bridesmaids and the groomsmen would probably help too. We will provide a light lunch both days."

"That plan sounds good. I also have another idea I want to ask you about. Do you think it would be okay for me to ask Elaine to help? She is an interior decorator and would have great ideas and that special touch. But I wouldn't want to take advantage of her."

"You two have become good friends, haven't you? Doesn't she usually stay with her folks when you are there for spring break?"

"Yes, and we get along great. This last visit she confided in me about how she is trying to find out about her ex-husband and get in touch. She feels Michael really needs to know his dad. She heard through the rumor mill he had been arrested at least once and supposedly spent some time in prison. His mother won't tell her anything about him or where he is now. She blames everything on Elaine—the pregnancy, her son having to marry her, the divorce, and his getting into trouble. She wasn't very nice the last time Elaine tried to contact her."

"Well, I think you two are close enough that it would be perfectly fine to ask Elaine to help with the decorating. She would probably be thrilled. When I met her at your graduation she didn't seem like the type that would feel put-upon. I thought it was very special that she took the time to come to your graduation. She probably had to take time off work."

"Yes, that was a great surprise to have her and Michael there. And Mrs. Carpenter, of course."

"The Davenports are so thoughtful and generous."

Bethany checked her watch. "Elaine should be home now. I think I'll call and ask her right now."

When she hung up the phone, she reported to her mom. "She sounded very enthusiastic, like she thought it was an honor to be asked! I think it's an honor to have her help!"

"That's wonderful, Bethany! I am sure she will have some good ideas. Oh, I forgot to tell you. I made arrangements Sunday with Mrs. Hadley and Mrs. Wells to meet this Thursday to finalize plans for the decorations. We have to be at the church by 9:00 a.m. After that, we can order exactly what we need from the rental company."

"Oh, good. I am getting anxious to have that all nailed down."

"Me, too."

Wednesday evening after the mid-week service, Bethany sat up late watching a DVD. It had been so long since she had been able to do that, and she had been planning for the last several months to watch her favorite movie as soon as possible when she arrived home. The next morning she slept in later than usual. By the time she rose, ate and dressed, they had to leave for the meeting at church. She did not have time for her personal devotions, but promised herself she would do them when she returned home. She had experienced problems in that area the year she worked for the Davenports, and she definitely did not want to start down that road again.

The meeting was very productive. One thing Mrs. Hadley shared was how she planned to decorate the arbor on the platform and the one that would be at the entrance of the gym. Bethany asked if she could add some tulle along with the artificial flowers and greenery. Mrs. Hadley told Bethany, "I would be glad to have your help and input while I'm decorating the arbors, or I can give you the flowers for it, and you can do the whole thing."

"You are sure you wouldn't mind?"

"Oh, of course not. I have plenty to do with the other arrangements—the pews, the pillars, and the baskets for the steps up to the platform."

"I have a friend coming who has agreed to help—she is an interior decorator. Maybe I'll ask her do the arbors."

"That would certainly work out just fine. But in all honesty, hearing that a professional is coming makes me feel nervous and a little inadequate."

"Oh, no. You do beautiful work with the flowers. Elaine won't be critical; don't worry about that."

When the meeting was over, they went home and fixed a quick lunch. After her devotions, Bethany phoned the rental company to reserve the pillars, arbors, and a fountain for the punch. She was relieved that they had what she needed and that everything was still available. That was a load off her mind.

Later in the week the box from Bethany's cousin Jessica arrived. Bethany was happy to see that the porcelain cake topper was as lovely as she remembered, and it had not been damaged in the mail. She called Jessica and thanked her for sending it so promptly and wrapping it so carefully.

―――

The rest of May and June went by quickly. John called her almost every day, and sometimes they would have long conversations. She also consciously attempted to spend some time with each family member alone as well as when they were all together. She pitched balls for Brian to practice batting, played badminton with Betsy, and went for walks with her mom. On weekends she tried to give her dad a lot of attention.

They had always spent time together around the piano, the family singing while Mr. Prescott played. Since Bethany and Betsy had become proficient, sometimes he asked them to play. One day he whispered to Brian and Margaret to stop singing, leaving the sisters to sing a duet. Bethany happened to be at the piano that day and had learned to sing along as she played. Soon they realized the others weren't singing and stopped in confusion, looking at the rest of the family with quizzical expressions. Their Dad spoke up. "I wanted to hear the two of you together. How about you try it with Betsy singing the alto?"

Betsy questioned, "Dad, what is going through that brain of yours?"

"Don't worry about that now, punkin'; just humor me, okay?"

"I don't think I'm going to like it if it's what I think it is. But okay."

She and Bethany started over, with Betsy singing the alto part. She had learned to harmonized when singing in a girls' ensemble her dad had led.

"Just as I thought! You two sound great together. How about doing a duet one of these Wednesdays at church?"

"Daddy! I knew that was what was coming. I haven't done anything like that. In the ensemble, I'm not the only one doing the part," wailed Betsy.

"Now calm down. I know you can do it. It's time you started using the talents God gave you. What did you think, Mother?"

"It was beautiful. Betsy didn't seem to have any problem with her part."

"But I wasn't in front of everybody, either. I would be so nervous…"

"You thought that about being in the ensemble too, but you did just fine—even the first time."

"Come on, Sis. You did great. Daddy is right, and I have perfect confidence in you," added Bethany.

"I wish I did," answered a doubtful Betsy.

Her dad said, "Everyone is nervous when they first start. You pray, get up there, forget about the people, sing to and for God, and do your best. That is all anyone asks."

"Please, Betsy? I would like to do it with you before I leave."

"Oh, okay. But we have to practice—a lot!"

"That's my girl," James exulted as he gave Betsy a hug. "I will put you two on the schedule for the last Wednesday in June. That gives you two weeks to practice. We will start right now. Here, let me accompany you—like we will do it that night."

After much practice, in spite of Betsy's jitters, the two of them sang a duet for the Wednesday night service. Betsy remembered her dad's suggestions, and Bethany prayed with her before they left for church that night. They kept their hearts and minds on the Lord and tried to glorify Him, which was exactly what their singing accomplished.

Bethany kept in touch with her bridesmaids and was relieved when they all reported that their dresses were ready and fit well. She and Betsy worked on putting together little boxes and decorating them with pink and black ribbons. Then they filled them with candy for favors for all of the guests. Bethany was glad to have her days filled with activities. She especially enjoyed her last Fourth of July celebration with her family and church friends. A potluck at church was followed by games until it was dark enough for the fireworks.

In mid-July the ladies of the church gave Bethany a bridal shower. She was overwhelmed with the love showed to her and for all of the wonderful gifts. Bethany had used the bridal registry at a local store, but she had been forced to limit her list because once they started traveling, she and John would be living in a trailer. Many of the ladies gave her cash or gift cards.

One day in July she took Brian to get his tuxedo fitted. He would be ushering and lighting the candles along with Kathleen Durham's brother, who was the same age. They went out for lunch, and Bethany allowed him to choose the restaurant. After eating, they went to a nearby park and took a long walk. They both thoroughly enjoyed spending the day together.

The Davenports flew into Sea-Tac Airport on the last Saturday of July. They were planning to do some sightseeing in the Seattle/Tacoma area before the wedding. They rented a van and drove to a hotel that all the out-of-town guests were using. Once they had settled in, George called James Prescott to get directions to their church for services the next day. After giving him that information, James invited them to have dinner with them after church. When Mr. Davenport protested, James assured him that Margaret had it all planned and under control and definitely wanted them to come. They hung up after George asked him to extend their appreciation to Margaret.

Sunday morning, Mr. and Mrs. Prescott and Bethany waited outside the front of the church for the Davenports. When they had parked and disembarked from the van, Michael rushed to greet Bethany. He did not give her his usual hug because too many people were around, and he was getting too grown up. He extended his hand, but his excitement and happiness to see her were evident in his face. After greeting him, Bethany gave Martha and Elaine hugs before taking Michael to his Sunday school class. She and Elaine went to the young adults' class, while the Prescotts escorted George and Martha to the couples' class. Later, during the morning service, Betsy and Margaret sat with the visiting adults while Bethany and her father were on the platform with the choir.

After a stirring message from the pastor, they introduced some of their friends to the Davenports. At home Elaine and Martha helped with the final touches to the dinner, and they all enjoyed the meal of lasagna, garlic bread, and salad. Brian entertained Michael during the afternoon, and Bethany showed Elaine her wedding gown and the items they had purchased for decorating. The older couples visited until time to go back to church for the evening service. Afterward, George Davenport treated everyone at a local coffee shop. Michael and Brian especially enjoyed the hot chocolate and pastry.

John was scheduled to arrive the next day, the first Monday of August. Bethany was filled with excitement, anticipating seeing John again. Betsy was almost as exuberant as Bethany. They had a hard time settling down and falling asleep the night before his arrival, but both awoke before the alarm on Monday morning. Betsy rushed through her morning preparations, so she was ready to go along to the airport early. She nearly drove her mother and sister crazy, asking "Isn't it time to go?"

Bethany was so concerned about looking her very best for John that she was barely ready in time to leave. Margaret drove the car, as she was more familiar with the airport and was needed as their chaperone. She commented to Bethany on the way, "Just a few more days, and you won't need a chaperone. I am sure you are looking forward to that."

"Oh, Mom, I am just so happy the time has finally come."

"I am happy for you, but I will miss you…" Margaret stopped, as she was getting choked up and did not want to spoil the day, or this week, for Bethany.

Bethany reached over and gave her mother's hand a squeeze.

Margaret took a deep breath and changed the subject. "It certainly has been a busy time, but I think we have everything well-planned and organized, don't you?"

"Yes, I don't think we have forgotten anything."

At the airport they parked in the cell phone lot and waited for a call from John. He picked up his luggage, and they met him outside of the terminal. When Bethany got out of the car, she had to restrain herself from rushing to him and throwing her arms around him. John was experiencing the same desire, but he also refrained from indulging it. Only a few more days and he could hold her for the rest of their lives!

They put his luggage into the trunk, and then Bethany sat in the backseat with Betsy so John could sit in the front passenger seat. The ride seemed interminable to both of them; they just wanted a chance to sit in the living room and look at each other and talk. When they arrived at the house, they finally had that chance for about an hour before Margaret called them for lunch.

In the afternoon they took John to a car rental agency and then led the way to the hotel where he had reservations. His parents and siblings would also be staying there after their arrival on Thursday. The Prescotts left him there with directions and a GPS to help him get back to their house. After freshening up and unpacking his suitcases, John headed back to their home. He and Bethany had some time to visit again before James Prescott arrived home from work. Then Bethany left the men to renew their acquaintance, while she went to help her mother finish dinner preparations.

After dinner, John went out with Brian and shot baskets while the women cleaned up from dinner. Then they piled into the van and went to a local park where they walked on trails for several hours. When they returned to the house, John was ready to get some rest and headed for the hotel.

On Tuesday Margaret and Bethany picked up John and took him to the tuxedo shop. He could have found it with the GPS, but Margaret knew the young couple wanted as much time together as possible. Afterward, they took him home for lunch. The night before he had told Margaret not to plan dinner for Tuesday, as he wanted to take the whole family out to dinner. That evening they went to an all-you-can-eat buffet where there were plenty of choices to suit everyone's tastes.

John and Bethany met at the church on Wednesday for the counseling session with her pastor. Afterward they stopped at a coffee house for a treat and then met back at the house. John played basketball with Brian until lunchtime. Then Betsy and Bethany joined them, and they went to a playfield for a softball game. When they felt too warm, they went home, enjoyed lemonade, and gathered around the piano for a sing-along. John had brought his church clothes to change into so he wouldn't have to go back to the hotel, since the house and church were some miles away in the suburbs.

They all freshened up and changed clothes before Mr. Prescott arrived home from work. They enjoyed a simple dinner before going to church.

Thursday proved very busy for everyone. The Prescott women headed for the church early with all of the supplies for decorating the gym. James, who was taking vacation from work until a week after the wedding, headed for the airport to pick up his parents and Margaret's parents, who were flying together from Texas. They were planning to stay after the wedding for an extended visit and sightseeing. He took them to the hotel, helped them get their luggage in their respective rooms, and then headed back to the airport to pick up the wedding party. Cindy Burgess had been able to schedule her flight from Georgia to arrive close to the time that the others from Indiana would arrive. They stopped for a fast-food lunch, and then he took them to the hotel. The women unpacked and rested, while James and the two men went to have their tuxedos fitted.

John was also making trips to the airport with the rental car. Between them, everyone was delivered to the hotel, and all of the men in the wedding party visited the tuxedo shop.

When the decorating of the gym was finished, the Prescott ladies went home for a short rest and a chance to freshen up. Then they took the car and Brian and James took the van to the hotel where everyone was staying. The men and boys went out together to get dinner. The women went down to the hotel dining room and ate together with the out-of-town bridesmaids.

While they were eating, Kathleen Durham arrived, which was a surprise to Bethany. She joined them for dessert as arrangements had been made with the chef for a sheet cake decorated for a bridal shower. Since the young women from out of town had not been able to be there for Bethany's shower, they were having their own. When they had finished the cake, they retired to one of their rooms, where gifts waited.

The grandmothers, the Davenports, and the Holmans had been in on the plan and had also brought gifts. This was a lingerie shower, and Bethany was happy and embarrassed at the same time. Because of the presence of the single women and girls, the ladies tried to be discreet with their comments about the items they had brought for Bethany.

The groomsmen treated John to a nice dinner at a restaurant, and then they went back to the hotel where they visited and played board games.

After dropping off the men and boys at the hotel, James parked the van in the hotel lot and took the keys to Peter, so he could drive people to church the next day. When the Prescott family members were finally back together and headed home in the car, they were definitely ready to head straight for bed.

Friday morning the Prescotts headed for the church to decorate the auditorium, after first going out in their yard to cut long-stemmed pink and white gladioluses. As planned, they would be used along with other fresh flowers to decorate the platform.

Everyone eventually ended up at the church to help with the decorations. Carloads of people arrived at different times.

All of the out-of-town ladies brought the dresses they would wear for the wedding, which they tried on for the wedding coordinator at 11:00 a.m. This procedure was followed for all of the weddings held at the church. Everyone's dress passed the inspection for modesty concerns. The bridesmaids hung up their dresses in the bridal dressing room and put everything else in the prepared storage bins, ready for the next day.

Another room had been set up for the mothers, the grandmothers, and John's sisters. The Davenport women were invited to join them, and they also left their dresses there. Everyone would look fresh; their dresses would not be creased or rumpled from riding in the car.

The men had also brought their tuxedos and left them in the room assigned for them.

Elaine decorated the arbor on the platform and then went to the gym to work on the second one there. To Betsy's great contentment, Elaine's immediate response on seeing the gym was "It looks like a castle!" At the entrance, framed by the arbor, was a table covered with a white linen tablecloth decorated with sparkly pink tulle. In the center was the knight statuette from John, surrounded by pictures of Bethany and John together. Sparkly black and pink tulle with strings of miniature lights had been draped around the perimeter of the room, strung from the basketball hoop framework, which had been pulled up.

In the center of the back wall stood a life-size suit of armor, the mascot for the Trinity Baptist Christian School. Behind it was a backdrop of castle walls, which were left over from decorations used for a youth conference.

On the tables were small round vases filled with pink-tinted water and floating candles along with the guest favor boxes and the black sparkly tulle with rose petals.

After lunch, while the younger women and groomsmen finished up last minute decorating touches and clean up, the older couples went to the Prescotts' home to rest.

That evening the rehearsal was followed by a delicious dinner at a local restaurant with banquet facilities, hosted by the Holmans. They had borrowed a shuttle bus from the church to use, along with several cars to transport the large party. The Holmans had graciously included the Davenports and the two sets of grandparents. When Bethany was leaving for home with her family, John whispered, "Just twenty-four hours to wait."

Bethany looked at him with shining eyes and answered with a warm smile.

― CHAPTER FOUR ―

The Wedding Day

"...she became his wife: and he loved her...."
(Genesis 24:67)

*B*ethany came to full wakefulness slowly. She stretched, wiggled her toes, and looked across the room to see if her sister Betsy was awake yet. She was still sleeping, so Bethany whispered, "Good morning, Lord." Then she mused, "What day is it?"

She gasped and bolted upright in her bed. Startled, Betsy awoke and sat up in her bed. "What?"

"It's my wedding day!"

"Oh!" cried Betsy. "Yes, it is. What's it like outside?" She rushed to the window and pulled aside the drapes to look out. "Sunny! You will have a nice day for your wedding. Oh, Bethany, I am so excited and nervous—all at the same time."

"You! How do you think I feel?" asked Bethany. She couldn't keep from giggling. "I have waited so long for this day. I try not to think about climbing the platform steps in my long wedding gown without tripping."

"Like the dream you had before your high school graduation," Betsy said, and she too giggled.

"And then I think about saying my vows without getting them mixed up or something, and most of all, singing the solo to John. I almost wish I hadn't planned that part!"

"Oh, no, Bethany! It was so beautiful when you practiced it yesterday. You will do just fine."

"I sure hope so."

"I know you will and won't John be surprised! He will love it."

They laughed and hugged each other. Betsy said, "Oh, it is all so exciting and romantic!"

"Well, we had better get going or it won't happen," laughed Bethany. "Let's get ready for breakfast. Knowing Mom, she will make something special today. And after breakfast, we have lots to do before the wedding starts." The ceremony was to be at two o'clock, and Bethany knew the morning would fly by.

Betsy dreamily said, "I still think an evening wedding would be more romantic."

"Well, when you get married, you can do it that way. John and I decided this would be better for us—it gives us time to greet people without being rushed and still have plenty of time to get to the airport. We'll be able to make our flight out this evening, and we won't be exhausted when we reach our destination."

"You still don't know where you are going?"

"No, he only said to bring clothes for a warm climate."

"Maybe he is taking you to Hawaii."

"Your guess is as good as mine. I don't care that much about where; I only want to be with him. Is it okay if I take my shower first?"

"Of course. It's your day, after all."

"Not really."

"What do you mean?"

"I read a really good article in a ladies' Christian magazine about wedding preparations. Every day is a day the Lord has made, and our wedding day is also important to John, our families, and our church family. I have tried to keep that in mind all summer while we worked on plans. I didn't want to get self-centered."

"You haven't. You have been so sweet and let us all help, and you stayed so calm."

"Sometimes that was hard. But I have made sure I spent time with the Lord every day. Now we have to quit talking and get moving!" exclaimed Bethany, and she left their bedroom laughing.

After both girls had showered and dressed in casual outfits, they spent some time in their Bible and in prayer. By the time they were finished, they noticed delicious aromas coming from the kitchen. Bethany was right; Margaret Prescott had made her oldest daughter's favorite breakfast for this special day. They sat down to eggs, bacon, and pancakes. While they ate, Betsy gaily chattered, Brian rolled his eyes at his excited sister, and Bethany tried to do justice to the delicious breakfast. But she found that she could not eat with her normal appetite. She tried to concentrate on Betsy's happy chatter, and she made faces at Brian, imitating his responses to Betsy. He grinned back at her, and she knew that he was happy for her, but it was not a guy thing to let it show.

After breakfast when Bethany started helping clear the table, her father gently removed a juice glass from her hand and led her from the room. When they had reached his study, he closed the door behind them. He pulled his daughter into a fatherly embrace and explained, "Your mother said I should say my goodbyes now instead of at the church this afternoon. I love you so much, Bethany, and I am so proud of you. You are fulfilling a dream your mother and I have always hoped would come true for all of our children; you are going to the altar as a pure young woman."

"I have never even been kissed, Daddy."

"I am so pleased to hear that, sweetie. I know this is a very special day for *you*, but *I* have to give my little girl to another man." They both laughed.

"Seriously, I am very happy with your choice of a life's mate. You will have an exciting life with John; but at times, it will be hard. I have every confidence you will be able to handle it because you have learned to rely on the Lord for your strength. John is getting a very special young woman for his wife."

"I feel I am getting a wonderful man for a husband."

"I certainly agree with that."

"Daddy, I feel very blessed to have been reared in this family." Bethany had to stop for a minute to get control. Then she continued, "You and Mommy are the best parents in the world. Everything I am is because of you, and the Lord, of course. But you introduced me to Him and reared me according to His commandments. Thank you so much. And Daddy…"

"Yes, sweetheart?"

"I will always be your daddy's girl. I love you so much." Bethany laid her head on his chest and cried for a few minutes. Then she straightened up, wiped her eyes, and said, "Please send Mom in. We have enough time before our hair appointments to say our goodbyes too."

"Let me pray with you first."

When her mother entered the room, Bethany put her arms around her. "Thank you…" She stopped until she had regained her composure and then continued, "…for the way you reared me and the things you taught me, for being a loving mother, for making my beautiful wedding dress, and many others through the years. I love you soooo much!"

Her mother whispered in a choked voice, "I am proud to be called your mother."

They kissed each other on the cheek, blew their noses, wiped their eyes, and left the room to rejoin the family.

Mrs. Prescott took charge. "Come on, girls, it's time for us to pick up Mrs. Holman and John's sisters and head for the beauty shop." Bethany ran upstairs to retrieve the pictures from the first Valentine's banquet she had attended with John. She had not forgotten her promise to him to have her hair fixed the same way for their wedding day.

Arrangements had been made early to reserve enough chairs in a large salon for all of the bridal party as well as Bethany, her mother, and the Holmans. They had made simultaneous hair appointments for all of them and were starting early, as Bethany's curls would take time. Mr. Prescott was treating his family and all of the bridesmaids to manicures as well.

As they arrived at the shop, Peter drove up with Cindy, Donna, Sarah and Carrie. Kathleen Durham pulled into the parking space behind them.

As the young women stepped out of the vehicles onto the sidewalk in front of the shop, a pervading, electric fervor caught the attention of people up and down the block. Girls were hugging, chattering, and fluttering from one group to another. Onlookers smiled indulgently, guessing instantly that romance was in the air; these girls were obviously getting ready for a wedding. They burst into the shop with a flurry. Mrs. Prescott had to quiet them and call them to order so they could go to their assigned chairs. Kathleen said, "Oops, sorry," and put her hand over her mouth. Her immediate demeanor change struck Betsy as funny, and she couldn't hold back her giggles, setting off several of the others, so the quiet was soon dispelled. But soon they were all settled and quietly chatting with those in chairs close by.

Bethany was happy to find Cindy in the chair next to hers. She was anxious to learn how things were going with Randy Connor. She was glad to hear he was still planning on going back to Crossroads Baptist Bible College for his second year. Cindy would be at home in Georgia, teaching in the Christian school she had attended all of her school years. So Bethany told her she and John would continue to befriend and encourage Randy at every opportunity. He had become comfortable around John during the previous school year, and they had developed a friendship. Bethany would be taking only a few courses, but John was still a full-time graduate student working toward a Master of Pastoral Theology degree.

Cindy went on to tell Bethany that Randy had spent a week visiting her and getting acquainted with her family. "That was so great!"

"I'm sure it was! But why didn't you tell me about this?"

"It was kind of a spur-of-the-moment decision. Randy found out he could take the time off and found an inexpensive fare. It was like the Lord planned it all. It was just a few weeks ago, and I have been so busy with preparations for coming here, plus getting ready for the school year…"

"And talking to Randy on the phone ever since he was there, right?" teased Bethany.

Cindy blushed and answered, "Yes. I'll tell you more later."

Bethany flashed her a smile and a look that conveyed, "I can hardly wait!"

The hairstylist finished Bethany's hair and gave her a hand mirror so she could see the back. The style had turned out just like she wanted. Now it was time for her manicure. Everyone else was finished and ready to leave for a nearby coffee shop. Her mother said, "Come over there when you get finished, Bethany. I'll order your favorite drink."

Bethany answered, "Okay, Mom," then quickly pulled Cindy aside and whispered, "I am dying to know more, and we might not have another chance. Please, quick, tell me."

"Randy had a long talk with my dad. He was very honest with him about his backsliding, which, of course, my dad already knew about. Then he asked my dad if he would object to our developing a serious relationship."

"What did your dad say?"

"He told him he had no problem with it since he knows Randy is now sincere about trying to stay in God's will." Bethany squealed and hugged Cindy.

"There is a little more. Before he left, Randy told me he loved me, and I told him I felt the same way."

"Oh, Cindy! Do you have plans about getting engaged?"

"Randy is taking it slow, but I am sure we are headed there. At least I hope so!"

"I'll be praying for you two."

"Thanks."

When Bethany's manicure was finished, and the light-pink polish had dried, she joined the others at the coffee shop. Mrs. Prescott had called Peter to let him know his passengers were ready to be picked up, and he pulled up just as Bethany went in to pick up her take-out drink. The Holmans joined the four bridesmaids from out-of-town in the van. Kathleen followed in her car, as they all headed for the church. Bethany was hungry and looking forward to snacking from deli trays her parents were providing for the bridal party. She knew some of them would also be enjoying pizza, but she did not think that would settle well with the butterflies in her stomach. She remembered her high school graduation night and how the butterflies had quieted when she had taken the first step down the aisle. She hoped it would be the same today.

Bethany had decided to follow the old tradition of the bride and groom not seeing one another until she started down the aisle. When they arrived on the church property, Bethany said, "Please take me over to the gym building first. I want to run in and see how it looks with the cake in place." Bethany waited while Betsy went in to be sure John wasn't around. She hurried back and cried, "The cake isn't here!"

What?" responded both Margaret and Bethany together. Margaret added, "It was supposed to be here several hours ago. We need to find Mrs. Wells. Get back in the car, Betsy. Hurry!"

They drove across the parking lot to the main building, and Bethany waited in the car while Betsy scouted out the route to the bridal dressing room and made sure John was not around. Bethany hurried in when she was given the all-clear signal. As she headed to the dressing room, Margaret went to seek out the wedding coordinator. Soon she came in and told Bethany, "The bakery called. The owner said she had people calling in sick so she was behind schedule, but she felt sure she would have it here in time."

"I certainly hope so! We better pray about it," answered Bethany.

The bridesmaids arrived and were informed that there were snacks for all members of the bridal party. Donna went to the church kitchen where the snacks were laid out and made up a plate for herself and one for Bethany. After pausing a few minutes to talk to her husband Peter, she took the plates of food to the dressing room and ate with Bethany. The other girls joined them—some bringing their food with them. Soon they were all busily engaged in touching up their makeup and carefully slipping on their dresses without disturbing hairdos.

About twelve-thirty Mrs. Wells knocked on the door and beckoned to Mrs. Prescott. Margaret glanced at Bethany, hoping she hadn't noticed.

Unfortunately, the bride had and asked, "What is it?"

"I'm sure it's nothing of importance. I'll just go see."

Outside the room the other woman spoke urgently to Margaret while trying to keep her voice low. "I don't want to upset you all, especially Bethany, but the cake has arrived, and we can't find the figurine you were going to use as a topper."

At that moment Betsy was returning from the restroom and overheard. "The figurine is missing? Oh, no! It's a…"

"Shush," whispered Margaret.

"Oops," said Betsy, putting her hand over her mouth and glancing at the door of the bridal room. "I'm sorry. I hope Bethany didn't hear!"

Margaret turned back to Mrs. Wells. "I thought we had everything together on one counter in the kitchen."

"Yes, I know. But it isn't there now."

"Oh, dear. What can we substitute if we don't find it?"

"How about some silk flowers to fill the space."

"Yes, that's a good idea. Can you please check with Mrs. Hadley?"

"I will. Hopefully, we'll find it. I have some people searching the kitchen cupboards."

The door opened, and Bethany asked, "Is something wrong? Did I hear something about the cake topper?" When no one could think of how or what to answer, Bethany persisted. "Mom?"

"I don't want you to be upset, sweetie."

"It is missing? Oh, no!" Tears filled her eyes.

Quickly Margaret handed her a tissue. "Now Bethany, don't cry. You don't want red eyes."

Bethany dabbed at her eyes and fought for control. "But Mom, that is a precious family heirloom. Where could it have gone?"

"Let's go back in and try to stay calm. Maybe one of the girls knows something about it."

Mrs. Prescott explained the problem and asked if anyone knew where the figurine might be. Everyone shook their heads and murmured words of sympathy and concern.

Margaret said, "We have to finish getting ready. Mrs. Wells has some people searching for it; she's going to see if Mrs. Hadley can use some leftover silk flowers in its place."

A few minutes later there was a loud gasp from Betsy. Everyone spun around to look at her. "I just remembered something! Oh, I can't believe I did it. This is all my fault."

"What?" asked Margaret.

Betsy looked at the other bridesmaids. "Remember? I moved the figurine to another counter to show it to you. I had just put it back in the box when Elaine called us to go look at the arbor she had finished decorating. I forgot to go put it back with the other decorations." Wincing, Betsy added, "The box looks kind of old—I hope someone didn't toss it in the garbage."

"Betsy, don't even suggest such a thing!" exclaimed Bethany, sinking onto a chair.

"Bethany, you'll crush your dress."

At her mother's words, Bethany sprang up. Donna rushed over to fluff out the back of her gown as Bethany suggested, "Find someone to send over to tell them to check the garbage cans."

"Okay," said Betsy, fighting back tears as she left.

Margaret said, "We need to pray again." As they all bowed their heads, she asked the Lord to help them find the figurine, but most of all not to let the situation spoil the day.

Betsy re-entered the room. "I found a teenage boy to run over there."

"Thanks, Sis."

"Oh, Bethany, Mommy, I feel so badly about this."

"I know you do, but try not to get upset. After all, it is just a material object. Everyone finish getting ready. I am going to go see if the photographer is here yet."

Bethany was slipping on her shoes when her mother came to say they were ready to take pictures with her family and the bridesmaids. After the ceremony, they would take some of her and John and also with the entire bridal party.

When they were finished, Bethany returned to the dressing room to wait while the guests arrived. A few minutes later, Mrs. Wells came to the room. "Everything's okay. We found the figurine."

"Oh, thank the Lord!" exclaimed Margaret. "Did you get it on the cake?"

"Mrs. Hadley had already put some silk flowers on it. If we took them off it would have smeared the frosting. So we nestled the figurine in the flowers. It looks lovely."

Everyone sighed in relief. Margaret said, "Thank you so much for taking care of it."

"Where was it? Who found it?" asked Betsy.

"It was up in a high cupboard none of us ladies could reach, so we hadn't checked it yet. Somehow Brother Prescott and John had found out about the situation and came to help. We didn't think anyone would have put it up there, but John said we might as well check. Sure enough, someone had stuck it up there."

Bethany quipped, "See, I knew he would come in handy to have around." Everyone laughed.

The next half hour was the longest of Bethany's life, but finally it was time to line up for the processional. The bridesmaids, followed by Michael as ring bearer and Angie, the flower girl, walked slowly up the aisle and onto the platform. Finally it was time for Bethany's grand entrance. As she stepped into the auditorium from the foyer, she looked at John's face as he waited at the front of the church and caught his look of happiness, pride, and approval when he saw her. Her dad whispered,

"Come on, little girl. John's waiting for you." She squeezed his arm as they stepped out together to walk down the white aisle runner, symbolizing walking on holy ground. Remembering this gave Bethany a real sense of being in the presence of God during the sacred ceremony that was about to begin. Silently she thanked Him for the wonderful, godly man He had brought into her life.

John was having similar thoughts. To him, Bethany looked like a beautiful angel. The material of the veil was thin enough that he could see her radiant face as she came down the aisle. It seemed to take forever, but at last it was time for him to descend the platform steps, give her his arm, and receive her from her father. Then he escorted her to both sides of the aisle to murmur expressions of love and gratitude, embrace both sets of parents, and give both mothers a beautiful long-stemmed pink rose, which had been lying on the front pew. Then they ascended the platform steps together.

As they stood before the beautifully decorated arbor, Bethany thought, "It is really happening, I am about to become Mrs. John Holman." She tried to concentrate on what her pastor was saying, wanting to cherish every moment of the ceremony. Thankfully, a friend with a camcorder was filming it for them so they could relive it together at a later time. Thoughts of the next thing coming up—singing to John before they said their vows—kept distracting her.

When it was time, she handed her bouquet to Betsy, and Donna handed her a microphone that had been hidden for her use. Her solo went well, and she could see how much it moved John as she watched his face. To her surprise, when she finished, he took the microphone from her and sang to her. Her father had helped John plan this surprise, just as John had been surprised that she had sung to him. They had not included either solo in the rehearsal.

Then they said their vows. The pastor had carefully explained the meanings to them. They were promising to stay together for life; divorce would never be an option. They promised to *love* each other—a deep, abiding caring as well as a passionate affection. They said they would *honor* one another (to respect and give deference to), keep, and *cherish* (to care for tenderly). In addition, Bethany promised to *obey* (yielding and submitting to John courteously; and lovingly complying with his wishes and requests). She knew this plan had been designed by God to be a protection for her.

After they exchanged rings and the pastor had pronounced them man and wife, John lifted her veil, leaned forward, and tenderly gave her the first kiss either had ever shared. He whispered, "It was worth waiting for." Bethany smiled and nodded in agreement, tears shimmering in her eyes.

While John's sisters sang, Bethany and John stepped forward and lit the unity candle together. The pastor then said the words they both wanted so much to hear: "Let me introduce Mr. and Mrs. John Holman." As joyful recessional music rang out, they descended the platform steps and walked down the aisle with Bethany on John's arm.

In the foyer, all of her bridesmaids hugged her and whispered congratulations to John. Noticing that Michael looked uncertain, Bethany beckoned him to her and gave him a big hug. John shook his hand and thanked him for the fine job he had done. They did the same for the flower girl.

Their parents were then escorted out of the auditorium and joined them in the foyer, and more hugs and kisses and congratulations were offered. In the auditorium the pastor was explaining to the guests that a few photos would be taken before the wedding party went to the reception. The guests were welcome to go on over to the reception area and help themselves to the snacks, or they could remain and watch the photos being taken. Since they had not wanted pictures taken during the ceremony, they would be reenacting parts of the ceremony.

When the photos were finished, they went to the reception area. Betsy took it upon herself to help Michael find Mr. Davenport, since his mother and grandmother were serving the cake. Then she took Angie to her parents.

John and Bethany enjoyed greeting their guests, cutting the cake, and opening their gifts. When it was time to leave, the single young ladies gathered for Bethany to throw her bouquet. Bethany was pleased to see that Carrie caught it.

Donna and Betsy went with Bethany to the dressing room in the main building so she could change into traveling clothes and gather her suitcases to be put into John's rental car. Donna was also changing into more comfortable clothes, as she would be accompanying Peter as he drove the newlyweds to the airport. After they were in the room, Donna said, "I have some exciting news to share with you and Betsy."

"Ooh, what is it?" asked Bethany.

"The day before we left, my doctor's office called. I am expecting!"

Bethany and Betsy both squealed with delight and hugged Donna. "That is exciting news. I am so happy for you and Peter!" exclaimed Bethany.

After Bethany had changed, Donna and Betsy took her suitcases out to John while Bethany said a final goodbye to her parents. They all returned to the reception area where Bethany hugged John's family members and her bridesmaids while the guests lined up outside the doors with bubbles to blow at the newlyweds. After passing through the floating bubbles amid shouts of good wishes, they headed for the waiting car. John helped Bethany into the back while Peter went around and opened the front passenger door for Donna. When they were settled into the backseat, John put his arm around Bethany's shoulders and drew her close as they looked out of the window and waved to all of their friends.

Bethany did not find out where they were headed for their honeymoon until they reached the airport. She was happy to learn he had booked a suite for the first four nights of their honeymoon at a beautiful hotel in Half Moon Bay, California, which was located right on the beach. Bethany loved walking on sandy beaches, but she had never been to one in California.

On the plane they held hands for the entire flight, except when they were served soft drinks and a snack. They enjoyed watching the sunset in the western sky as they left the Seattle area and the way it reflected on the snowy top of Mt. Rainier to the east and turned it pink. After they had landed at the San Francisco Airport, they rented a car to drive to the hotel. Bethany's heart began to beat faster with excitement—soon they would actually be alone together. The ride seemed indeterminable, but at last they drove up to the beautiful entrance. Bethany gasped as she saw the gorgeous building that reminded her of a palace. It seemed to sparkle as all the lights glowed against the darkened sky. John squeezed her hand as she turned toward him, her gratitude showing in her eyes. Soon they were being escorted to their suite by a bellman, who carried their luggage.

When they had tipped him and he had left, they stood and simply gazed at each other for several minutes. Then John drew a long breath, sighed, and closed the gap between them. Gently he put his arms around Bethany. She relaxed and put her head on his chest, and she too drew in and expelled a long, shuddering breath. She felt his warm breath on her ear as he whispered, "Oh, Bethany, I have waited so long for this. To be alone with you at last and be able to hold you in my arms seems like heaven on earth. Sometimes it felt like we would never make it to this wonderful moment!"

"I know. I have felt the same way, sweetheart—especially since we were engaged. I have had some real problems with patience," Bethany answered with a soft laugh, tipping her head up to look into his eyes. She heard John catch his breath and asked, "What?"

"You are so beautiful; it still takes my breath away," he whispered, before bending his head to meet her upturned lips.

— CHAPTER FIVE —

The Honeymoon

"Set a watch, O LORD, before my mouth; keep the door of my lips."
(Psalm 141:3)

Sunday morning at the hotel, they had room service bring their breakfast. They sat by the windows facing the ocean, enjoying the beauty of the waves breaking on shore. Later they drove to a nearby Baptist church for the morning service. John had used the Internet to locate a church and learn the times of the services.

They took a much-needed nap in the afternoon, recuperating from all of the excitement and activity of their wedding day. Then the newlyweds went down to the dining room for dinner before heading back to the church for the evening service. On their way, they discussed what activities they would like to do during their stay. At the top of Bethany's list was roasting hot dogs and making s'mores over a bonfire on the beach. John said they could go shopping the next day to get ready to do that in the evening. Bethany was grateful and showed it by giving John a big hug as soon as they were back in the privacy of their suite.

The next morning after breakfast, they drove the rental car to a grocery store to buy the needed supplies for the planned hot dog roast as well as items they could fix in their room for other times. After everything was put away in the mini-kitchen area, the couple went for a walk on the beach. They found a sheltered area where there was evidence that other people had built fires and decided that would be "their spot" in the evening. After lunch and a rest in their room, they prepared to go down to the beach and find some driftwood to use for their fire. Before leaving the room, he pulled a blanket from his suitcase. "Knowing we would be at the beach, I borrowed this from my mom."

"John, you are so sweet and thoughtful. I really appreciate the way you think ahead to provide for my comfort. You really are a gallant knight," she said while rising up on tiptoe to plant a kiss on his lips.

John encircled her with his arms and returned the kiss before they left the room. At the beach, Bethany helped John carry some wood to "their spot," and then he asked her to stay there to "reserve" it while he went back to the hotel for the food supplies.

Bethany had barely spread out the blanket and settled herself, when John returned, empty-handed. He came over to where she was sitting and extended his hand to her. She took it, and he pulled her up; then he quickly gathered up the blanket. In a quiet voice, he said, "Let's forget this for now and go back to the hotel."

"What's wrong, John? Don't you feel well?" She saw him cringe as she spoke.

John answered very quietly, "Let's not talk right now. Just hurry, please." He gave her no explanation.

His response, coupled with her intense disappointment, caused Bethany to feel very frustrated. She did what he asked, but her body language showed she was not pleased. As they quickly and quietly walked back to the hotel in a rather roundabout way, Bethany's frustration grew into resentment. They had planned this evening's activity, bought the necessary supplies, and John knew how excited she was about it. *So what is this all about? And why is he not even answering my questions?*

They reached the hotel and entered the elevator, along with several other people. John did not want to discuss his actions in front of others. He placed his hand on Bethany's shoulder tenderly, but when he felt her stiffen, he removed it. When they reached their floor, Bethany resolutely stepped out and headed down the hall toward the suite, not even looking back at John, let alone holding his hand, as they had been doing wherever they went together.

Once in the room, Bethany could not restrain herself a minute longer. In a strained, irritated tone she asked, "Why did we come back here? Would you mind telling me what this is all about?"

"Please don't be angry, Bethany. I'll explain."

"Who's angry?"

John ignored her terse response and went on. "On my way back to the hotel, I overheard a bunch of guys talking. They were obviously drunk and using unacceptable language. And they were talking about you!"

"What do you mean?"

"I heard one say something about 'the gorgeous blonde,' and he was wondering if they might see her on the beach. He would like to get 'better acquainted,' and comments like that. Another one answered that he had seen a big guy with her. They started laughing and talking about how there were enough of them to 'take him out' so he wouldn't be bothering them, and they could have her to themselves. I was shocked, and I thought they must have been talking about us. So I hurried back to get you and came back a different way so as not to run into them. I didn't want to spend time explaining. I didn't want to frighten you, and I didn't want them to hear us. I am sorry, darling, I didn't know how else to handle the situation."

"Oh, John," cried Bethany and threw herself into his arms. "I am so sorry. How could I be so stupid and get so upset? I should have known you had a good reason for acting like that. You were protecting me, and I got angry! Oh, please forgive me. I love you so much! How could I?" Bethany broke down and sobbed.

John took her by the shoulders and held her at arm's length. Bethany buried her face in her hands and continued to weep. John cupped her chin with one hand and lifted her face. "It's okay, sweetheart. Please don't cry. It's not that big of a deal. Honestly, I am not upset with you. I can understand why you were put out with me. Shush, honey, stop crying. It's okay. I love you, Bethany." John continued to murmur endearments and soothing words until Bethany was finally able to stop crying.

She was still very upset with herself. "How could I be angry with you when we've only been married two days? You are probably wishing you hadn't married me! You are probably thinking, 'What have I gotten myself into?' "

"I am not thinking any such thing, I promise you. I don't expect you to be perfect because I'm not. Anyway, you didn't do anything that serious—you didn't yell, or swear, or hit me…"

"I should hope not!" Bethany answered, horrified.

Her reaction made John laugh. Bethany looked at him with surprise, then relaxed and joined him.

John pulled her close and whispered in her ear, "Remember when I invited you to visit my home when I was planning our engagement? You asked me if my parents knew about the plan, and I was a little upset with you."

"Yes," she whispered back, although no one else was around to hear.

John continued, "I told you then that if we were married, we would have to kiss and make up." He proceeded to do exactly that. Later they fixed a simple meal from the food items they had bought.

The next day John was relieved to spot the rowdy bunch of young men carrying their luggage to a car and leaving the hotel. He was happy to report to Bethany that they should be able to fulfill her wish for a bonfire and cooking on the beach that night.

After a breakfast of cereal and toast in their room, John and Bethany drove to a small shopping area, full of small shops designed for tourists. They bought a few souvenirs for themselves and loved ones and then returned to the hotel for lunch. Their afternoon was spent relaxing in their room for a few hours before going to the beach for a long walk. They found the same sheltered spot and were happy to see the wood they had collected still remained. Bethany settled on a big log and watched the ocean while John went to the room for their supplies.

Soon they had a bonfire going and roasted their hotdogs, satisfying their ravenous appetites they had worked up on the beach walk. A little later they roasted the marshmallows and made s'mores. They both enjoyed the roasting and the eating, the smell of the driftwood fire and the ocean, and the music of the ocean's constant movement.

Life had been busy for both of them for many years; it was good to have a chance to relax and unwind. This time to learn more about each other and simply be alone together was important and precious. Joy, gratitude, and love for their Saviour constantly welled up in their hearts. Now it spilled forth from Bethany's lips in a spontaneous burst of song. John enjoyed listening to her sing a praise hymn, then he started another, and she joined in. They fell silent again for a few minutes, and then softly, tenderly John sang the song he had sung to her during the wedding. Bethany followed suit with her song to him. They spent another hour at the bonfire, singing, talking, and listening to the night sounds. Feeling very contented, they gathered up their belongings, put out the fire, and walked back to the hotel.

On Wednesday, right after breakfast, they repacked their belongings and checked out of the beautiful hotel. After some sightseeing and a lunch of fish and chips, they checked in at a less extravagant motel where John had made reservations for the remainder of their honeymoon. Since their room had a small kitchenette, they cooked the leftover hotdogs and heated up canned vegetables. They ate fruit for dessert and then went to the local Baptist church for the evening service.

Thursday, after a day spent mostly on the beach, they bought some fast food and took it to the beach to eat by another bonfire. The honeymooners slept in Friday, had brunch out, and did more sightseeing in a different direction. After enjoying dinner at an Italian restaurant, they stopped at a store and bought microwave popcorn to eat in the evening while watching a DVD that John had thought to bring.

Saturday they stayed at the motel, spending their time divided between the beach and their room. They still had some food that they could prepare in their room. In order to fully enjoy this last day, Bethany pushed away thoughts of the end of the honeymoon coming the next day.

After attending the local Baptist church on Sunday, they drove four hours to his parents' home. On the way to church for the evening service, they dropped off the rental car at the agency. John's mother followed them to the agency in John's car, which he had left at their house when he flew to Tacoma for the wedding. The three of them met the rest of the Holmans at the church. After the service, they met back at the Holmans' home for a visit and snack. Then John and Bethany retired to the downstairs room Bethany had used on her visits to their home.

On Monday morning after enjoying breakfast with his family, the newlyweds left to drive back to Tacoma, Washington. Bethany was going to serve as the matron of honor for Kathleen's wedding the following weekend. She would be marrying Bob, the young man Bethany had once dated casually, who was now a medical school student.

As they drove north, John and Bethany stopped twice—once for a quick lunch and once for a gas/bathroom break. At 6:00 p.m. they found a motel, and after checking in, went to a nearby restaurant for dinner.

They retired soon in order to get an early start the next morning. Consequently, the Holmans were able to arrive at the Prescotts' home in Tacoma on Tuesday in time for dinner. Bethany was thrilled that both pairs of her grandparents, who had flown out together from San Antonio, Texas, were still in town. Mr. and Mrs. Prescott had grown up together in the same church, and their parents had been friends before their children started dating.

That evening the newlyweds drove to the motel where they were staying, promising to return for breakfast with the family in the morning.

The next morning after breakfast, John sat down in the living room with Bethany's grandparents to get better acquainted. Bethany and her mother visited while they cleaned up the kitchen. Bethany shared about her reaction to the spoiled plans for a hotdog roast on the beach. "Mom, I still can't believe I was so angry at John so soon and over something so petty! I feel terrible. It wasn't a very good start to a marriage. I thought I was more mature than that and so much in love with him that nothing would irritate me! I was so anxious to be with him, and then I went and spoiled it." The memory caused tears to well up in her eyes.

"How did John respond?"

"Oh, he was very loving and forgiving. He said we had to kiss to make up." Bethany laughed nervously with embarrassment.

Margaret Prescott pretended not to notice and said, "You need to forgive yourself. You should pray about it and confess one time your lack of reverence and respect for your husband, and then put it out of your mind. Your reaction wasn't anything serious, Bethany, and not that uncommon. You are making many adjustments, and you had just gone through an emotional, exhausting time. Don't be too hard on yourself."

"You really think it's not that uncommon?"

"Yes, I have even read stories in Christian publications about newlywed brides getting frustrated by something their new husbands said or did."

"What about you? It seems like you never get angry at Daddy."

"I simply try not to let my children know about it. We talk the matters over in our bedroom before going to bed if there has been any disagreement between us."

"I bet you didn't get upset at him on your honeymoon."

"I don't remember for sure, Bethany, but I know it has happened through the years—even right at the beginning of our marriage. And it works both ways—sometimes your father gets irritated with me."

Bethany sighed. "I'll try to do what you said. It really scared me."

"Scared you? Why?"

"Because it makes me think I will have a lot of problems with my attitude and with submission."

"Let me share some thoughts that might help you. The man is not meant to complete a woman, but you were created to complete him. A woman has to learn to give up her way more than a man. We are to respect and submit to our husband as unto the Lord. The weaker vessel surrenders itself to the stronger. Actually, if a wife doesn't submit to her husband, she is rebelling against God. A wife cannot fully reverence God if she doesn't respect and reverence her husband. Any woman can find some things to respect and be grateful for in her spouse. You need to make the decision to be a submissive wife, then simply keep asking the Lord for help, read your Bible daily, and stay close to Him. Continue doing all of the good habits you have made in your life."

"I thought I had made that decision, but when the real test came, I blew it."

"Bethany, how many times have you blown it with other things that you have made decisions about?"

"Lots."

"Exactly. You confess it and then go on. But remember this, even though you made that decision and sincerely want to be a good Christian wife, you cannot do it in your own strength. You have to continually surrender your own will and depend on the Holy Spirit."

Giving her mother a hug, Bethany said, "Thanks, Mommy."

Later that day John and Bethany looked again at their wedding gifts. They had opened them at the wedding reception, but much of the wedding day was like a blur of activity in their memories. Now they could take time to really appreciate what people had given them. They found a few more to open, which had arrived in the mail after the wedding. Then Bethany's maternal grandmother presented her with a special gift she had made. It was an embroidered wall hanging of a pickup truck pulling a travel trailer with the words, "Home is where the heart is."

Bethany exclaimed, "Oh, Grandma, it is perfect and especially precious because you made it. It will definitely be displayed in our trailer. I love it! Thank you so much."

Bethany made a careful list of all the wedding gifts so that she would be able to write thank-you notes. Then they started packing the gifts into larger boxes and suitcases, hoping everything would fit into the car. Bethany was looking forward to setting up housekeeping in their apartment in Indiana.

They had to leave some of the packing for another day. Dinner was ready, and they needed to freshen up for church that evening.

Pastor Noble of Trinity Baptist Church had asked John to preach on Wednesday night and share his future plans of traveling as an evangelist and camp speaker. At the end, the pastor asked the congregation to consider supporting John as a part of their home missions, which was enthusiastically agreed upon by the people. This auspicious beginning of their deputation warmed Bethany's heart. A special offering was also received for them. John and Bethany planned to add this gift to a fund John had started saving in order to purchase a truck and travel trailer, which would also be their only home for a time.

Thursday Bethany took John to the Pike Street Market in Seattle, and John surprised her with lunch at the Space Needle. They returned to her parents' in time to finish packing the gifts before dinner and then spent the night at the motel. On Friday, they visited the Museum of Glass and some other places of interest in Tacoma before going to the rehearsal for Kathleen and Bob's wedding. After the rehearsal they enjoyed a barbecue dinner in the Durhams' backyard. After eating and fellowshipping, everyone gathered on the patio or sat nearby on the ground and joined in a sing-along. It was a relaxing evening, and Bethany reflected that it probably helped soothe any tension or nervousness the bride and groom might be feeling.

Saturday morning they joined her parents and grandparents for breakfast at a restaurant. Bethany said goodbye to her grandparents there. James and Margaret were going to take them to the airport and be back in time for Kathleen's evening wedding. While Bethany was getting her hair done professionally, John went to hang out at the Prescotts with Betsy and Brian.

When Bethany's hair was done, John picked her up; and they returned to the Prescotts where she helped Betsy get lunch ready. James and Margaret arrived while the others were eating. They had stopped to window shop at a mall close to the airport. After lunch Bethany cleared out her things from the room she had shared with her sister. Betsy could not stand to watch and went downstairs to keep her mind off the coming departure of the newlyweds. John and Bethany would start their trip back to Indiana the next day after the morning service. They would be doing some deputation on the way. The first church on the schedule was in Ellensburg, Washington; they would arrive there in time for the evening service.

Bethany enjoyed serving as Kathleen's matron of honor. Whenever she thought about that title, she was reminded of giving John a good laugh by telling him it made her feel "old." By the time the reception was over, she was ready to return to the motel and immediately fall into bed. After such a busy week, she was glad John had planned to make their return trip to Indiana a leisurely one with some sightseeing stops along the way.

In the morning they went out for breakfast and met her family at church. After the service they said their goodbyes in the parking lot. James Prescott prayed for them, standing by their fully loaded vehicle. Betsy hated saying goodbye to her sister, but she managed to control her emotions so as not to be embarrassed in front of her friends. Still, a hint of tears glimmered in her eyes. Bethany and Margaret were in the same condition.

Although she also found it hard to say goodbye, Bethany was filled with excitement about her future life with John. Starting deputation now to gain some support helped make it seem real and not some distant goal. Since she was vivacious and outgoing, Bethany was looking forward to visiting churches and meeting new people. Now they needed to get on the road in order to make it to Ellensburg in time for John to present his plans to be an evangelist and a camp speaker, and to preach for the evening service. After hugs all around, John honked the horn as a goodbye to all as they pulled out of the church parking lot.

— CHAPTER SIX —

Beginning Married Life

*"Through wisdom is an house builded;
and by understanding it is established."*
(Proverbs 24:3)

After wiping away tears she had finally allowed to fall, Bethany turned to John with a smile and said, "I feel like this is the REAL beginning of our married life."

"What about when we get to Indiana and get the apartment set up? Won't that be the real beginning?"

Bethany laughed. "I also thought it was the beginning when we started the honeymoon. I guess we will have lots of beginnings."

"Yes, like next year when we actually start traveling full-time."

Somewhat shyly, Bethany added, "And in the future when we start our family."

"And then when we become grandparents."

"Ooh, will you stop rushing us into old age?" cried Bethany, giving him a playful slug on the arm and laughing.

"Hey, no fair, I can't defend myself when I'm driving. And we can't kiss and make up right now. So, my fair lady, you will have to give me extras later as interest for having to wait."

"Gladly, Sir Knight," said Bethany with a happy grin.

For a wedding gift, John's grandparents had given them a GPS, which proved to be a tremendous blessing and help that evening. They arrived with time to spare at the church in Ellensburg, early enough to check out the sound system and location of the piano. They determined that it would be possible for Bethany to play and sing along with John. When John explained to the pastor that he was a "singing evangelist" and asked if it would be acceptable for them to do a musical special before he preached, the pastor had no problem with his request.

After the service, the pastor and his wife took them out for coffee and pie. He told John that their singing was a real blessing and asset to John's ministry; and he advised them to use their talents and abilities whenever possible. His compliment and assurance meant a great deal to Bethany. She had long cherished the hope that she could make a tangible impact, in addition to being John's help meet.

They were glad to get to the motel after such a long, emotional, and eventful day—but a blessed day. Following the evening service, one young woman had gone forward for salvation, and a young man had surrendered for full-time ministry.

After checking in, Bethany and John took their suitcases and their hanging clothes from the back. Even more clothes and their wedding gifts were left in boxes and suitcases in the trunk. Knowing they would be traveling across country with all of their belongings, John had taken the precaution of having an alarm system installed in the car. After they had put their things in the room, John went to move the car so they could see it from the window of their room and set the alarm.

As they were leaving their room the next morning, they saw a maid working in the room across the hall. John whispered to Bethany to try to witness to her when she came back to the cart in the hall. Bethany waited, handed her a tract, and said, "I have a Gospel tract here I would like to give you. It will tell you how to be sure you will go to Heaven some day when you die."

The young woman started to hand the tract back to Bethany. "I don't think I need this. I go to church sometimes, and I haven't ever done anything real bad."

"Please, just keep it and read it later when you have a chance. You see, we can't be good enough on our own to earn our way to Heaven. We are all sinners. That is why Jesus died on the cross for us to take our punishment. That paper will explain it all to you. Some churches don't teach that we all need to be forgiven and take Jesus as our Saviour. Will you read it later?"

"Okay. I haven't heard anything like that before."

"Everything in there is copied right from the Bible. It is God's Word, and it is true. Here, let me put our phone number on it. Please call us if you have questions."

"Thank you."

"You are very welcome. Have a good day."

"You too."

They left then, not wanting to interfere with the maid's work. In the car they prayed for the young woman and then went out for brunch before starting on the road. While they ate, Bethany noted the time and laughingly commented that they would have to be careful about making sleeping-in a habit. Once they arrived in Indiana, there would be few, if any, opportunities for that. Bethany planned to take a few courses and to join a ladies' soul-winning group, which met on a weekday. She was also hoping to give private piano lessons to a few pupils, as well as learning to be a homemaker and a wife. John was going to join a youth work ministry, take college classes for his master's, and hold down a part-time job. They would both also participate in church music groups. In addition, they would be doing some deputation to obtain financial support for John's evangelistic ministry.

John laughed with her and then added, "We need a little time to spoil ourselves. We will get back into the routine once we get there. We've done it for many years, after summers that were more laid back."

"That's true. It only hurts for a few days," Bethany observed, putting on a dejected look.

John leaned across the table and whispered, "But now I'll be there to kiss away any hurt." Bethany blushed, knowing that was exactly what he had intended. He continued whispering, "You won't mind how early it is when you have me to wake up to."

Bethany pretended to be horrified. "Wow! We don't think highly of ourselves, do we?"

"Well, I know how impatient you were to be my wife."

"I should never have told you that," Bethany groaned. "When will I learn to be careful what I say and not to give you ammunition to use against me?"

John simply grinned at her.

When they had finished their meal, they left a tip and a tract, then climbed back into their fully loaded car and navigated back to Interstate 90. John was treating this trip as an extension of the honeymoon, so he was keeping his plans a secret. Monday night they again stayed at a motel along their route, but rose earlier on Tuesday morning. As was their custom, they left a tract in the room for the maid to find.

This motel offered a continental breakfast, which saved them time and money. They had brought a few items in an ice chest, so they stopped long enough to make their lunch. After that, they had only bread and fruit left. Later they stopped for gas and a restroom break and were able to purchase some deli items for sandwiches for the next few days.

That afternoon they left I-90 and headed south. Signs clued Bethany in; they were headed for Yellowstone National Park. Later they stopped for dinner and then drove on to a motel. Bethany was so filled with anticipation for the next day's activities that she had difficulty settling down to sleep. She had never been to Yellowstone and had always wanted to visit the famous park.

In the morning, after a quick breakfast and about an hour of driving, they reached the park entrance. They stopped first at the Mammoth Hot Springs and then drove to the Petrified Tree. From there they drove to the Old Faithful geyser area. They had lunch before watching the geyser spout and enjoying other tourist attractions.

As they were walking on a trail, they were startled to hear a weak call for help, followed by groaning and gasping sounds. They stopped and looked around, but saw no one. John whispered to Bethany, "I'm going to check behind those bushes over there. Be ready to run back to the Visitor's Center if I yell, 'Run.' "

Bethany whispered back, "Be careful, John."

John nodded to her, and quietly skirted around some high bushes. He saw a young man, lying on the ground. He was gagging, but nothing was coming up. John moved toward him and could tell that he was having difficulty breathing. He called to Bethany, "I'm okay. Someone appears to be ill. Wait there a minute." He moved to the young man and said, "You look like you need help. Are you seriously ill? Your breathing doesn't sound too good."

The young man gasped out, "Friends…gave me cigarette…said… 'Try this.' I…asked…'What…is it?' said…'Something…give you a buzz.' I…have pains…here," pointing to his chest.

"It was a cigarette dipped in something?"

The young man nodded.

"Then when you started feeling badly they ran off and left you?"

Again he nodded.

"Hold on," John ordered. "Try to stay calm so you don't make your breathing worse. I'll be right back."

John went to Bethany and said quietly, "Run to the Visitor's Center and tell them a man needs medical help. Ask them to send for a MediVac helicopter. Bring a ranger back if you can."

Bethany did not ask questions, but left to do what John had asked. While Bethany was gone, John spoke quietly to the young man, trying to keep him calm. "We are trying to get you some help. Your so-called friends gave you something that is making you sick. It can even destroy your brain. You need to stay away from those guys who gave it to you and then ran away when you had this bad reaction."

John continued, "Have you heard about Jesus?"

The young man nodded.

John continued, "I'm a Christian. I don't know why you are running with the wrong kind of guys, but Jesus can help you with any problem. He died so you can have forgiveness. God loves you, buddy." John pulled a Gospel tract from his pocket and wrote his cell phone number on it. "Read this when you feel better. Feel free to give me a call if you have questions or want to talk about Jesus. Okay?" John stuck it in the young man's pocket.

The young man gave a slight nod. He could not spare what breath he had to try to speak.

John heard the sound of footsteps and voices. Bethany was returning with help. He put his hand on the young man's and prayed for God's watchcare over him and that he would see his need for salvation.

Bethany and a ranger, carrying a stretcher, appeared. John helped to get the sick man on the stretcher and then helped carry him back to the ranger station to await the arrival of a MediVac helicopter.

The young man managed to gasp out, "Thank you," as John turned to leave after setting down the stretcher.

"You're welcome. Please look at the tract I gave you and think about what it says," said John as he pulled out another to hand to the ranger.

When he and Bethany resumed their hike in a much-subdued mood, she asked, "What was going on? What was wrong with him?"

"His so-called friends gave him a cigarette most likely dipped in formaldehyde."

"Formaldehyde!" gasped Bethany. "Isn't that what they use to embalm bodies?"

"Yes. People can be so stupid or ignorant. No 'buzz' is worth frying your brains. I once talked to a police officer who knew of a guy who had used it for so long that he didn't even know enough to stay out of the street. About all he knew at that point was that he wanted more of the stuff!"

"Oh, how sad!"

"Yes. And this poor sucker—I don't think he knew what they had dipped the cigarette in."

"Oh! They should be arrested."

"Yes, I hope that happens. And I hope that poor guy will be okay and not suffer too much permanent damage to his body or his brain."

From Yellowstone National Park, they took a Wyoming state highway south toward the Grand Teton National Park. They began to see antelope and watch them with excitement, as neither of them had ever before seen them. Soon watching them was no longer a matter of great interest because they had seen so many. When they entered the park they spotted bears, elk, and deer. They drove through part of the park, enjoying the mountains and animal life before turning north to stay in a tourist cabin in Yellowstone for the night.

The next day they traveled east across part of Wyoming on a two-lane road that eventually intersected with I-90, stopping at points of interest along the way. The long road stretching across flat land seemed like it would never end. After a while, the repetitive landscape and even the frequent antelope no longer held their attention. They were listening to a Christian music CD when Bethany's cell phone rang. When Bethany answered, she heard a hesitant female voice shyly say, "Hi. This is Mary."

"Mary?"

"Mary Crawford. I am a maid at the motel you stayed at in Ellensburg. You gave me a paper with your number on it."

"Oh, yes, of course. I am glad to hear from you, Mary."

When Bethany mouthed to John, "The maid," John immediately started praying as he drove.

Bethany continued, "Did you have a question, Mary?"

"Not really. I mean, I am confused about this. I always thought I was okay—about going to Heaven, I mean. This paper scares me." She started to cry. "I don't want to go to Hell."

"That's good, Mary. God doesn't want you to go there either."

"Then why did He make it and send some people there?"

"He made it for Satan. He doesn't send anyone there. People make the choice. He sent His own Son Jesus to earth because He loves us so much. If we believe that Jesus died for our own personal sins (as well as everyone else's in the world), and that He rose from the dead, we can be saved."

"That's all? That sounds too easy."

"God wanted it to be easy. But you do need something else. You must repent—be sorry for your sins and be willing to turn from them."

"That's kind of a problem for me."

"Why is that?"

"Well, I am living with my boyfriend. God doesn't like that, does He?"

"You are right."

"So what should I do?"

"You truly want to be saved? To know you would go to Heaven if you died?"

"Yes."

"So what do you think you need to do?"

"Move out?"

"Or else get married."

"What if Jimmy doesn't want to?"

"Get married, you mean?"

"Yes."

"Then I think you already said the alternative. I know it would be hard. You have to decide what is the most important thing to you. Is it being saved?"

After a pause, Mary answered, "Yes. I want to be sure I will go to Heaven. But there is another problem. Jimmy and I have a baby."

"Mary, do you want to do what pleases God?"

"Yes."

"Let me pray for you, Mary." Bethany prayed that Mary would truly put her trust in the Lord and then live for Him. She prayed that Jimmy would also be saved and that he would be willing to get married. "Now, Mary, are you ready to ask forgiveness and trust in the Lord?"

"Will He let me while I'm still living with Jimmy?"

"You don't get cleaned up first and then come to God. You come to Him, and He helps you make changes and clean up your life. I asked you those questions because you have to be willing to obey God. You seem to be."

"Yes, I am. And I'm ready to trust Him as my Saviour."

"I am so happy to hear that. Do you want me to help you pray?"

"Yes, please."

Bethany led her in a simple prayer, asking for forgiveness and accepting Jesus into her heart and life. "Now, Mary, you need to tell Jimmy what you have done. Don't nag him about doing it too or about getting married. Just mention those things when the time is right. But do start going to church—an independent Baptist church, if you can find one. Hopefully, Jimmy will go with you."

"I hope so."

"Pray about it. You are God's child now, and He wants to answer your prayers. My husband and I will be praying too. Okay?"

"Oh, thank you so much. By the way, what is your name?"

Bethany laughed. "I guess I never told you that, did I? I'm Bethany Holman, and my husband's name is John. We are newlyweds."

"I suspected that."

Bethany laughed. "That obvious, huh? It's been great talking to you, Mary. Feel free to call us if you need to talk or have other questions. Okay?"

"Thank you, Bethany. I will."

When the conversation had ended and Bethany had filled John in, they prayed together for Mary and Jimmy. Then they entertained themselves with guessing games and a word puzzle book.

After a long day, they spent the night at Sturgis, South Dakota, so they could visit the Black Hills National Forest and Mt. Rushmore the following day, which were places Bethany had always hoped to see. They also visited the historical Wall Drug Store in Wall, South Dakota, before spending the rest of the day driving to Mitchell.

On Saturday, the newlyweds enjoyed sightseeing at Mitchell, drove to Sioux Falls, had lunch and did more sightseeing. Then they drove on to Worthington in southern Minnesota where they had dinner, went shopping for lunch items, and found a motel. The next morning they drove to the Baptist church where they were scheduled to present their plans for their future ministry and provide special music during the service. Afterward, the pastor and his wife took them out to lunch. He told John he was very impressed and would recommend their work to his church for support. He asked them to contact him when they were ready to start evangelism. They continued their homeward journey toward Sparta, Wisconsin, and found the church where they were scheduled for the evening service. This pastor had asked John to preach. Afterward, he too took them out for a meal and indicated he hoped to be able to support them when the time came.

They left early Monday morning. This last day of the trip was hard on Bethany's patience. She had enjoyed their leisurely vacation and sightseeing opportunities, but now she wanted to see the apartment John had rented for them. Even though he had paid for several weeks when they weren't occupying it, he felt it was worth the expense to have someplace ready for them when they arrived. He had already moved his belongings there before leaving for the wedding. He had purchased some secondhand furniture—a bed, a chest of drawers, a table and chairs. They would have to do some shopping for living room furniture, a desk, lamps, and odds and ends. They had received most of the things they would need for both the kitchen and bath and had cash and gift cards that would help them purchase the other items they needed.

Bethany was anticipating the whole process with great excitement—even though they would be rushed to finish before John had to go back to work and college. They would concentrate on the larger items first—Bethany could finish getting the smaller items on her own.

Before they reached the town where their apartment was located, Bethany's cell phone rang. She heard Donna greeting her and answered, "Hi! How is the mother-to-be?"

"I'm fine. I haven't had very much morning sickness, but I am a little more tired than usual. How was your trip?"

"Fantastic! I'll have to tell you all about it."

"I'd love to hear about it. How about tonight? Come to our place for dinner."

"Oh, Donna, that is very kind; but it wouldn't be fair to you on such late notice."

"I'm way ahead of you. I planned to cook extra in case I could talk you into coming."

"I hope you didn't go to a lot of extra trouble."

"Don't worry about it. Just ask John if it's okay, would you?" Donna tried to sound impatient, but ended up laughing. "Peter says to tell him to say yes; he is almost as anxious as I am."

"Hang on." Bethany put her hand over the receiver and told John about the invitation. She asked him, "Would you like to go?"

"Yes, I really would, but what about the apartment? We will have to do a few things to be ready to sleep there tonight. What time would she want us for dinner?"

"John wants to know what time you would want us."

"Would six o'clock be okay? If not, I'm flexible. It can be later."

After telling John Donna's answer, he checked his watch. "I think it would be best to go to the apartment first to take in our suitcases and get the bed made up. We can unload the things in the trunk tomorrow. Six-thirty might be better for us—if that's not too late for them."

Donna answered, "Six-thirty will be fine!"

Bethany had hardly hung up when her phone rang again. This time it was Sarah. "Hi, Bethany. Paul and I want you and John to join us for dinner tomorrow night."

"This is weird! I just got off the phone with Donna. She invited us for tonight!"

"I know. We planned it together. I even know what she is fixing, so I won't fix the same thing."

"You two! You've been conniving behind our backs!"

"Well, we know what it is like getting an apartment set up for the first time. You will be real busy tomorrow, and this way you won't have to worry about stopping to fix dinner."

John was sending questioning looks her way, so Bethany said, "Just a minute" to Sarah and put her hand over the mouthpiece. "This time it's Sarah about tomorrow night. She says we will have lots to do, and she wants to fix us dinner. She and Donna planned this together."

"How thoughtful. Tell her we gladly accept."

"John said to tell you we gladly accept. It is very thoughtful of you two to plan this. Can we bring something? And what time shall we come?"

"Just bring yourselves about six o'clock, if that is convenient."

"That will be perfect. Thanks, Sarah."

Bethany hung up with a relieved sigh. "That's a load off my mind. I was already thinking about what I could fix that would be fast and easy. I'm sure we will get better meals this way—not to mention fellowship." They laughed together.

"That only takes you off the hook temporarily. I'm expecting something great from you on Wednesday."

"You are only saying that because you think I can't cook and everything will be horrible. You may be surprised! Anyway, I hope you will! I have done some practicing this summer."

"Well, it looks like your family survived, so maybe I'll do okay." Bethany playfully punched his arm. He made a big act of being hurt by the punch. "Ooh, don't be beating me when I'm defenseless. It's not fair when I'm driving."

"Oh, poor you, so delicate!" laughed Bethany.

"We probably need to stop at a store for a few things for breakfast and lunch, right?"

"Yes, we better do that before getting to the apartment. Oh, I am getting so anxious to see it; I can hardly stand it. Our first little 'home.' "

"That's a good description, since it is only an apartment."

"And you still haven't told me anything about it—not even how many rooms."

"I thought you liked surprises."

"I do."

"So, I'm saving it for a surprise."

"Not even a little hint?"

"Nope."

"Oh, you are cruel."

John just laughed and squeezed her hand as he turned into the parking lot of a grocery store. "Don't worry, my little homemaker. We are only about ten minutes away from our first little home, and then the suspense will be over."

"Ooh, seriously, John? I am soooo excited!"

Laughing, John answered, "I never would have guessed it!"

In the store they bought some staple items, as well as some meat, milk, bread, eggs, and a little fresh produce. "This will get us by until I make my menus for the rest of the week," commented Bethany as she put the last item in the cart.

"So that's how you are going to do it?"

"That's what my mom suggested, plus a few extra things for an emergency shelf, in case of last-minute changes in plans or unexpected guests or something."

"Sounds like a plan."

When they had paid for the groceries and were in the parking lot, John said, "And now, my little princess, into your royal coach you go for the short ride to your castle. Do I need to tie you down so you don't float away on clouds from anticipation?"

"The seatbelt should serve nicely, thank you."

When they pulled up in front of an apartment complex, Bethany said, "It certainly looks nice on the outside."

"I hope you like it, Bethany. If you don't, we can move. I talked the manager into letting me rent it for one more month. If you like it, we will lease it for a year."

"I'm sure it will be just great."

John opened the car door for her and then grabbed a bag of groceries from the back seat before leading the way to an outside door, which he had to unlock.

Bethany exclaimed, "This is great! I will feel much safer when I am here alone."

Once inside John led the way up the stairs and down the hall to their apartment. As he set down the bag he was carrying, he commented, "I was glad I could get this apartment on the end. That way we only have neighbors on one side."

"I'm happy you chose the second floor. That way we won't hear footsteps and other noises from above."

John inserted the key, unlocked the door, and then scooped up Bethany in his arms and carried her into the apartment. Surprised, at first Bethany could only gasp. Then she whispered in his ear, "That is one of the many things I love about you. You are both romantic and old-fashioned."

He set her down, and she looked around as he picked up the grocery bag he had set down in the hall. "Oh, John, this is really nice. I was afraid to hope it would be this big and this clean."

"Come and see the rest."

Bethany needed no urging. "Which way is the kitchen?" John led the way and set down the bag of groceries on the counter. Bethany was happy to see it was a good-sized kitchen with many cabinets and much counter space. She briefly walked around the kitchen before hurrying out to find the bedroom. She was delighted to find two bedrooms and one and a half baths. She threw herself into John's arms. "It is beautiful—so roomy. I did not expect it to be so big! You did a marvelous job of picking it out. Are you sure it isn't too expensive?"

"I'm sure."

"I see you already have your laptop computer in the second bedroom. You must have made the bookcase using boards and bricks? Do you plan to put a desk in there and have it for a study?"

"Yes. We can rent a rollaway bed if we have company. I imagine my folks might come out for graduation."

"That would be nice."

"Shall I start bringing in the rest of the groceries and our clothes now? We are going to have to hurry to get some things done here and get to the Agnews by six-thirty."

"Oh! I got so interested in the apartment I forgot all we need to do. Yes, please do. I'll start putting away the groceries." John kissed her before hurrying out to the car.

When John came back with the first load, he asked Bethany, "What about the sheets and some towels? Do I need to find some among all the things in the trunk?"

"My mom was thinking ahead. One small bag marked 'First night in apartment' is in the very front of the trunk. We can get by with just that one."

"That's a relief. God bless your mom!"

"Why don't you bring it next? I can start making up the bed while you bring in the rest of the groceries and our clothes."

"Good idea," John said. "Remind me tomorrow to show you where the laundry room for our floor is located."

"You mean I don't have to go to a Laundromat? What a wonderful surprise! I guess there are definite advantages to being married to an 'old' man."

"Hey, you little imp, I'm only five years older." He gently grabbed her and started tickling her ribs. Bethany squealed and tried unsuccessfully to get away. "Aha! You ARE ticklish."

Bethany was squealing and laughing so hard she could hardly speak but managed to say, "I'm sorry; I'm sorry."

Laughing, John stopped tormenting her and kissed her instead. Bethany finally pushed him away to remind him, "We have to get to the Agnews."

"Oh, yes, I better hurry."

John brought the specially marked bag first and then made several more trips with groceries and the clothes from the back seat that they had been using on the trip. Each time he brought a load, John kissed Bethany before going out for the next one. Finally she commented, "Wow! You sure are in a kissing mood—not that I'm complaining."

"I'll explain later. I think I can empty the inside of the car with one more trip. We'll unload the trunk in the morning. Are you almost done in here? We need to be leaving soon."

"I got the perishables put in the refrigerator, have the bed made, and the towels hung up. I have to finish putting away the groceries."

"I think the rest will have to wait until tomorrow."

"Okay."

John gave her another tender kiss and hurried out for the last bunch of clothes. When he came in Bethany helped him hang them in the closet. Then they both hurried out to the car. Glancing at his watch, John said, "Whew! That was some fast work. We should make it right on time. Thanks, Bethany."

"It was a joint effort. Now how about that explanation?"

As they drove the short distance to the Agnews' apartment, John answered, "I was just getting myself in the habit of kissing you goodbye every time I leave. I want to establish good habits from the beginning."

"My wonderful knight. What an extremely good idea!"

"I'm glad you approve, my little princess."

"Oh, I more than just approve," she said with a twinkle in her eye and her tinkly, feminine laugh that John loved so much. "That is one habit that I will find intensely satisfying."

John asked, "What exactly did you mean about the advantages of being married to an older man?"

"With your business degree, you have a better paying job than a lot of the men here. Also, you have learned to be frugal and having savings helps, so we can have a nicer apartment than most of the married students. I know Donna and Sarah both have to go to Laundromats, and that can be a real bother! I don't take any of it for granted, that's for sure."

"You do realize that you will have to do that when we are traveling and living in a trailer?"

"Yes, I have thought about it. All the more reason for me to be happy that I don't have to do it now!"

John laughed and then changed the conversation to discussing all that they needed to accomplish in the upcoming week. They talked and planned until they reached the apartment complex where the Agnews lived.

In answer to their knock, Peter greeted them warmly and invited them in. Donna came from the kitchen, wiping her hands on a towel. She greeted John and gave Bethany a hug. Bethany hugged her back and said, "This was such a good idea. We are tired. It is a little warm for all that rushing around."

"Oh, I hope I didn't make it too early for you."

"Too early?" responded John. "I have worked up an appetite and wouldn't want it to be satisfied any later."

"Good. Everything's ready."

They enjoyed Donna's delicious dinner and the fellowship, but at 8:30 John commented that it had been a long day, and they had several busy days ahead of them. Bethany agreed that she was ready for some rest. After thanking Peter and Donna profusely, they headed for "home."

"It feels good to have our own little home to be going to."

"Yes, it does. That bed is sounding very inviting."

They did not set an alarm, so they slept until 8:00 in the morning. They showered and dressed, ate a quick breakfast of cereal, and had their morning devotions. Then they worked quickly and steadily for several hours. While John started lugging in boxes and suitcases from the trunk of the car, Bethany put away the rest of the groceries from the previous evening. She placed everything in one cabinet, as she had not yet had time to study the kitchen and decide how to organize it.

Then Bethany went to the bedroom and organized the closet. She put her clothes on one side of the closet and John's on the other. As he brought in containers marked "clothing," she unpacked them and either hung them up or put them in the chest of drawers. When she came across her heavier winter items, she took them to the spare bedroom closet. She asked John if he wanted to separate any items for that closet since he too had both winter wear and sportswear he wouldn't be using often or soon. He agreed that would be a good idea.

He again "practiced" kissing her every time he left for another load. He soon noticed how her side of the closet was filling up much faster than his, which led to a lot of teasing.

They stopped to make sandwiches for lunch. While they ate, John told her he only had a few more things to bring in. "Then we can go shopping," he announced.

"For what?"

"Whatever you want to look for first. More groceries, appliances you need for the kitchen, or for some of the bigger items."

"It would be fun to look for living room furniture. Where do you plan to go?"

"Do you mind looking at thrift stores, since we won't be using those things for very long?"

"Not at all. Sometimes you can find some nice pieces there."

"I scouted around some and know which ones have the most and in the best condition. In fact, that is where I bought the bedroom furniture."

"It is in good condition. It will work for us for the short time we'll be here." Bethany did not mention the scratches and dents she had noticed or that she did not care for the dark-colored wood. They were on a tight budget, and his choices were definitely serviceable.

"I'm glad about that. I was a little nervous about getting it on my own."

"You did a good job. The table and chairs are nice too."

"I'm sorry the chairs don't all match."

"It's okay, John. They aren't so rickety that we will end up on the floor!"

He laughed and said, "I bought them from a married couple who were leaving after he graduated. College students often advertise items for sale on a bulletin board at the college in the spring."

"We could do that with our furniture next year."

"Exactly what I was planning. So, what do you want me to do?"

"How about moving the containers marked 'Kitchen' in here? That way they will be out of the living room when we do find furniture to go in there."

"Your wish is my command, my princess," he said as he stood up, bowed to her, kissed her, and headed for the living room.

She smiled as she cleared the few dishes and put them in the dishwasher and then headed for the bedroom. She had finished with the clothing, so she started unpacking the bathroom items and dividing them between the linen cupboards in the two bathrooms. She also found the other set of sheets they had been given and put it away in the master bath cupboard. John had finished moving containers marked "Kitchen" onto one of the counters, so they left to go shopping.

"Well, my little homemaker, are you exhausted?"

"No. Only a little tired. I have been thoroughly enjoying myself."

"You have had all the fun—organizing and putting things away. I have to fetch and carry."

Bethany immediately responded with a contrite tone, "Oh, John, I am so sorry. I've been selfish."

John hastened to assure her, "I was only kidding, my sweet. I would not have had the foggiest idea how to arrange and organize things—or the patience for that matter. Besides, the exercise was good for me."

She playfully slugged his arm again. "Will I ever learn? I can never tell when you are joking."

"Hey, haven't you learned yet that if you hit me while I'm driving, you have to pay up with extra kisses?"

"Maybe that's why I hit you," she teased back.

They arrived at one of the thrift stores. After parking, John went around and opened her door. He took her hand as they walked across the parking lot and into the store.

"Is this where you found the bedroom set?"

"Yes."

Bethany found a couch that she felt would be suitable, which was in relatively good condition. However, John suggested they wait and look some more: they might find a set with matching couch and chair somewhere else.

They tried several other places before finding such a set in even better condition, and they both liked the fabric better. But when John looked at the price tag, he frowned. "This is priced too high for a used set—even if it is in good condition." Bethany's heart sank.

A salesman approached. "Nice set, isn't it? Are you folks interested in it?"

"Sorry, not at this price," John answered, honestly. Bethany felt a little embarrassed.

"Well, let me see if I can do anything about that. Would you mind waiting while I talk to my manager?"

"Not at all."

When he had disappeared into the back of the store, Bethany said in a low tone, "Oh, I hope he can lower the price. I really like it."

"I know, sweetheart. When he comes back, let me handle it, okay?"

"Sure, John," Bethany agreed, while secretly thinking, "In other words, he wants me to keep my mouth shut." This thought rankled her a little.

The salesman came back. "My boss is in an agreeable mood today. You are lucky," he whispered. "If you can seal the deal right now and pay for it, it's yours at 20 percent less than the marked price."

"Well, I will have to think about it," John answered.

"You are making a big mistake. This will probably go fast, and if you come back another day, he probably won't let you have it at the marked-down price. We are closing in about five minutes. Are you sure you don't want to grab it now? It's a good deal. I would if I were you."

John answered seriously, "But you aren't me," and laughed softly to soften his words. "We may be back tomorrow. Come on, sweetheart. We don't want to hold them up at closing time."

John took Bethany's arm and steered her to the door.

Bethany's thoughts were turbulent as she pondered. "Why is he being stubborn? It sounded like a good deal to me. And I really like that set. But I don't want to act like I did on the honeymoon. Like Mom said, if I resent my husband's leadership and decisions, I am actually resenting God for putting women under the authority of their husbands."

Silently she prayed, "Father, help me. My flesh is feeling irritated at my wonderful husband. I surrender those feelings right now. I need the Holy Spirit's help to obey your commands."

In the car John said, "Thanks, Bethany."

"For what?"

"For not saying anything and being patient. I know it was a nice-looking set, and you really wanted it."

"Well, yes, but I figure you have a reason for what you did."

"I wasn't really sure about the price—even after the reduction. But most of all, I don't like high pressure. I don't like being told I have to decide right now or lose out. I want to pray about it. Maybe we will have to wait a little longer to get something. I think we have visited nearly every store. I am sorry. But it is a principle I plan to live by—my dad taught me that way."

"That makes sense," answered Bethany after a few minutes of thinking over his words. "We aren't desperate for furniture. We have the kitchen chairs to sit on."

"You are great, Bethany. I know you were hoping we'd find something soon. You are anxious to get the apartment set up and looking nice. And we don't have a lot of time before I go back to work and school."

"Like you said, we will pray about it." Inwardly, she was thanking the Lord for helping her hold her tongue and have the right attitude.

John said, "You know, we were concentrating so much on the couch that we didn't pay much attention to the other things we need. I want to go back to one of the stores tomorrow where I think I saw some nice lamps."

"Okay. For now, let's go to the apartment and freshen up a little before we go to the Norbergs' for dinner," suggested Bethany.

"Good idea. I am really looking forward to spending the evening with them."

"Me too. Even though Sarah is the quiet type, she can be a lot of fun. And I am anxious to see their apartment. She is so creative and organized that I am sure it will look gorgeous even though she is working on a limited budget."

Back at the apartment, before Bethany could do anything else, John "demanded" that she pay up the kisses she owed him—one for arriving home and one for hitting his arm while he was driving. She happily obliged, and then laughing, she pushed him away and said, "I have to check my hair and makeup. We have to leave soon."

John made a sad face. "Maybe I should have thought about it longer before I agreed to go to the Norbergs for dinner." Bethany just grinned at him as she headed for the bedroom. He followed her, came up behind her as she stood in front of the mirror, and put his arms around her.

Bethany laughed. "You don't exactly make this easier," gesturing toward the eyeliner she was holding.

He answered contritely, "I am so sorry," but he made no move to change his position.

Bethany whispered, "You are so bad," as she turned in his arms and put her lips to his. After a few minutes she sighed, gently pushed him away, and turned back to the mirror.

John looked at his watch and playfully scolded, "Look at the time! Aren't you ready to go yet? You women take so long!"

Bethany answered, "Yeah, right," while she dashed by him, scooped up her purse, and ran to be at the front door before him. "Well come on, slowpoke. What are you waiting for? I am ready to go. We don't want to be late."

John opened the door for her as he commented, "You think you are pretty smart, don't you, me wee one?"

As they were going down the stairs, she asked, "What's this 'wee one' about?"

"My Scottish ancestry coming out in me, me bonnie lassie," he answered in a Scottish accent. "Besides, you are a wee one—I get a crick in me neck trying to bend down far enough to reach your lips."

"Well, I guess you will just have to give up kissing me."

"I'll take the crick in me neck." They laughed together as they reached the car, and he held open the door for her.

The banter between them continued until they reached the Norbergs. When she opened the door for them, Sarah asked, "What's so funny? You both look like a little kid who just stole a cookie."

"We have just been joking and teasing all the way here. How are you?" said Bethany as she hugged Sarah.

"I'm great. How about you two?"

"We are enjoying married life," was John's response. "That about sums it up."

Paul had come up behind Sarah and joined in the laughter.

"It was so nice of you to ask us over. I've been glad I didn't have to think about cooking dinner these last two days."

"But I told her she's not off the hook for tomorrow night. I'm expecting a gourmet dinner," said John.

"You will probably still be 'expecting it' after you eat what I fix."

When the laughter had again subsided, Sarah ushered them to the table. "We don't want the food to get cold. Sit down, and then I'll pour the drinks and bring in the food."

Bethany started to protest, but Sarah assured her everything was under control, and she should just sit down.

As they enjoyed the dinner Sarah had prepared, Bethany and John shared their experiences during the honeymoon and their cross-country trip. Sarah and Paul expressed their enjoyment of visiting the Pacific Northwest for the first time.

After dinner the men went to the living room to visit while Bethany helped Sarah clean up the kitchen. Bethany asked her about where they had bought their furniture and told her about their unsuccessful search for living room furniture. Sarah said, "I think we just saw an advertisement for that nearby high-class neighborhood; they have a giant yard sale day throughout the whole area every year." Drying her hands as they finished up, she added, "Let's go ask Paul. I think it is happening this coming weekend. We found some of our things there last year. Those people have really nice items which are usually in very good condition even when they get rid of them."

"What a good idea! We hadn't thought about that possibility."

When they entered the living room, Sarah waited for a break in the conversation between the two men and then asked Paul about the yard sale. He answered, "It's this coming weekend. Why?"

"Bethany and John are looking for furniture and things for their apartment."

John asked, "What is this giant sale you are talking about?"

Paul explained, and then Sarah took them around the apartment showing them what they had found the previous year.

"We will have to check this out."

Paul said, "Why don't we go too? If you tell us what you need, and we take our cell phones, we can cover twice as much ground. It is a big area."

"Oh, I can't ask you to give up your Saturday for us."

"You didn't ask; I volunteered," laughed Paul. "How about it, Sarah, would you like to do that?"

"Sure, I'd love to. Maybe we will even find some things for ourselves."

Paul tried to act horrified and severe. "Now wait a minute. That is not what I had in mind."

Knowing her husband well, Sarah only laughed.

"Afterward we can go somewhere for dinner—my treat," added John.

"Sounds like lots of fun," said Bethany. "I do hope we find some things in our price range."

Sarah said, "We will all pray about it between now and then."

They visited a little while longer; then John decided they had better head for home. Bethany was ready, as theirs had been another busy day.

At the door, Sarah said, "I'm looking forward to going with you on Saturday."

Paul added, "Why don't you meet us here?"

"Sure. Around 1:00 p.m.? That will give me time to finish with the youth ministry and grab a bite of lunch."

"That will work for us. See you then."

"Goodnight, and thanks again for the delicious dinner."

"You are welcome. Goodnight," said Sarah.

Wednesday morning John and Bethany had breakfast, cleaned up the kitchen, and then settled at the kitchen table with their Bibles. After reading for a while they each shared something from the portion of Scripture they were currently studying, then they worked on a memory verse together and prayed together. Then each had a private prayer time. After their devotions, they left the apartment to go to some of the thrift stores. Later Bethany was happy to return home with a set of matching lamps for their bedroom and a framed print for the bedroom wall.

They had stopped for lunch at a fast-food restaurant so Bethany could spend a few hours in the afternoon going soul winning. When she returned, she had a few minutes to put another purchase in place. They had used one of their gift cards to buy decorative pillows for the bed that matched the comforter set they had received. Bethany liked the way the bedroom was shaping up after placing them. She would only need a silk flower arrangement to complete the room's décor.

That night at church Bethany spotted Carrie and Doug sitting together. She asked John if they could join them. Carrie was delighted to see them and asked about their honeymoon and trip back to Indiana. Bethany gave her a quick synopsis before the service began. After the service Doug told them how excited Carrie had been to be in the wedding. He kidded her about it, and she took it well. Bethany remembered what a shy, insecure girl Carrie had been when she first met her and silently praised the Lord for the growth she saw in her.

Bethany awoke with excited anticipation Saturday morning—an hour before the alarm was set to go off. She rose early, had her devotions, and made a breakfast of homemade biscuits and scrambled eggs, much to John's astonishment and delight. When John had left to meet up with his ministry group, Bethany made phone calls to both sets of parents, filling them in on the week's activities.

When John returned and they had eaten some sandwiches, they left for the Norbergs' apartment and then followed them to the area of expensive homes where the annual giant yard sale was being held. Each couple went in a different direction.

When Sarah called to say they had found a nice living room set, Bethany was anxious to see it. She and John drove to the address Sarah provided. When Bethany saw it, she realized she liked this set more than the one in the thrift store, even though it showed some wear. The set was priced lower, which was an extra bonus. Bethany was surprised, until the seller explained they had priced things low because they had to move in a hurry. Bethany was so glad that John had decided to wait. She thanked the Lord that He had helped her trust her husband's judgment, and now she had received the reward!

John had a friend with a pickup truck, so he called to make arrangements to borrow it that evening. They paid the homeowners for the set, received a signed receipt, and exchanged contact information. They arranged to return at 7:00 p.m. to pick it up. Then the two couples split up again to continue looking for other items on Bethany's list. When the Norbergs found something, they would call the Holmans so they could go check it out. By the end of the day they had found many items at low prices, including two end tables, a set of lamps to set on them, a computer desk and floor lamp, a framed picture for the living room and several decorative knick-knacks.

"Wow! What a haul," said John with a big grin. "We have our work cut out for tonight, but I think we found about everything we need!"

"I know!" exclaimed Bethany happily. "It is great! God is so good!"

"I'll come along tonight to help load everything," said Paul.

"Thanks, I appreciate that. Now, let's go get some dinner."

The two couples enjoyed dinner in a nearby restaurant. Sarah suggested that she and Bethany go to the Holmans' apartment to be ready to supervise the placement of the furniture when the men returned with it. So the men went in the Holmans' car to pick up the truck while Sarah drove with Bethany back to their apartment. During the ride Bethany shared with Sarah about the struggles she had at times in submitting and keeping her mouth shut. She told her about how she had felt at the thrift store, and how glad she was that the Lord had helped her. "Because I stayed quiet, God gave us an even better set of living room furniture!"

"Don't feel you are alone, Bethany. I have also had my share of struggles and defeats in that area."

"I was surprised when my mom also admitted having that same problem. I never heard her argue or question my dad's decisions. She said they privately discussed what she called 'differences of opinion' in their bedroom."

"That is an excellent thing to remember when we have children. I hope I can pull it off."

"Me too."

Bethany was happy to show her apartment to Sarah. She mentioned that she wanted to get a silk flower arrangement for the bedroom. Sarah asked, "Do you want to get the flowers and put them together yourself? I would enjoy helping you, if you want."

"Oh, Sarah, that is a great idea. I'd love to do that!"

The young women moved things in the extra bedroom to clear a space for the desk and lamp before the guys arrived. Then they went to the kitchen and made a pot of coffee and set out dessert bowls to have ice cream after the truck was unloaded.

The men arrived with the couch first, unloaded it, and drove back for more of their purchases. At last everything was in the apartment with the desk set up in the spare bedroom and living room furniture tastefully arranged. John and Paul left to refuel and return the pickup and get John's car.

Sarah and Bethany hung the pictures and placed the lamps and the knick-knacks on the end tables. Bethany also brought out a few of their wedding gifts, as well as the crocheted pillow Mrs. Carpenter had made for her before she started college. She lovingly placed it on the couch. Sarah commented, "Oh, I remember that. You had it on your bed at college. Didn't Mrs. Carpenter make it?"

"Yes. That makes it extra-special for me."

When the men returned, they enjoyed the coffee and ice cream before the Norbergs called it a night and headed for home.

Bethany took a last, satisfied look at the living room before heading for the bedroom. She gave John a big hug and thanked him for all he had gotten for them as well as his work to haul it into the apartment. "I love you, John; I am so glad we did not rush into buying that set at the thrift store. I have learned a lot this week about waiting on the Lord and my husband and keeping my mouth shut. It pays to be patient and trust."

"You are doing a great job, me wee one. I am very proud of you and love you more and more every single day!"

Bethany laughed at his Scottish accent and commented, "Next week we have to get into a routine again. It is going to be hard for me when you are gone to classes and work."

"You have enough planned to fully occupy yourself—you won't have much time to be lonely or bored. I just hope you won't try to do too much. You don't have to have piano students if it proves to be too much."

"I know, but I would like to be able to help a little with our fund for buying an RV."

"I understand your feelings, but I don't want you to feel like you have to. I intend to support this family."

Fearing that John was hurt, Bethany was quick to say, "I never questioned your ability or desire to do that, John; I won't do piano lessons if you don't want me to."

"Is the money for our RV fund your only reason for wanting to teach piano?"

Bethany thought about his question before answering honestly. "No, I want to try it to see if I can get children started. If I succeed, I will know I can do it with our children. It will be good practice, and I love children."

"Okay, love, then it is fine with me."

Bethany was relieved to hear his answer. She had been prepared to give up her plan if John told her to, but she really did not want to have to do so.

"By the way, how will you do it with our children when we are traveling around in an RV?"

"I will have to use a keyboard and hope they can practice on church pianos occasionally."

"Why don't we put your earnings in a special account to go toward a keyboard? Then you will also have something to practice on."

"That's an excellent idea, John."

Bethany went to bed in a contented mood. They had worked things out in a way that pleased both of them and had done it without an argument.

— CHAPTER SEVEN —

Adjustments to Married Life

*"...It is not good that the man should be alone;
I will make him an help meet for him."*
(Genesis 2:18)

*R*egistration day at the college came the first week of September. The clock radio woke John and Bethany at seven that morning. Bethany bounced enthusiastically out of bed. Today she was going to make waffles from scratch for breakfast. She hurried through her shower and preparations for the day and had her devotions. While she prepared breakfast, John helped by setting the table. He complimented her after his first bite, "You keep surprising me. You are a good little cook."

"I'm glad you think so. There will probably be disasters in the future, but so far everything has turned out okay."

"I have enjoyed every meal you have prepared so far."

When they had cleaned up the kitchen (Bethany had been happily surprised that John did not mind helping with kitchen chores), they left for the college. They went their separate ways to register for classes. Bethany had decided to take only one course this first semester—"Woman the Completer" from the Department of Marriage and Motherhood. She discovered that she could not register for that course until after chapel. When she met John for the chapel service, she found that he also had to do more registering after chapel. So after the service, they again went in different directions.

To register for the one class should not have taken Bethany very long, but she kept running into friends and stopping to chat. She was still in the registration line when she looked at her watch and was horrified to see that she was already late for meeting John. She took out her phone and opened it, then returned it to her purse in frustration. Since she was already close to the front of the line, she stayed and registered for the class. Then she practically ran to the meeting place. She knew John had to go to work that afternoon, and since it was a Wednesday, there wouldn't be time for their usual dinner meal in the evening. She had planned to fix him a nice lunch and send a sandwich with him to eat later.

When she approached she saw that he was scowling, looking at his watch, and looking around for her. She rushed up to him and said, "I am so sorry to be late. I didn't realize how long I was visiting with the friends I ran into."

"Well, you are here now. We better hurry, so I can get something to eat before I go."

"I have been thinking about that. I feel so badly—I won't have time now to fix what I had planned." Bethany was practically running to keep up with John. He was usually very aware of the difference in their strides and would slow his steps or shorten his strides to accommodate her.

They reached the car and, without a word, John opened her door, waited for her to be seated, shut the door, and went around to the driver's side. He started the car and headed for home, still without saying a word to her. When they were almost to the apartment, Bethany could stand it no longer.

"John, please don't be angry. I said I was sorry; I didn't mean for it to happen."

As if coming out of a fog, John said, "What?"

"I don't want you to be angry…"

"Bethany, I'm not angry. Why do you think I am?"

"Because I was late, and you aren't saying anything…"

He interrupted her again. "I know you are sorry, I heard you. I'm not angry with you. I am sorry you got that impression."

"Then what is wrong?"

"I just heard something today about someone's backsliding, and it really upset me."

"Oh, no! It wasn't Randy was it?"

"No, no. I haven't seen him yet, but I assume he is back and everything is okay. No, this is about Jack McCauley. Do you remember him?"

"Yes."

"I guess he started hanging with some old buddies and decided he didn't want to be a pastor after all, so he joined the Army. I respect and appreciate our military, and indeed, not everyone is meant to pastor. But Jack told me he felt God had called him to be a pastor, and I believed it as well. I am so disappointed."

"Me too. It's sad for anyone to leave God's best for them." She sighed, and then glanced at John sheepishly. "But I am relieved. I thought you were mad at me."

John asked, "Why didn't you just text me that you'd be delayed?"

Bethany winced. "Dead battery. I forgot to charge my cell phone last night."

When they reached the apartment, John parked, got out, went around to her side, and opened the door. He said softly, "Come on, honey. Let's go in."

As soon as the apartment door shut behind them, John took her in his arms, held her close, and then tipped her face up so he could kiss her. "Thank you, John," she whispered as soon as his lips left hers.

He grinned at her. "Are you convinced now that I wasn't angry?"

"Yes, but you better let me go to the kitchen and fix you something to eat."

"Um, I guess I should…" as she started to pull away, his arms tightened around her, "…but you feel so soft and smell so good. Oh, I wish I didn't have to go to work!"

"Me, too, but the fact is, you do, so let me go get you something to eat. Time is getting away." John sighed heavily, but he finally let her escape from his encircling arms.

Bethany hurried to the kitchen, put on an apron, and washed her hands. She put on a frying pan to heat while she formed two hamburger patties. While they were cooking, she quickly made a salad. John worked in an office, so he didn't have to change clothes. He simply freshened up and then joined her in the kitchen where she was putting snack items in a bag. "I'll have to make a sandwich for you later. You can eat it in the car on the way to church."

John answered, "That's fine. It won't be the first time I have had to do that."

At the table, after asking the blessing, John said, "I'm sorry I worried you."

Bethany asked, "Do you get like that often? I never saw you like that before."

"Not real often, but it does happen when I am concerned or upset. Sometimes I am just concentrating on something I am trying to learn or understand."

"How will I distinguish between that mood and your really being upset with me?"

"Why are you worried? I haven't been upset with you yet."

She softly answered, "I know. That amazes me because I am so far from being perfect."

"None of us is perfect."

"Oh, I know, but what I really meant to say is that I have a long way to go to be the kind of wife I want to be."

"Well, I'm not complaining."

"I know. I appreciate that. You are very patient."

"Really, Bethany, you are a great little wife. You have made me very happy. You don't try my patience."

"What about when I was upset on our honeymoon, and today when I was late meeting you? You had to have patience with me at least those two times, and I am sure there have been others."

"Well, you have had to be patient with me."

"For instance?"

After thinking for a moment, John responded, "When I didn't buy the furniture you liked at the thrift store."

"But that was different. I was supposed to be patient with you because you were making decisions as the head of the home. That is different from being patient when the other person does something wrong."

John looked at his watch and rose from the table. "Well, don't be hard on yourself, my sweet. And just wait—there will be things I do or say that you will have to be patient and forgiving about."

"I doubt that."

"Don't be putting me on a pedestal. I'm human too, and I make mistakes." He kissed her and said, "I have to go. Hope you have a good afternoon. Lock the door after me."

Once classes began, Bethany saw that John had prophesied correctly about trying her patience! After the first day of classes, when John had finished studying, he left his books on the couch. Bethany came into the living room to turn off the lights before going to bed, noticed the books, and picked them up without thinking. She stacked them on the computer desk next to her own book. John was already in the bedroom getting ready for bed.

John was still getting used to his new schedule and was tired the next morning. After Bethany had been up a while, she realized she did not hear him moving around. She discovered he had fallen back asleep. After she awakened him, he had to rush to get ready on time. As he was heading for the door after kissing her goodbye, he went to grab his books from the couch. "Bethany, where are my books?"

"On the computer desk," she called from the kitchen where she was cleaning up from breakfast. She heard him dashing back into the computer room and then a thud.

"Sorry, I knocked your book off. No time to pick it up," he called as he dashed out the door.

That evening Bethany again saw his books lying on the couch. They bothered her; she liked the living room to look neat and orderly. Recalling that morning, she decided she better not move them again.

After several days, she couldn't stand it any longer. She brought up the subject while they were driving home from the college. "John, do you think you could leave your books in the computer room and pick them up from there when you are leaving in the morning?"

"Why, Bethany? They are real convenient for me on the couch."

"I know they are, but it bothers me. I like everything to be neat and orderly before I go to bed."

John laughed. "My little homemaker. But why does it matter when we are in bed? No one is going to see them—not even us."

Bethany sighed so quietly that John did not hear and said, "I guess that makes sense."

Thinking she was convinced and agreed with him, John continued the habit. Bethany decided she needed to be patient, but his habit still bothered her.

One Sunday afternoon John finished studying just before time to leave for the evening service. He piled his books on the couch, so they would be ready to grab Monday morning. At church they met Donna and Peter, and John asked them over to share what was left of a cake Bethany had made on Saturday. When they arrived home, Bethany immediately grabbed the books and took them to the computer room while John waited at the door for the Agnews, who were coming up the stairs behind them. After the company had left, Bethany remembered to move the books back, knowing John would be expecting them to be in the usual place in the morning. She had to bite her tongue to keep from pointing out that she was justified in not wanting them left there.

A few weeks later Sarah invited them over again for dinner. Bethany noticed an attractive large basket sitting next to the door, which held Paul's books. Instantly, a light bulb went on in her mind. Later in the car when they were on the way home, Bethany asked John, "Do we still have a little money left from wedding gifts?"

"Yes, did you have something in mind that we need?"

"Yes, I want to go shopping for something in particular."

"Is it a big, dark secret? Let me think—it is still a little early for Christmas and my birthday. Soooo…it must not be something for me."

Bethany laughed. "In a way it is, but it is also for me."

"So are you going to tell me?"

"No, because I'm not sure myself what I am looking for," she answered with a mischievous grin.

"You are really being mysterious. Mysterious women are always interesting," he added with a wink at her.

"Well then, I will definitely keep it a mystery."

The next morning Bethany prayed about finding something to meet her need. This was a day when John did not have to drive for the car pool, so she had the use of the car. That afternoon she left the apartment shortly after John and shopped for several hours. She went to several stores but found nothing that shouted, "I'm it; buy me!" She did find a large basket similar to Sarah's, but she really wanted something a little different. She did not want to copy Sarah and also felt the basket idea did not match her décor.

On Saturday afternoon after John finished working with his ministry group, Bethany told him she wanted to look for garage sales; she had even found some advertised in the paper. He decided to go with her—even though he had no idea what she was looking for. They went to one that had been advertised and found nothing. On the way to the second address, they passed another house with a sign up and decided to stop. Bethany spotted a small end table with two shelves and instantly knew it was perfect. With a little negotiating she got the price down close to the amount they had left from wedding gifts. She asked John if they could spend the small amount over and he agreed, still not guessing why she wanted it. Since her purchase was a nice looking table in good condition, he did not mind.

Bethany was excited. She could hardly stand the ride home. Knowing this, John teased her and stopped at a Dairy Queen for a treat. Deciding to go along with his little game and not give him any satisfaction, Bethany calmly enjoyed her treat and pretended not to be anxious to get back in the car. When they did get home, John continued teasing her. He opened the car door for her, took her arm, and started walking toward the stairs leading to their apartment. Realizing what he was doing and still determined not to give him any satisfaction, she said nothing about the table in the trunk and began a conversation about something that had been discussed in her class the previous day. Finally, John took pity on her. As soon as he had opened the apartment door, he returned to the car and brought up the table.

"Now, my love, what is this for?"

Bethany took the table and without a word placed it by the door. She took out a figurine that she had never found a place for and set it on the top shelf. Then she went in to the computer room, got her book and John's books, and stacked them on the second shelf.

John grinned. "That will be convenient. What a good idea! Hmm, I seem to remember a conversation we had about my books being on the couch. But you never said anything else, so I thought you agreed that it didn't matter. But I guess it did matter to you. I'm sorry, honey. Why didn't you tell me it still bothered you?"

"It wasn't worth making a fuss over. The idea came from Sarah. Remember, she had a big basket by the door."

"Oh, yes. But I like our little table better."

"I'm glad you do," responded Bethany as she hugged him.

He wrapped his arms around her. "I recall another conversation."

"Oh? What about?"

"I predicted you would have to be patient with me about some things. You have certainly been patient over this. Thanks, little one." He grinned down at her. He enjoyed teasing her about how short she was, but he actually loved her small frame.

"Oh, you…" she paused to think, "Big hunk! I am not little." She stretched as tall as possible and rose up on her tiptoes.

John laughed, grabbed her up, and glided around the room holding her in a dancing position.

For a few days, John kept forgetting about the new table. Bethany quietly and patiently went behind him and moved the books. When he saw her do it, he said, "Oops. Sorry, honey. I have to break the old habit and make a new one."

"Do you mind if I move them? I don't want to be stubborn or…"

"No, of course I don't mind," he said interrupting her apology. "I told you I thought it would be very convenient, and it is. If you see me put them on the couch, simply remind me. If I move them myself, it might help me remember," he said in a gentle tone.

He continued, "I am glad you keep a neat and tidy home. I was reared that way. My mom was particular about keeping the house clean and orderly. 'A place for everything and everything in its place' was her motto. She inspected our bedrooms regularly. I remember when I was just a kid…"

Bethany took the opportunity to tease him, "You can remember back that far?"

"You little minx," he said as he started toward her with the look in his eye that she knew meant he would grab her and tickle her or hold her down while he blew on her neck and ear, which drove her crazy.

She ran and said, "You were saying something about your memories as a kid?"

She couldn't escape, and he grabbed her and held her with her feet off the ground. "Now what do you have to say, little smart aleck?"

Bethany was laughing so hard she could barely get out the words. "I am so sorry, Sir Knight."

Her affectionate title for him caused him to give her a gentle kiss instead of a tickle. He set her down, laughing. "That wasn't fair. As I was saying before I was so rudely interrupted," he teased "when I would go over to some of my friends' houses, and we would decide to toss a baseball around, they wouldn't be able to find their ball. Their rooms were an absolute mess with clothes thrown everywhere and stuff shoved under the bed. I was actually glad my mom made me keep things picked up. Of course, I didn't always feel that way while I was doing it."

"It was the same way at my house."

The next time Bethany saw him put his books down on the couch, she said, "John, the table."

"Oh, thanks," he said and picked them up and moved them. With only a few gentle reminders, he soon developed a new habit.

A few days before their first-month "anniversary," John had asked Bethany, "Did I ever tell you about my family's tradition that started with my grandparents?"

"No. Is it something special?"

"I am quite sure you will think so."

"Oh? Sounds interesting. Do you plan to continue it for another generation?"

"Yes. My paternal grandparents and then my parents have always done something every month on the date of their marriage. Usually they go out to dinner. When my grandparents didn't have enough funds for that, they would simply go out for a treat—like ice cream cones. So, my love, our first month will fall on Tuesday, and I have to work that evening. So we will go out to eat for lunch. We won't have time for a leisurely sit-down meal; we will do that next month. But for this week, I thought we would go to a coffee shop for a special drink, a sandwich, and a dessert. Does that sound okay to you?"

"Sounds great! I could kiss your grandfather for starting that tradition!"

John laughed. "You can kiss me instead."

Bethany was again grateful that John had taken his grandparents' tradition as their own when their second month anniversary came, and they celebrated with the promised dinner date.

Shortly after the school year had begun, several families who had seen Bethany's advertisement on the college note board contacted her regarding piano lessons for their children. Since she did not have a piano, she would give the lessons in their homes. Bethany would have to work around John's carpooling schedule, which left her four afternoons a week from which to choose. However, she decided she would only use two of them for piano students. She could study and do housework during the other two.

After several weeks she had fallen in love with her pupils and made new friendships with their mothers. She had a busy schedule, but it was not overwhelming. She soon found she could manage all of her different roles efficiently—at least most of the time. At times she ended up doing laundry late in the evening in order to keep one of them from running out of clean essentials. At such times she would be disgusted with herself. She had experienced problems with this same area when she lived in the dorm as a student.

She expressed her frustration to John, "Don't I ever learn anything? I feel like I make no progress at all. I get so discouraged."

"We all have struggles with old habits and sins rising up to haunt us," said John while hovering over her.

"I'm serious, John."

"I know, sweetheart. I am only trying to lighten your mood a little. Maybe you are trying to do too much. You might need to give up some of your piano students."

"Oh, no! I don't want to do that if I can help it. I will have to work on scheduling my duties better."

For the next few weeks, Bethany did better at keeping things done on time. Now something else was bothering her, and one evening as she and John settled into bed for the night she told him about it. "John, I don't feel like I am serving the Lord enough. I think I need to do some other church work."

"I don't know about your adding more, sweetheart. You're already quite busy. You are doing the most important thing that the Lord expects all Christians to do—soul winning. And you are actually serving the Lord with your piano lessons—helping to prepare children to serve in music ministries."

"But I get paid for that, John."

"That is true, but you know those parents could never find another teacher at the rate you charge."

"I still feel I need to do more—like maybe teaching a Sunday school class. I love working with children."

"That would take preparation time. You have homework from your class plus being ready for your piano students. Let me think and pray about this for a few days. Okay?"

"Sure. Thanks, John."

A few days later John brought up the subject. "I think I have a solution about finding you another place to serve. I was talking to another married student who happened to mention his wife works in a nursery. You wouldn't have to prepare a lesson for that responsibility. Would you enjoy doing that?

"Oh, yes. That would be perfect. Shall I inquire about any openings?"

"Yes. Go ahead."

Bethany learned that in a few weeks a lady working in the two-year-olds nursery would be moving away. Bethany was told she could be the replacement worker. She was delighted. She fixed a special meal the evening she had gotten the answer and gave John an extra big hug and extra kisses when he came home. "Wow! What is the occasion?" asked John after enjoying the welcome and smelling his favorite dinner cooking.

"I wanted to thank you for caring about my feelings and coming up with a solution for me. I found out today that there would be a place for me in the two-year-olds nursery in a few weeks. I am really happy about it."

"Well, good. I am happy for you too. Especially when it causes you to make meatloaf."

"Oh, you!" Bethany laughed, giving him a playful slug on the arm. Bethany felt that they were settling into the married state quite well. She remembered her frustration after the honeymoon about being submissive and the ensuing conversation with her mother. She was happy that it was getting easier for her, but there were still trying moments and issues as two people adjusted to living together. Even though John was quite considerate, tender, and romantic, she could see some things would always be done "his way."

However, where possible they found ways to compromise. One area involved the age-old problem of "how to squeeze the toothpaste tube." Bethany agreed with John that the tube had to be squeezed and used up from the bottom; but when the tube was brand-new, she found it easier to squeeze the middle for a while. She would begin correcting it and push and roll up the bottom after some was used, and she could get a better grip. John found her practice very irritating and was constantly fixing the tube. One day he happened to be shopping with Bethany when they needed a new tube. She noticed he picked out a different flavor than she had been buying. "That's not the right one, John."

"For me it is; I like this better."

"I didn't know that. You haven't said a word."

"I didn't want to make you feel badly. But I'd really rather get this kind."

"Why don't we get two? Then we can each have the kind we like, and we won't be bothering each other by the way we squeeze the tube."

"How did you know the way you squeeze it bothered me?" asked John, surprised.

"It was obvious—you were always going behind me and 'fixing' it. Besides, a few times I even heard you muttering about it."

"Okay, let's get two. That's a great idea."

Bethany laughed.

"What is so funny?"

Adding her choice of toothpaste to the shopping cart, Bethany answered, "Oh, I was only thinking about how little things can cause frustrations; I am happy we can usually find compromises."

"Usually?"

"Yes."

"What do you mean? I can't think of anything we haven't compromised on!"

"Well, there are…but never mind."

"But I don't mean to…"

Bethany interrupted him. "That was the last thing on our list. Let's check out. When we get to the car, I'll explain what I mean."

When they were in the car and on the way home, John said, "Like I said, I don't mean to be uncompromising."

"I know, John, and because you are sensitive and loving, it makes it easier for me to submit to you. God tells me to do so in His Word, and I want to obey. I know in the long run that we'll have a better marriage, and I will be happier for doing it God's way.

"You have certain principles you use to make decisions. I know that it is good and sensible for you to do that. Most of the time, that is," she added and laughed. "There have been times and will be others, I'm sure, when I forget that, and I just want my way. Later, I will probably realize you were right. But even if I never agree with your decision, I am glad, in principle, that you don't give in to me or let me sway you under those circumstances."

John answered, "I appreciate that you feel that way and let me lead, sweetheart. It makes me want to care for you with tenderness and never to walk all over you. It is obvious that you have a true inner strength that allows you to be gracious, feminine, and submissive. That is much of the reason why I love you and wanted to make you my wife. I'm sorry if I am stubborn or overbearing at times."

Bethany had seen women intent on dominating their husbands—never a sight she could respect. She wanted the joy and beauty that God had intended for her through a Godly marriage. She said, "Don't worry, I trust you as head of our home. And I don't want you to let me walk all over you either—even if I get frustrated and try sometimes."

"Little ol' you?"

"Yes, little ol' me. I still have a battle with submission. I suppose I always will. But I do find it is getting a little easier."

"Well, that's good."

"You would think so," she answered, pretending to be serious and put out about it.

John hastened to pacify her. "I meant it was good for you…"

Laughing, Bethany interrupted him, "I know what you meant. I got you on that one."

"You little scamp," he responded.

One day after this conversation, John came home and was quiet and distant. At first Bethany thought he was angry with her and then remembered the incident on registration day. She asked him, "What are you worried about?"

Bethany was totally surprised and dismayed at his response as he answered her sharply, "Are you correcting me? I'm supposed to be your spiritual leader—not the other way around." He turned away and walked into the kitchen to begin rummaging in the refrigerator.

Bethany was stunned into silence and then broke down into tears. John had never spoken to her in that way or used that tone of voice before. She hurried to the bedroom, shut the door, and threw herself on the bed. She began sobbing uncontrollably and pulled a pillow over her head in an effort to muffle the sound.

John heard her and then thought about how he had answered her. Remorseful, he went to her and gathered her in his arms. "I am so sorry, sweetheart. I should not have spoken to you that way."

When Bethany could speak, she said, "I don't understand what I said or did to upset you, John."

"I thought you were reprimanding me for the sin of worrying."

"I honestly wasn't thinking in those terms at all. I guess I used the wrong words."

"No, I overreacted. I think you put me under conviction because I really was worrying."

"Want to tell me about it?"

"It's not that earth-shattering. I am having a problem learning something I am going to be tested on. I guess I set too high a standard for myself at times, and I haven't even prayed about it. So I guess I needed to be reprimanded."

"But not by me."

"It wasn't really you. The Holy Spirit used your words, that's all. Excuse me, please, sweetie. I need to go do that praying right now."

One afternoon while Bethany was giving a lesson to a boy named Jimmy, his mother Nancy had a friend visiting. After the lesson Nancy introduced Bethany to her friend Molly. After the introduction, Molly asked Bethany if she would be interested in teaching another student.

"Oh, I am flattered by your request, but I don't see how I can add more to my schedule. It takes time to drive between houses."

"I don't have a piano, but Nancy has kindly offered to let me bring my son over so he could have a lesson right after Jimmy. It would only be the extra half-hour since you wouldn't have to drive to my house. Oh, please say yes. I can't afford the other teachers I know about, and David is really interested. Come here and meet Mrs. Holman, David."

"Hello, Mrs. Holman. Are you going to give me lessons? I really want to play the piano."

Bethany already had all of the piano students that she and John had agreed on. She answered doubtfully, "I don't know yet, David. I need to ask my husband."

"Please tell him I really, really want to take lessons. Okay?"

Bethany laughed. "Okay, but don't get your hopes up too much."

Very seriously David answered, "I will pray that he says yes."

As she drove home, Bethany had conflicting thoughts. She hated to disappoint David who seemed genuinely sincere about wanting lessons, or Molly, who had practically begged her to take him on. It would just be another half-hour, but she did still have a struggle keeping up with everything. She just did not know what to do.

That night when she told John about the situation, she could see the hopeful faces of David and his mother in her mind. She found herself begging John to let her do it!

"I don't know, Bethany. We have discussed your struggles to keep everything done. I don't want you stressed and overtired."

"But like Nancy said, I wouldn't have to drive somewhere else. It would only be another half-hour. Little David was so sweet, and he is praying you will let me. I hate to disappoint him."

"I want you to think carefully about the opportunity and pray about it. I will leave the final decision with you, but my personal opinion is that adding another student is not a good idea. You have told other people you couldn't take on any more students."

"I am sure if they even hear about it, they will understand that these circumstances are different."

"You sound like you have already made up your mind."

"No, no. I will do what you asked."

John sighed. "Sweetie, your heart is simply too tender."

Bethany did try to pray about it and consider John's words, but always David's little hopeful face rose up in her mind. In the end, she agreed to give him lessons.

To her dismay, beginning with the first lesson she discovered that Molly was a talkative person who always had questions about David's progress or simply wanted to chat. Bethany had a hard time getting away from the house, so the extra half-hour usually became at least forty-five minutes. Then she would be rushed to get grocery shopping and other errands done. John wanted her to be home before dark. She had to admit she should have listened to John's advice. She asked God to help her remember this lesson in the future.

— CHAPTER EIGHT —

Celebrating the Holidays

"And Levi made him a great feast in his own house…"
(Luke 5:29)

When November arrived, Bethany decided she had better get serious about the upcoming holidays. She had to finish Christmas shopping for her family and get the packages mailed early. She and John also needed to make their Thanksgiving plans. The Davenports had invited them to spend it with them, but Bethany really wanted to have it at home and do the cooking. She had thanked the Davenports for thinking of them but graciously turned down the invitation, explaining that the following year they would probably be living in a travel trailer, so she wanted to take advantage of the nice kitchen she presently had.

Knowing some college students couldn't go home for Thanksgiving, she suggested to John that they invite a few to join them. She especially wanted to invite Randy and also John's sister Ruth. John was enthusiastic about the idea.

"Ruth will be excited to come," he said. "She'll be flying home for Christmas and was probably hoping to spend Thanksgiving with us. Altogether for dinner, I'd say we could handle four extra people easily. Since we only have four chairs, we may have to borrow two or buy some folding ones—which might not be a bad idea. We could use them to sit outside once we are living in a travel trailer."

"Good thinking!"

John took a bow. "Thank you, my fair lady. On a serious note, are you sure you will have time for all of the preparations?"

"I have already thought about that. I will tell my piano students that there won't be any lessons that week. That will give me extra time to make some pies."

"You can make the pies?"

"You doubt me? I guess I haven't made you one yet. I'll practice on you this weekend. Then you can be the judge. What kind do you want?"

"For Thanksgiving, let's have a pumpkin and an apple. But this weekend, if you are serious, I would like a cherry."

"Okay. One cherry pie coming up."

Bethany was fairly confident about her pie-making abilities. She had practiced at home and had learned how to make a flaky crust almost as good as her mother's. She was a little nervous about the turkey and made several calls home with questions for her mother.

The following Saturday Bethany made a cherry pie, and John was very happy with the result.

Bethany left the inviting up to John and concentrated on planning for the items she would need. She was happy that Randy had gratefully accepted the invitation and had told John of others in the dorms who were not going home for Thanksgiving. It was not difficult to come up with four guests, two other men and Ruth. Actually, Ruth would spend the entire Thanksgiving break with them.

The week before Thanksgiving, the season's first big snowstorm hit their area. Bethany enjoyed the beauty but not the driving in the deep snow. She was grateful that during her senior year of high school there had been a heavier snowfall in Washington than usual. The schools were shut down, which usually happened in that area even though the snow was rarely very deep and did not last long. People in the milder western side of Washington were definitely not experts at driving in snow. Mr. Prescott had anticipated that Bethany might need to know how to navigate in such conditions at some point in her life and had taken her out in the family car to teach her and let her practice. Now she remembered those lessons but still did not feel really confident. At least John had put tire chains on the car—in Washington most people did not bother to put them on since there were so few days when it snowed.

Bethany thought of her friends, Donna and Sarah, who had to take their laundry to a Laundromat. It reminded her that she was blessed to be able to live in an apartment with laundry facilities down the hall from her apartment. Very few of the students' wives had that advantage.

In spite of her trepidation, she had to go to the store on the Monday before Thanksgiving to get the groceries she would need and to buy a set of folding chairs. She was relieved when she had safely navigated the roads and had returned to the apartment. After everything was put away, she made up a bed for Ruth in the computer room. John had brought home a rented rollaway bed in the morning. He picked up Ruth in the early afternoon after chapel. That Tuesday she helped Bethany with some house cleaning. Bethany found a tablecloth among the wedding gifts, which Ruth pressed and carefully draped over the chair they used in the computer room.

Wednesday morning she and Ruth made the two pies. That night after midweek service, Bethany went to bed early with the alarm set for early rising to get the turkey in the oven. John rose with her and helped her truss up the turkey and then carried the roaster pan to the oven for her. They had a quick breakfast, and then the two young women began the other food preparations. Ruth proved to be a good helper, and she and Bethany did a lot of catching up on their respective activities while they prepared and cooked the food, set a festive table, and set out snacks.

After their guests arrived, everyone enjoyed a few snacks and visited until they sat down to a delicious feast at three in the afternoon. The men proclaimed John a lucky man to have a wife who could cook so well. After the apple and pumpkin pies were served, they were even more enthusiastic.

Randy stayed after the other guests had left. "I just heard from Cindy. She plans to come out this spring for the teachers' conference held at the same time as the pastors' conference. It will be great timing—I've been saving up for a ring and will have enough by then. I have already talked to her dad, and he is fine with our getting engaged."

"Oh, Randy! That is great," exclaimed Bethany.

"Thanks. I was wondering if you two could help me?"

"We would be happy to," said John. "What do you have in mind?"

"Well, we better ask Bethany first because it would involve some work for her."

"I don't mind, Randy. Just tell me what you want me to do. This is so exciting. I'd be glad to help make it special—I have such great memories of what John did."

John said, "I do too, even though it didn't happen quite the way I had planned. But it was better, I think."

Randy outlined his plan, and Bethany and John were so enthusiastic they even made suggestions to do things more elaborately than Randy had dared hope for.

After Randy had left, John took Bethany in his arms and told her how proud he was of her and how much he had enjoyed the day.

On Friday the three of them went to Sarah and Paul's apartment. The men visited while Sarah helped Bethany make the silk flower arrangement to decorate their bedroom. Bethany was happy to learn how and liked the result as they positioned the silk blooms and greenery in a wall holder Sarah had helped her choose. Ruth watched for a while and then settled down with a book she had brought along. They went home after dinner and immediately mounted the new arrangement over their bed. It brightened the room pleasingly.

That evening Bethany received a phone call from Cindy. In an offended tone, Cindy said, "Thanks a lot, Bethany!"

Astounded, Bethany blurted, "For what? What did I do wrong?"

Cindy laughed. "Nothing. That's just the point. Randy called and was bragging on your wonderful dinner. Now I'll have to live up to it!"

Bethany laughed. "You had me going for a while. I thought you were really mad at me! I'm glad Randy enjoyed it. I really didn't do anything that hard. I had lots of fun."

"I guess I will have to get my mom to teach me more and do some practicing."

"That's how I learned. By the way, Randy told us you plan to come out this spring for the pastors' conference. That's great! I'm looking forward to seeing you."

"Yes. It is the same week as our school's break. I am looking forward to seeing all of my friends."

"Of course, you're not at all excited about seeing Randy."

"Not at all," laughed Cindy.

"We will have to have you two over for dinner while you are here, so you can see our apartment."

"I would love that, if you are sure it won't be too much trouble. I know you have a very busy schedule."

"It will be a perfect time. We won't have classes that week, and I will also cancel piano lessons so I can go to the sessions."

"Okay, then. The time will crawl by for me with the anticipation."

Bethany thought, "Oh, if you only knew what is in store for you! Randy is the one who is really going to be having problems waiting."

The next few weeks were extremely busy for Bethany as she began preparing for Christmas, adding decorating, shopping, wrapping, and mailing to her already full schedule. When the packages that had to be mailed were sent off, she added baking to her list. She enjoyed every bit of it but did feel robbed of some sleep. When the college's Christmas break arrived, she was able to sleep in a few mornings to get rejuvenated. She had everything ready by the last day before Christmas Eve. She had time to relax and contemplate the meaning of the Christmas season. To really make the season a time of joy and blessing, she received a very special phone call.

"Hello?"

"Is this Bethany Holman?"

"Yes."

"This is Mary, the hotel maid in Ellensburg."

"Oh, yes. I am so happy to hear from you."

"Do you have a few minutes to talk? I know this is probably a busy time for you."

"I was just sitting here, relaxing and thinking about the blessing of the birth of Jesus and how God has blessed me in other ways. I am thrilled to hear from you."

"Well, I just had to let you know what has happened in the last few months. It is all so amazing and awesome. I told Jimmy about getting saved, and I was so surprised when he told me he had gone to a Baptist church when he was a young boy. He had gotten saved and baptized. When he was a teenager, he backslid and dropped out of church. He was fine with my wanting to go to church, and he went with me the day I was baptized. Then he started really getting under conviction. He surprised me a few weeks later and told me he was going with me. At church he went forward to rededicate himself. Then he set up a meeting with the pastor and told him he knew we should get married! I didn't even have to bring up the subject. Isn't that great?"

"It is! I am so happy for you. Did you get married yet?"

"Yes. I am now Mary Miller. We are getting involved at the church, and we are both really happy. He told me to tell you thank you. It is all because of you."

"Not really. God did it. He just used me as His spokesperson."

"Well, you had a big part in it, and we will never forget."

"That means a lot to me. Is this your own number that came up on my cell phone?" Mary told her that it was, and Bethany said, "Is it okay if I save it to my phone so we can stay in touch?"

"Sure. That would be great."

Christmas morning John read the Christmas story from the Bible before they emptied their stockings. Bethany had put in fruit; John had gotten nuts and candy, and they had each bought the other a small gift. After breakfast they opened their gifts from their families. John suggested they make the fun last longer and wait until that evening to open the big gifts from each other. They called home to their families and then went to Donna and Peter's apartment. Donna had invited them and the Norbergs for Christmas dinner. Sarah and Bethany had both insisted on bringing something to contribute to the meal. They exchanged gifts after dinner and then enjoyed pie. When Bethany shared with her friends about the phone call from Mary, they all rejoiced with her.

Bethany and John had agreed earlier that they wanted to have the other two couples over for a New Year's Day dinner. They extended the invitation, which both couples were happy to accept. Sarah and Donna both offered to bring something to help with the meal.

When they had gone home and each opened their last gift, Bethany sighed with contentment. "What a wonderful first Christmas! It was perfect."

Bethany enjoyed entertaining their friends on New Year's Day. After dinner they played games and visited. The guests did not stay late, as they had all stayed up the night before to welcome the new year. After the last busy weeks, Bethany was ready to go to bed early.

The next morning John asked her, "Do you feel a little bit of a letdown now that the holidays are over, and we have to get back to our usual schedule?"

"A little," she admitted.

"Well, don't forget, my love, it is only about a month and a half until Valentine's Day. Would you like to go to the Valentine's banquet again? Married students are allowed to attend. Doug said he and Carrie would like us to join them again."

"Oh, yes! I would like that very much."

"Good. I will make our reservations. Would you mind wearing the blue dress that you wore at that Christmas party where I first saw you? You look really nice in blue."

"Sure, and thanks for giving me something special to anticipate."

Bethany had only a few days off from classes. She enjoyed sleeping in a little later, but she also used the time to catch up on some extra chores around the apartment. The rest of the month was busy as classes were finished up and final exams held. Again she appreciated a few days off before the next semester began.

John would be finishing his master's degree. Bethany decided to take a course on abnormal adolescent behavior since John was planning to do a lot of preaching at youth conferences and camps. She was also continuing to give piano lessons.

Besides finishing the courses for his master's degree, working, and helping with the youth ministry on Saturdays, John was having phone conversations with the evangelist, Ralph Gibson, discussing plans about traveling with him for about six months. Brother Gibson was preaching at a youth camp in August and hoped John and Bethany could join him. That would mean selling furniture and moving from the apartment as well as buying a truck and travel trailer between the last week of May and the beginning of August. But the plan would work out well as far as their lease on the apartment was concerned.

One day they were discussing their plans and Bethany asked, "When are we going to get the trailer?"

John paused, looking troubled. "I don't know yet. I need someone with experience to help me make such an important decision."

Bethany thought about it for a while then snapped her fingers as she thought of a possible solution. "The Davenports have had travel trailers. Maybe Brother Davenport would be willing to go shopping with us. There are probably plenty of sales lots in Detroit."

"Well, me wee one, you've got a brain in that little head of yours. What an excellent idea! I will contact Brother Davenport and ask him if he would be willing to do that. He is a very wise man; I know I can trust his opinions. If he is willing, we can go there in early June."

"What about selling the car and buying a truck to pull the trailer?"

"I guess we can mention the truck to our friends. When it gets closer to graduation, I will post a notice on the bulletin board at school about the furniture and the car. We'll take photos of them and print them from my computer, and if we don't get enough response from the college bulletin, we might put ads on the Internet. We also have to raise some support from churches. I have put my name in with the college for availability to fill pulpits—sometimes pastors or churches contact them asking for names."

"This is going to be a busy time! I guess it's good that I am going to have fewer piano students."

"When did that happen?"

"Just this morning one of the mothers called saying her family will be moving from this area because of her husband's job. I was teaching two of their children."

"I am glad to hear that, Bethany. It will give you extra time to start sorting and packing things."

"Already?"

"Yes. Then it won't be so hard at the last minute. You can start sorting clothing, and as soon as spring comes, then pack our winter clothes in suitcases or boxes. You need to leave some suitcases to use for our trip to Detroit. I don't know how much storage space we will have in the RV. I am sure we will have to thin out our wardrobes."

"Oh, yes. I have been thinking about that already. I am going to ask around about my formal dresses and also ask Betsy if she wants any of them. I won't have any more need for them, and we certainly won't have room for extras like that."

John took her in his arms and whispered against her ear, "You are being so brave and cooperative about this whole thing. It just makes me love you more and more."

"It's not a great sacrifice in comparison to what many of the Christian martyrs have gone through over the centuries."

Bethany took John's advice and started sorting their clothing. She gave away some of her clothes, knowing she would still need some clothes for every season and climate as they traveled. John went through his things and made piles to give away and others to be packed.

One day Bethany realized that the Valentine's banquet was only a week away. She pulled out the blue dress and pressed it and also brushed and pressed John's best suit. She experimented with her hair until she came up with a style she could do herself—curls pulled back with a comb.

The day of the banquet John came home with two surprises—a tuxedo with a blue tie and a cummerbund to match her dress and a beautiful corsage of white roses and blue ribbons in a slightly darker shade than her dress.

Bethany exclaimed, "Oh, John, I hope you always stay this romantic. You make me feel so special and loved."

"That's exactly how I want you to feel! I am sorry you went to the trouble of pressing my suit unnecessarily, but I wanted to surprise you."

"Oh, that was no big deal. Besides, it needed it anyway."

"Well, I will be putting it to good use. Next weekend I have a preaching engagement. The pastor of a church in a nearby town called and asked me to fill his pulpit for the entire Sunday while he is on vacation. In the course of the conversation, he asked what I was planning on doing after graduation. When I explained my plan, he said he wanted me to tell the congregation about it so they could possibly consider supporting me. Oh, and we need to practice some numbers that you could play and sing with me—I told him about that part too, and he said we should do it for his congregation."

"John, that is great. Wouldn't it be wonderful if they decided to support you?"

"Us, my love. You are also a part of this ministry."

"Okay, us."

"Now, let's get ready for the banquet and enjoy a relaxing evening."

When they arrived at the banquet, they met Doug and Carrie. Carrie was especially excited because she had on her own, brand-new dress, which she had been saving for this occasion since Mrs. Davenport had bought it for her during the previous year's spring break. Bethany was enthusiastic and sincere in her compliments to Carrie, which boosted Carrie's self-confidence. Bethany's opinion was almost as important to her as Doug's.

They also saw John's sister Ruth and her date. She looked very pretty in the pink gown she had worn for their wedding and was radiant with the excitement of her first formal dating occasion.

Later, on their way home, Bethany expressed her gratefulness for a wonderful first Valentine's Day with great warmth. "This evening will be a wonderful memory, John. Thanks so much."

"My pleasure, sweetheart."

— CHAPTER NINE —

Blessings From the Lord

"And the heavens shall praise thy wonders, O LORD.…"
(Psalm 89:5)

The following Sunday they drove to the nearby town and found the Baptist church where John had been asked to preach. One of the deacons was waiting to greet them. After introductions, he took them to the auditorium. He knew how to work the sound system and turned it on so they could practice the special music they would be sharing during the service. Bethany was grateful for his thoughtfulness. It helped her to be more confident and at ease when she had time to warm up and become acquainted with the instrument and the acoustics of the building. John also liked the opportunity to warm up and use the microphone.

John taught the adult Sunday school class that morning and included a brief testimony and explanation of their plans for their future ministry. He mentioned that they would be using a truck and travel trailer and asked the people to be praying for the Lord's leading in meeting these major expenses.

During the break between Sunday school and church, a man approached John and asked him to step away from the crowd where they could talk more privately. He introduced himself as Andrew Sorenson. He asked John what he was currently using as a vehicle. When John told him, he said, "I thought so. I saw it parked outside and did not recognize it as belonging to a church member. I took the liberty of looking it over a little. Could we meet after church for a little spin in your car? After I see the inside and know a few more things about it, I may have a proposition for you."

"You surely have my curiosity aroused now. Sure, that should be no problem."

"I just thought of another idea. I'll take you and your wife to dinner. That will make me points with my wife too," he joked. "After church I'll have her take your wife to a local restaurant so they can hold a place in line for us; it is popular, but worth the wait. We'll join them there."

"Sir, that's not necessary…"

"I really want to do that, Brother Holman."

"Thank you. My wife and I really appreciate it."

John went to inform Bethany of this plan, and Andrew explained to his wife. Then he brought her over to the Holmans. John introduced Bethany to them, and Andrew introduced his wife Becky.

Andrew said, "Brother Holman, I am in the choir, so I'll go with you to show you where to line up to enter the platform for the service." Turning to the ladies, he added, "We will leave you two to get acquainted now."

Becky invited Bethany to sit by her, and she introduced Bethany to a few ladies sitting nearby. Becky's daughter Jessica, who had just come in after leaving her baby in the nursery, joined them. Jessica sat on the other side of Becky, leaving enough space for their husbands to sit with them when the choir left the platform and sat in the congregation.

As they took their seats, Bethany mused about being in the morning service instead of the two-year-old nursery. Earlier in the week she had made arrangements for a substitute. It was going to be exciting to have a part in this service, but she missed the little ones.

After John was introduced to the congregation, he made some introductory remarks and then asked Bethany to come to the platform. He introduced her and gave a short account of her Christian upbringing and how they had met. He had done that at the church where he preached at the beginning of their trip from Washington State to Indiana, and he had discovered that people enjoyed hearing about their encounter at the library on a slippery winter morning. He told how he had been thinking about her since spotting her at a party, where neither one of them had fit in or had been comfortable.

While he did that, Bethany quietly moved to the piano. At a signal from him, she began the introduction of the number they would be doing. Many "Amens" from the congregation when they finished the number assured them that their duet had been a blessing.

Bethany left the platform while John prayed and returned to her seat next to Becky. After the service, Jessica complimented Bethany on her playing and singing and excused herself to retrieve her baby. Becky asked Jessica to bring little Rachel so she could show her to Bethany. Jessica complied, and after arriving with the six-month-old child, Becky asked Bethany if she would like to hold her. Bethany looked at Jessica questioningly, and the mother was quick to assure Bethany that she did not mind. Bethany cuddled the little girl and discovered a motherly longing growing in her heart. She was a little surprised—she had been so busy that she had not even thought about starting her own family. She knew it would be a little longer before she and John were ready for that step. She wanted to be used to their new lifestyle before introducing a child into the picture. But she certainly enjoyed holding this darling little girl!

After a few minutes, she gave the baby back to Jessica and moved to the back to stand with John as he shook hands. When everyone else had left, the deacon whom they had met at the beginning brought John an envelope with a check enclosed and thanked John and Bethany for coming. After Andrew told the deacon he was treating the Holmans to dinner, they headed for the parking lot. As Bethany got in the car with Becky, John took Andrew to his. The two women went on to the restaurant as planned.

As Becky and Bethany waited in line to be seated, they visited. They discussed their families and shared their personal salvation experiences.

In the meantime, Andrew had directed John to drive to his home. When he had told John where to park, Andrew said, "This is my home. I want to show you my truck. It is only five years old and has very few miles. I thought I would use it more than I have." John was very impressed with its extended cab, which provided a second seat for passengers. Indeed the truck would definitely fill his needs, but it looked to be beyond his budget. He wondered what Mr. Sorenson had in mind. After looking at the truck Andrew asked, "Would you mind letting me drive your car to the restaurant where our wives are waiting?"

John answered, "Not at all."

The men arrived right as their turn came to be seated. After they had ordered, Andrew told them what he had in mind. "I have been thinking of selling my truck for some time, and we need a car for our teenage son. You haven't met him because he helps on a bus and in junior church. He rides after church to take the children home, and then he stays for the afternoon program. They bring back some of the teens for the afternoon, feed them, and have a program for them until time for the evening service. Because he helps with that, he eats lunch with the bus teens."

John said, "He sounds like a dedicated young man. I am sure you are proud of him."

"Definitely. If he continues in this path, I believe the Lord will greatly use him someday. He is saving money for Bible college.

"Anyway, I would like to make an even trade with you—my truck, which can pull anything you end up buying, for your car."

"Oh, Brother Sorenson, your truck looks like exactly what we need, but it's surely worth more than our car."

"But your car would be a perfect first car for my son. An even trade is my offer. What do you say?"

"I'm—speechless!"

Andrew reached across the table and shook John's hand. "Then it's settled. All we have to do is transfer ownerships."

Bethany could say nothing. She was so surprised and moved by Andrew's kindness, her tear-filled eyes had to speak for her.

After the meal, they went to the Sorensons' home and exchanged addresses and phone numbers and took care of paperwork arrangements for transferring vehicle titles. Andrew insisted on giving them the keys and having them begin driving the truck immediately. They followed the Sorensons back to the church for the evening service. John preached, and the couple did another musical special. Afterward, the awestruck couple drove the truck home. The next day, John would take care of changing the ownership and mail the car title to Andrew. They went to bed feeling like they were already dreaming.

At the beginning of March, Bethany and John were busy preparing for mid-semester exams. Once that was behind her, Bethany started thinking about the surprise for Cindy that they were helping Randy plan. She was going to cook and serve a fancy dinner, restaurant-style, to make a romantic setting for Randy's proposal. He had wanted to buy all of the groceries, but they told him they wanted to provide the meat. They ate more simply than usual the week before in order to save up to buy tenderloin steaks to serve. That purchase would be a surprise for Randy as well, for Bethany had told him she was planning to make a meatloaf. She gave him a list of items she needed for the rest of the meal, and he had them to her a week in advance.

As the pastors' and teachers' conferences neared, Bethany also needed to do the baking she had signed up for to help with snacks that would be provided for the delegates. After that, since there were no college classes during conference week, she completely focused on making Randy and Cindy's dinner look and taste special. She pressed a tablecloth with matching linen napkins and bought pink candles to match the flowers in the border design on the tablecloth. For a centerpiece, Bethany used a vase of pink silk flowers from their wedding. She bought two curtains she found at a thrift store and enlisted John's help to put up a makeshift clothesline on which to hang them in order to separate the table from the kitchen. She had pressed a white shirt and black slacks for John and a white blouse and black skirt for herself.

The day before the dinner Bethany baked a brownie torte. The next morning she made sweetened whipped cream to top it. She set aside two of the napkins and tied them with pink ribbons. One had the diamond engagement ring fastened with the ribbon. Other napkins were already at each place setting.

One of their wedding gifts was a top-of-the-stove grill, which Bethany used to grill the steaks. She made twice-baked potatoes, bacon-seasoned green beans, and a fancy salad.

The conference was to begin that evening, so John and Randy picked up Cindy at her hotel about 4:30. Randy had told her the Holmans had invited them to come early to visit before eating a dinner. That way they could arrive at church on time. John acted as chauffeur and drove to the apartment. When they arrived, he hurried ahead and knocked on the door to warn Bethany, carefully shielding his actions from Cindy's view. Bethany hurried to the door and opened it, revealing her server's outfit, complete with a white apron. As she was greeting Cindy and Randy, John slipped into the kitchen and wrapped a white dishtowel around his waist. Then he and Bethany escorted an astonished Cindy to the curtained-off dining area, pulled back one curtain, and revealed the beautifully set table with lighted candles. Randy helped her to be seated as Bethany and John pulled the curtain back into place and disappeared into the kitchen. Randy said grace, and the couple started on their salads.

About fifteen minutes later, Bethany and John cleared away the salad plates and then brought in the main course. Cindy tried to express her gratitude as well as compliment Bethany on the cooking and decorating. Bethany answered, "You relax and enjoy it. I loved doing it."

Randy was astounded when he saw the steaks. He started to say something, but John motioned for him to keep still. Bethany and John departed to the kitchen where they enjoyed grilled hamburgers and potatoes and beans. Bethany had the desserts, the other set of napkins, and clean forks on a tray. Every so often they peeked into the curtained off dining area to see whether the two sweethearts were ready for the dessert. When they were, they entered to clear the dishes, silverware, and napkins.

Then John carried in the tray, and Bethany brought fresh coffee to refill their cups. John put the desserts in front of them and laid down the clean forks wrapped in fresh napkins. He made sure to place Cindy's down so the ring was on the bottom of the napkin. Then they quietly retired to the opening in the curtain where they could watch unobtrusively. Cindy was talking to Randy. Bethany and John were breathless with anticipation. Finally Randy unwrapped his napkin and said, "Let's eat our dessert, sweetheart. We don't want to be late for the preaching."

"Oh, yes. I'm sorry. It seems like there is so much to catch…" She stopped mid-sentence and gasped as she saw the ring tied to her napkin.

Immediately Randy slipped to one knee and said, "Cindy, I love you and want you for my wife, to be mine for always. I have your father's permission to propose. Will you accept my ring and my hand in marriage?"

"Of course!" Cindy shrieked with her customary exuberance as she jumped up from her chair, tipping it over. John was able to jump forward to grab it before it hit the floor and then retreated again.

Turning to Randy she exclaimed, "I had no idea! I didn't know you were ready for this, and I didn't know you had talked to my dad! You are downright sneaky, Randy Connor," she added with a laugh. Her sparkling eyes showed her excitement and joy.

"Oh! I was so surprised I haven't even looked at the ring." She picked up the napkin and tried to untie the ring, but she was quite jittery from the surprise. Randy pulled out his pocketknife, cut the ribbon, and dropped the ring into Cindy's hand. "It's so beautiful! Here, Randy, put it on my finger."

In her excitement she reached toward him with her right hand.

"Uh, sweetheart, I think it's supposed to go on your left hand?"

"Oh, my goodness!" exclaimed the distracted Cindy and then burst into giggles.

They all laughed uproariously with her. Finally Randy regained control, and Cindy was able to hold her left hand still long enough for him to slip on the beautiful diamond solitaire. Then he pulled out a ring box, opened it and held it out for her to see a beautiful wrap ring of diamonds and sapphires. "The wedding band, Cindy. I hope you can wear it before too much longer."

"Oh, me too, Randy! That is going to look so amazing when we put them together. I couldn't have picked anything I liked any better. And you put my birthstones on it. What a special touch! They are beautiful sapphires. Thank you so much. Let me show it to Bethany and John."

Their friends stepped back inside the curtains, and Cindy held out the ring box to Bethany. "Isn't that the most gorgeous wrap?"

"Yes, now let me see the diamond ring."

"Oh, yes," she said, laughing. "He's got me so flustered!" She held out her hand to Bethany and then to John.

After they had both admired the rings, John said, "Now you two better eat that dessert. We need to leave fairly soon to be on time for the preaching service."

"Oh, yes! It looks delicious, Bethany, and fattening. I'll eat every bite and then diet for two weeks to pay for it!" Cindy threw her arms around Bethany, "You knew he was going to propose!" she accused. "What a wonderful surprise! You made it all so special and romantic! Thank you, thank you."

They all laughed at the irrepressible Cindy, and then Bethany and John retreated to the kitchen. They agreed on eating their dessert later and worked together to load the dishwasher and clean up the kitchen. In spite of their host's protests, Randy and Cindy helped clear their dessert dishes and take down the curtains. Then they grabbed their Bibles and went out to the car. They all sat together during the service and were also joined by Donna and Peter. Cindy threw her arms around Donna in greeting and then impulsively patted her stomach. She declared, "Donna, you are a beautiful mother-to-be!"

"Thank you, Cindy. I am glad to see you have not changed. Just as enthusiastic about life as ever!"

"That's a nice way to say I am high-strung," said Cindy with a laugh.

"*High-spirited* would be a better description. I like that you are so passionate about everything. I would love to see you in action in your classroom. I bet those kids adore you."

Randy whispered, "I don't know about the kids, but I sure do! Show her, Cindy."

Cindy held out her hand for Donna to see the ring. Now Donna grabbed her in a bear hug. "I am so happy for you two."

They all settled into their seats as the instruments began the prelude.

Elaine had written a letter telling Bethany that she and her parents, the Davenports, would also be attending the conference. As Bethany and John sat with their friends waiting for the service to begin, Bethany looked for them in the large crowd of people, but she had not yet spotted them. Elaine had said her father wanted the Holmans to meet them at their hotel for breakfast the next day. Bethany thought, "Even if we don't see each other at church tonight, we will still be able to get together."

At another location in the huge auditorium, Elaine and her parents had found seats. Elaine was looking around trying to spot Bethany and John. Suddenly, a young man who reminded her of her ex-husband, Mark Briscoe, arrested her attention. She told herself she was crazy and continued looking for the Holmans, but her eyes kept straying back to the young man. Her body tensed as she stared, hoping to get a better, clearer view of his full face. Mr. Davenport noticed her tenseness and asked, "What is it?"

"That man over there—he looks like Mark."

"Where?"

"The third row back in the far section."

"Oh, I see him now. You're right. I see a strong resemblance. Let's check him out at the break."

Elaine had a hard time concentrating on everything that went on before the first break. Then she and her dad quickly left their seats, asking Martha to save them. They didn't have time to explain what they were doing. The two of them moved as quickly as possible in the direction where the young man had been sitting. Because of the crowd, it took considerable time to reach the place, and by then, he had moved out of the auditorium.

They exited out the nearest door and split up. As Elaine moved through the crowd, all at once she was looking straight into his face. Their gazes locked, and now she was sure—it was Mark!

He made no move, but Elaine hurried toward him. "Mark, I didn't expect to see you here."

Surprised that she was even speaking to him, he guardedly replied, "I am definitely as surprised as you are. I had heard about you getting saved and changing your life completely."

"What brings you here?"

"I was saved in prison. I was recently released and joined a church. My pastor suggested I come here with him. So here I am. It's been great so far, hasn't it?"

With embarrassment, Elaine answered, "I have to admit, I haven't been able to concentrate much. I spotted you at the beginning, although I wasn't positive it was you. It was such a surprise to see you here, I mean, I didn't know…"

"I understand. I am pretty surprised about it myself," he remarked, with a small chuckle.

"It is so great that you are saved. We'll have to get together when we have more time to talk so we can share our experiences."

"I would like that."

Right then, George Davenport found them. "Mark, it really is you!"

Just then the lights blinked, indicating the break was almost over. Elaine quickly asked, "What hotel are you staying at?" She found a piece of paper and pen in her purse and wrote down the name. "Is it okay if we call you?"

"Of course, I hope you will."

"Okay. Talk to you later then."

They hurried to their seats. Martha Davenport asked, "What have you two been up to?"

"Sorry about rushing off with no explanation, Mother. We didn't mean to be rude. You will never guess who we saw and talked to."

"Who?"

"Mark!"

"Are you kidding?"

"No. We are going to call him and get together."

There was no more time to talk, so Martha just smiled at her daughter to show how happy she was that their prayers had been answered.

In the morning, when John and Bethany reached the hotel and joined the Davenports in the breakfast room, they were surprised to see that Elaine was sitting at a different table with a young man. Mr. Davenport explained in a low tone, "We ran into Elaine's ex-husband last night at the church. What a surprise and answer to prayer! He has recently been saved, and his pastor brought him to the meetings."

"Praise the Lord!" exclaimed John. "Bethany and I have been praying about that."

"Hopefully, they will join us in a few minutes. You'll have to excuse them. They have a lot of catching up to do," explained Martha.

"That is certainly understandable," Bethany assured her. "We are just very happy for them." She glanced quickly in the direction of the other table and saw Elaine holding photographs—Bethany was quite sure they were photos of Michael.

When the waitress came to take their orders, Elaine heard her, so she and Mark hurried over to join them. They sat down and ordered along with the others. When the waitress left, Elaine made introductions. Bethany and John greeted Mark warmly. It was quite evident that he was overwhelmed with surprise and gratitude at the response, especially from the Davenports.

Mark said, "Thank you for your kindness. I am still getting used to the warmth and openness of fellow Christians." Turning to the Davenports, he added, "I guess I was expecting you to react like my parents. In spite of my protestations, they insist that everything was Elaine's fault. She was just telling me that my mom would not give her any information about me. Even though Elaine is too polite to say so, I suspect my mother was pretty rude to her over the phone. I am very sorry. The problem is, they also need to find the Lord."

"Of course," George Davenport agreed, "and I think I am safe in saying that everyone here will be putting them on their prayer list."

There was a murmur of agreement around the table. John pulled out a notecard and pen and asked, "What are their names?"

Mark answered, "Charles and Betty Briscoe. Thank you all so much."

George Davenport spoke up again. "Elaine, we all understand that you two have a lot of catching up to do. We won't be offended if you go back to that other table. It is still empty."

"Oh, are you sure?"

Martha answered with a warm smile, "Of course, dear. Make good use of the time you have together."

They excused themselves, stood up, and returned to the other table. When the waitress came with the food, George asked her to take Mark's and Elaine's to them at the other table. They were talking so much that they didn't finish their breakfast before George went over and told them they needed to be leaving for the church. Mark had told his pastor he would meet him at Crossroads Baptist Church, as Mr. Davenport had told him over the phone he would give him a ride after breakfast. Mark had walked a few blocks from the hotel where he was staying to meet them earlier.

When he met up with his pastor, Mark told him, "I can't believe it's the same woman to whom I was married! And her parents—what a change! They have been very accepting and forgiving. She gave me a picture of our little boy and told me he also is saved. I'll show it to you later," he whispered as the musicians started playing.

During the first break, Mark took his pastor to meet Elaine and her parents. They shook hands and agreed to meet for the lunch break.

Bethany and John were also planning on joining them. Over lunch Mark explained he had gone to prison for a drug offense and heard the Gospel from a member of the church he was currently attending. He was planning on joining the prison ministry group in a few years—after he had proven he had been truly converted and could hopefully get clearance to go into a prison. He needed to grow spiritually and get used to life on the outside before he could help others.

George asked him whether he had any training and if he had found a job. Mark explained that he had done some correspondence courses in computer science, and one of the men in the church had helped him get a job in his company. After a trial period of six months he would be considered a permanent employee, eligible for benefits. "The Lord has been blessing me through other Christians—in ways I don't feel I deserve."

"None of us deserve God's grace and blessings, Mark. Don't be too hard on yourself," responded John.

"I am ashamed of being in the drug scene."

Quietly Elaine commented, "I have things I am also ashamed of. I was a spoiled brat who partied most of the time and wasn't much of a mother to our child. My mother was stuck with most of his care."

"Until we hired Bethany and all of our lives were changed," said Martha as she smiled at Bethany.

"Elaine told me a little about that, and I can definitely see a big change in all of you."

George asked, "When are you coming to visit and meet your boy?"

"We haven't gotten that far," Mark answered as he glanced at Elaine. "Frankly, I didn't know if I should…" He faltered and tried again. "If I would…"

Elaine rescued him. "Why don't we keep in touch for a few months? When you are feeling a little more confident and feel ready for another big step, let me know. We will make arrangements. I don't want to keep you away…" she paused, blushed, and hurried on, "…from our son."

Martha and George both had to hide knowing smiles. They had seen a new animation in Elaine since the previous evening and suspected that old feelings were being stirred in her.

Mark's pastor spoke up. "I agree with that idea. I think it is an excellent plan."

George said, "That arrangement will also give us time to prepare Michael. Mark, lately he has begun showing some curiosity about you."

"Yes, he also asked me several times about his father," added Elaine. "We haven't had enough time to talk for me to tell you all of this, Mark. He asked me why his father left and why he doesn't come to see him. Now I can tell him that I have seen you. How do you want me to answer his question?"

"I definitely want to see him and establish a relationship. You two have been on my mind a lot. I just hadn't gotten up my courage to try to contact you. I am trying to go slowly, one thing at a time. Finding a place to rent was a challenge because of just getting out of prison. I don't blame people. They don't know whether or not I really have changed just because I tell them that now I am a Christian. I finally found a Christian landlord who was willing to take a chance on me, for which I am very grateful—to him and to the Lord."

"Okay. Here is my phone number. Maybe in a few weeks you and Michael will be ready to talk over the phone. After that we could arrange a face-to-face meeting."

"That sounds good to me, Elaine. You are being more than fair, and I appreciate your generosity. Here is my phone number and address. I hope Michael will be able to accept me."

"I am sure he will—even if it takes a while. He has had a lot of changes in his life in the last few years and seems to be handling them quite well. We will have to bathe the whole thing in a lot of prayer."

John spoke up, "Bethany and I will be praying. If there is ever anything we could do to help, like talking with Michael, just let us know."

"I will keep that in mind," said Elaine. "He likes you and respects you a lot. You might be a big help…and Bethany also." She turned to Bethany. "He still adores you."

During the last two days of the conference, Mark spent every meal break with Elaine and her parents. They crammed in as much conversation as possible. Mark was anxious to hear all about Michael, as well as the details of Elaine's life since their divorce. She told him about her trip to Europe, and the Davenports described the happenings in their home during that period. Mark marveled at how the Lord had worked.

Bethany and John returned to meeting their other friends for lunches during the rest of the conference. Friday morning they picked up Ruth, who was going to spend spring break with them. At the college they saw the Davenports again, as they had traveled there to take Carrie to their home for the break. Carrie had matured so much that she felt comfortable going without having Bethany along for support. Bethany knew the Davenports would spoil her and make her stay very pleasant.

John had a brief conversation with Mr. Davenport about their plans to shop in Detroit for their trailer with George's help and advice. They decided on four weeks after commencement. Mrs. Davenport reminded them that they wanted John and Bethany to stay with them while they were in Detroit.

Bethany and John's sister Ruth enjoyed the time together during the spring break. While John was at work, she and Ruth went shopping or prepared special treats. On Thursday, they took her back to campus. They all had a month and a half of classes and then final examinations. John's family would be coming out for his graduation, when he would receive a Master of Pastoral Theology degree. They would stay for several days, and then Ruth would travel home with them for the summer.

Bethany tried not to think about the busy time they would have after that until they joined with Evangelist Ralph Gibson. Instead, she concentrated on finishing her course work and being prepared for the final exam. During this period people contacted them who were interested in buying furniture and decorative items that they had advertised. Bethany took their names and addresses so they could do the transactions later.

The next exciting event was the birth of Donna's little girl, Elizabeth. Bethany went to the hospital a few hours after the baby's arrival and was thrilled to be able to hold the newborn. Again she felt the stirring of her motherly instincts and a distinct longing for a child of her own growing in her heart. Donna's parents came from Detroit to help out for the first week. John and Bethany visited Donna and Peter and the Cornells when the baby was three days old. Bethany made a casserole and some cookies for them, which Donna and Mrs. Cornell appreciated. John took a turn holding little Elizabeth, and Bethany caught her breath at the sight of her big brawny husband tenderly looking down at the little bundle in his arms. It only confirmed what she had always known—John would make a great dad.

Finally the middle of May came—time for final examinations. Both were happy when that was behind them. Bethany was glad she only had one class and when that exam was done, she could concentrate on getting ready to entertain John's family.

John's parents, his sister Naomi, and his brother James arrived the afternoon before commencement exercises. Bethany had dinner going in a slow cooker so she could go to the airport with John to greet them. Bethany enjoyed entertaining but was a trifle nervous about cooking for her mother-in-law. Mrs. Holman remembered how she had felt as a newlywed and worked at putting Bethany at ease. She was kind, complimentary, and helped her daughter-in-law without taking over. Bethany soon relaxed and enjoyed the visit.

They were all very proud of John when he received his advanced degree. Carrie sat with them during the ceremony and was teary-eyed when Doug also received his degree. Carrie had one more year to finish, and she was hoping that after that she and Doug could get married. In the meantime, he was going to start working in a youth ministry in Chicago, trying to prevent young people from falling prey to gangs.

The next day all of the Holmans went to the campus to clean out Ruth's belongings from the dormitory. They put some things in storage for her to use the following year and shipped some to California. After that they relaxed and did some sightseeing.

When John's family had left for California, Bethany and John started sorting the items in their apartment: things to keep, things to sell, or things to give away. Their pickup truck came in very handy as they delivered some things to other married students and took other items to thrift stores. They wanted to be ready to vacate the apartment easily in case they were able to buy an RV while in Detroit.

Before the time to go, they were down to the bare necessities—bedroom furniture, table and chairs, and the four folding chairs they would keep to use in the RV. John knew of a student who was getting married during the summer and was currently looking for an apartment. He and John made arrangements with the landlord for him to take the apartment when the Holmans were ready to vacate. Since a new renter was lined up, the landlord would not hold the Holmans to their lease or penalize them.

The young man also wanted to buy the bedroom furniture and table set. He was happy to get those items at a good price from the Holmans. The purchase would make things easier for both families.

During this time John had also sent out letters to the churches they had already visited. Bethany's home church as well as John's immediately sent them checks. The church in Ellensburg wrote that their work would be presented for a vote to the congregation at the next quarterly business meeting. The pastor of the church in Minnesota wrote back that he was presenting it to the deacon board, and if they agreed, it would go before the congregation in a few weeks. The church in Wisconsin said they would take them on for support beginning in January, as did the one in Indiana.

A week before they were scheduled to go to Detroit, Michigan, Pastor Butler of Faith Baptist in Detroit called and asked John to preach and do a music special on the Wednesday evening following their arrival. John said he would be happy to, but he would have to check with the Davenports about staying longer. When he called Mrs. Davenport, she enthusiastically assured him they would be happy to have them stay as long as they liked. John said, "I guess it will give us more time to shop if we don't find an RV on Saturday."

"Yes, you will probably need time to get paperwork done too. Some places only have models on hand; you might have to order what you want."

"Actually, I am hoping to find a used one in good condition."

"Well, whatever happens, you and Bethany are always welcome to stay here as long as is necessary. We enjoy having you. I think Michael needs some time with you too—maybe for that little talk you offered to have with him at the pastors' conference. Elaine has brought up the subject of Mark, and Michael has mixed feelings. He is struggling with accepting his dad after all these years of absence."

"Of course he is. That is only natural. I hope I can help somehow. I will be in prayer about that matter. We have been praying about the situation since pastors' conference. Could you have Elaine contact me before we get there so I know what she has told Michael so far?"

"I will pass on that message to her."

"Thanks, and thank you for your overwhelming generosity."

"Don't mention it."

John called Pastor Butler and accepted the invitation. John gave his notice at his part-time job. The following Thursday would be his last day of work.

Sunday afternoon, Elaine called. After catching up on each other's latest happenings, Elaine asked to speak to John. "Mother said that John asked me to contact him before you come to Detroit. He wanted to talk to me about Michael. This is a good time for me, as Michael went to eat with them after church."

"Yes, I know John wants to try to help. I'll give him the phone."

"Hello, Miss Davenport."

"Hello, Brother Holman. Thank you so much for offering to help Michael with this situation with his dad. Mark and I are communicating quite a bit. Some of the old feelings are stirring, but we are taking it slowly and cautiously. I have told Michael that we were married young, and neither one of us was saved. We couldn't get along so we divorced. I didn't hide the fact that we both did wrong things, and his dad ended up going to prison. I could tell that bothered Michael a lot. I assured him that God had forgiven Mark and that Mark had changed. I left the subject alone after that and prayed until Michael brought it up again. He said, 'You have been talking to…my dad on the phone, haven't you?'

"I told him, 'Yes, we have talked quite a few times since we ran into each other at the pastors' conference. Does that bother you?' I could tell he had a hard time saying, 'My dad.'

"Then he asked, 'Well, why is he calling? What does he want?' So I told him Mark wanted to come for a visit because he really wanted to see his son."

"How did he react to that?"

"He exploded and shouted, 'I don't want an ex-con visiting me. I want him to just stay away!' "

"Oh, my!"

"I know! I asked him where he had learned that word. He said he had talked to one of the older boys at school."

"The other boy probably also gave him the idea that he didn't want to see Mark. I will try to talk to him," John said. "It will take time. I am glad you and Mark aren't rushing him. It is not surprising that Michael would be upset."

"What really concerns me, Brother Holman, is that he is getting back some of his old rebellious attitudes. He doesn't want to obey me and is talking back. I even had to spank him the other day, and I haven't had to do that for almost a year."

"We will be arriving next Saturday to shop for the RV. Are you planning on joining us?"

"If you don't mind, I would enjoy looking at them with you, and Michael would spend every waking minute with you if he could."

They both laughed. John suggested that he and Bethany take Michael out for dinner Monday night. "Maybe we can also play miniature golf or something. When he has had fun and is relaxed, maybe he will open up with me."

"That sounds like a good plan. I hope he will share his feelings and listen to you. My dad has tried to talk to him, but Michael just clams up."

"We will see you next Saturday, Elaine. Don't worry—I think this attitude will pass."

"Thanks, Brother Holman."

The following Friday they luxuriated in the knowledge that John did not have to go to work, and they had a day completely to themselves. They slept in and then enjoyed a delicious brunch of omelets and biscuits. John took Bethany shopping and bought her a new outfit. Then he took her out for dinner. "John, you are completely spoiling me," she protested.

"I love doing it. Besides, you spoiled me with that delicious breakfast this morning. So we are now even."

"We won't be even unless we buy you some new clothes. Please, honey. You could use some new shirts and ties. Couldn't we afford that?"

"I guess so. I really hadn't even thought about it. Some of my shirts are getting a little worn."

"Good. As soon as we finish dinner, we can go back to the mall. I saw some sales in some of the stores. Maybe they will have some men's clothing marked down—like my outfit was. Even if there is no sale, I would still like to get you something. Remember, we won't need grocery money for the time we stay with the Davenports."

"Okay, okay. I surrender to your wishes," John teased, holding his arms up in the air.

"John, quit that. People are staring." Though Bethany tried to sound firm, she couldn't help laughing at his antics. "Just hurry up and finish your dinner so we can go shop for you."

"Yes, my little shopping fanatic."

"I am not a fanatic!"

"Well, you must admit you love to shop."

"Yes, and you love to tease. Now would you please finish your dinner so we can go shop for you?"

John finished his last few bites, and as they rose from the table, he whispered, "Have I ever told you how cute you are when you get frustrated?"

"No. Is that why you keep going with your teasing? I will have to hide it better!"

John's only response was a chuckle as he reached for her hand and walked with her to the front counter to pay.

Even though John continued teasing Bethany, they accomplished some "serious shopping," as Bethany called it, and found some good buys for John's wardrobe.

Bethany managed to get her "revenge" for his teasing on the way home. John stopped at a gas station to fill up the truck for the drive to Detroit the next day. When he got out, leaving the keys in the ignition, Bethany locked the doors. After he finished and tried to open the truck door with no success, he looked questioningly at Bethany. She gave him her sweetest smile and made motions that he was to beg for her to let him in. When he was convinced she could wait longer than he could, he looked around to see if anyone was watching, and then put his hands together and gave her a pleading look. Bethany shook her head.

He mouthed, "What?"

Bethany made pointing motions toward the ground. John kept pleading—but to no avail. Looking around again, he finally got down on his knees, keeping his hands in the begging position. Bethany relented and unlocked the truck, but not before people they knew from the college let their presence be known by honking their horn, pointing, and laughing. Red-faced, John got in the truck and drove away as fast as possible. "You little imp. I'd say you got me back for anything I have ever done!"

"Oh, I don't know about that!" Bethany managed to answer in spite of laughing so hard tears were rolling down her face. "That turned out even better than I had hoped. What perfect timing that the Hancocks happened by!"

"Oh, yeah! Perfect timing!"

Bethany laughed harder. Finally, John couldn't keep from joining in. They were still laughing when they reached the apartment. After unlocking the door, John swept Bethany up in his arms, carried her inside, and dumped her on the couch. "I should turn you over my knee and spank you!" he joked, as he bent down and gave her a kiss instead. She caught him around the neck and pulled his head down to get a second.

Getting serious, John said, "You know I wouldn't ever do that. I don't believe in a husband spanking his wife."

Bethany could not help laughing. "Well, that's a relief!"

John grinned and kissed her again.

Saturday morning, they put their suitcases in the truck and headed for Detroit. They had packed enough clothes to stay a week, if necessary. They would have to return the following Saturday, as John was to be ordained on Sunday, along with others who were about to start in a ministry.

Ever since John's phone conversation with Elaine, they had increased their prayers for Michael. John had given much thought to what he could say to the young boy to help him accept his long-absent father. As always, Bethany was also looking forward to seeing Michael. They were both excited about getting a trailer and beginning this new phase of their lives. They didn't know much about trailers and were very grateful that Mr. Davenport would be helping them with the decision.

When they arrived at the Davenports' home, Michael rushed out of the house to greet them. John shook hands with him, then Bethany grabbed both of his hands and said, "It is so great to see you again, Michael."

"I am really happy to see you!" he exclaimed. "I miss you so much. I have been learning to draw at school. I want to show you what I have done."

"We should have time before lunch—after I greet everyone else."

"Oh, thank you, Bethany. I will get them ready." He hurried back into the house while Bethany greeted the adults who had come out to welcome them.

Martha Davenport said, "I heard that exchange. Michael has talked all morning about showing you his pictures and playing basketball with John. We were all getting anxious for you to arrive!"

Bethany laughed and greeted her with a hug. "Hello, Mrs. Davenport. Thank you so much for again inviting us into your lovely home."

"My pleasure, I assure you."

Bethany hugged and greeted Elaine and turned to George Davenport. He grasped her dainty hands with his and greeted her warmly. Smiling, he told her, "Go on in and make yourself comfortable. I'll help John with your luggage. You better look at those pictures before Michael has a conniption fit, as my grandmother used to say."

Laughing, Bethany went on in to find Michael.

She was impressed with his drawings. "You are very talented, Michael. I can't draw anything!"

"Thanks, Bethany. I really like it! Maybe I'll grow up to be an artist. I could draw Bible stories and give Jesus short hair, like He really had."

"What an excellent idea! What is your favorite story?"

"Well, I really like David and Goliath. And in the New Testament, I like when Jesus and Peter walked on the water. I want to try those as soon as I get better at drawing people."

"You must send us some of your drawings or scan and e-mail them to us."

"Okay."

"How would you like to go out with John and me for dinner Monday night?"

"Do you mean it? I'd like that. Do you mean just me or is Mom coming too?"

"Just you."

"Sweet!"

Martha came into the room to inform them that lunch was ready, so they went to the morning room. Bethany was glad they were using the very room she had always enjoyed with its French doors looking out on the beautiful garden, which had many flowers blooming now. She knew they would be eating dinner in the more formal dining room.

She and Michael had eaten breakfast and lunch in this room. She remembered an incident when Michael's temper had resulted in his throwing his glass of orange juice at the wall.

As she entered she saw that the room had been redecorated. She suspected it was Elaine's work, and she liked the new, updated look. The wallpaper had been stripped from the one wall, which was now decorated with press-on letters that spelled, *"As for me and my house, we will serve the LORD."* The room was painted a slightly brighter yellow than before. She exclaimed, "Oh, Mrs. Davenport, I love the new look!"

"So do I. Elaine did it for me. Wait until you see the guest room you will be using."

Turning to Elaine, Bethany complimented her.

John entered with George Davenport, and they sat down at the table. George asked John to return thanks.

After enjoying a delicious lunch, George pushed back his chair and said, "We better get going on shopping for your trailer. Martha and Elaine, are you coming?"

They both answered, "Yes."

"All right. We will all meet in the front in fifteen minutes. I'll inform the chauffeur."

When they were all seated in the limousine, George said, "I did some inquiring about the best place to buy an RV. I hope you can find something there. It's only about five minutes away."

"Thank you, Mr. Davenport," answered John. "I appreciate all of your help as well as your insight because I know you are a busy man."

"I hope I am never too busy to help special friends."

When they arrived at the lot, John sought out the used trailers. After looking at a few, the owner of the dealership came out. Bethany and John both recognized him; he was a member of the Faith Baptist

Church where they had both attended before going to college. George Davenport introduced them. "John, Bethany, you remember Brother Milton from the church?"

"Yes, of course. It's nice to see you again, sir. It is a relief to know we will be doing business with a fellow Christian."

He directed them to the new trailers, explaining that he was going to sell one to them at cost, taking no profit for himself. He ignored John's protests, merely asking how much he had intended to spend. He went with them and gave advice as to which manufacturers he thought produced the best products. After looking at several, they agreed on a model that both Bethany and John liked.

At that point Mr. Davenport spoke up. "Let's go look at the fifth wheels."

John said, "I don't have enough saved up for one of them."

"Well, let's just look for the fun of it while we are here."

"Oh, I would like to see them, John," added Bethany.

"Okay." Turning to the dealer, he said, "I will be in to sign the papers on the trailer in a little while."

"That's fine. There's no rush. Just look around as much as you like. Do you mind if I walk around with you?"

"Of course not. Your expertise and advice are very much appreciated," answered George Davenport.

"Come on, then, Bethany. I have wanted to see these new ones for a long time. Coming with us, Mother?" asked Elaine.

"Yes."

Michael stayed with the men, and the three ladies started looking in the fifth-wheel trailers. They looked at a number of them and discussed the pros and cons of each different model. The men walked at a more leisurely pace, listening to Mr. Milton's technical information. Finally Elaine said, "I think I like this one the best. I would get this if I were buying one."

Bethany agreed that it was nice. "But I think the last one had a better kitchen area; it had a little more room and a better design."

"Let's go back to it again, then. I didn't notice that. It is hard to keep them all straight."

"Yes, isn't that the truth?" added Martha. When they were inside the previous one again, Martha said, "Oh, yes. I see what you mean, Bethany. The kitchen is an important consideration—especially since a woman spends a lot of time there."

"Look up here at the bedroom section," called Elaine. "It's nicer, too. This slide out with a large closet would really be a blessing for someone living in it full-time."

"This would definitely be my choice," laughed Bethany.

"Then it is yours," said Martha Davenport.

"Wha…What?"

"My husband wanted Elaine and me to find out which fifth-wheel trailer you liked the best. He will pay the difference between the other trailer and this one."

"Oh! Mrs. Davenport. No, that is too much…"

"You know you won't be able to talk him out of it, Bethany. We decided this some time back and made arrangements with the dealer."

Tears came to Bethany's eyes. "I don't even have words to thank you and your husband properly for this."

Martha gave her a big hug. "Just accept the gift. It makes George uncomfortable if you say too much. Besides, it is his way to give an extra gift to the Lord and to have a part in your ministry."

"Well, it is very generous!"

"Come on, now. We have to stop that husband of yours from signing papers on that other trailer; although, I know George won't let him."

When they met up with the men, George shot a questioning look at his wife. Martha nodded yes to him and handed him a note with the model number of the fifth-wheel trailer on it.

George asked, "Show us." As Elaine and Bethany started leading the way back to the fifth wheel trailer that Bethany liked, George explained his intentions to John.

John tried to protest, but Martha drew him aside and said, "He has made up his mind. He wants to have a part in your ministry. Just let him do this for you. It makes him uncomfortable if you protest or thank him too much."

Though John shrugged his shoulders in resignation, he could not hide his joy and gratitude. "Okay. Thanks, Mrs. Davenport."

When they were inside the fifth-wheel trailer, John was impressed. "This one is made by the company that Brother Milton recommended."

Bethany explained that they had checked out all of the models, and this was the one she liked best. "Do you want to see all the others?"

"No. I trust you ladies. It looks great to me. I am in shock—I still haven't taken in all of this. This definitely has more room than the trailer. What a great blessing! Praise the Lord! Thank you, Brother and Mrs. Davenport."

George answered, "You are welcome. Let's go sign the papers."

The dealer explained that they had seen the lot model, and he would have to order one for them. It could take several weeks to get it. John remarked that they did not have to be out of the apartment until the end of August. They could go back to Indiana and wait until the fifth wheel was ready. Fortunately, he had not set a definite date to meet up with Ralph Gibson, the evangelist.

They left the dealership, and Mr. Davenport told the chauffeur to stop at a coffee shop. "Let's celebrate your new home. My treat."

John started to protest, "But Brother Davenport, you have already done enough."

"I want to do this. Everybody order your favorite drink."

After enjoying the treat, they headed back to the Davenports' home. While John, George, and Michael went out to shoot baskets, the three women relaxed and visited until dinner was ready.

After dinner they played a game of dominoes until Michael's bedtime. He and his mother were also spending the night. The plan was for Elaine to return to the apartment Sunday after the evening service, while Michael came back to the Davenports'. That way he could spend Monday with John and Bethany. After dinner Monday night, they would take him home to the apartment.

After saying goodnight to Michael, John and Bethany excused themselves, explaining that they wanted to share their good news about the fifth wheel with their families. John called his family from the guest room they were using, while Bethany went downstairs to the library. Both families were surprised and overjoyed to hear of the blessing they had received.

On Sunday Pastor Butler took the Holmans out to dinner after the morning service. During the meal he gave them some wonderful news; he had lined up two other churches in the area for John to preach, share their plans, and do a music special for their Wednesday night services. "I have already told George Davenport about this. They are already prepared for you to stay with them. Do you still have an apartment in Indiana?

"Yes, but it is almost bare," answered John, laughing. "We had expected to move into a trailer fairly soon, so we only have a few necessities left and a little bit of furniture."

"When do you have to be out?"

"Since another couple is waiting to take the apartment as soon as we are out, there is no set time."

"Then I suggest you go back to Indiana Thursday. You can pick up the things you are keeping and do whatever else you have to do to tie up your affairs there. Do you think you could accomplish that in a week?"

"It sounds like a workable plan, don't you think, honey?" asked John.

"Yes. There isn't that much left to do. I don't think it will even take a whole week."

"We really appreciate all the time and effort you have put into this for us, Pastor."

"You are welcome. I remember the days of leaving college and getting started in a ministry. Glad to be of help."

After the evening service, Michael said goodbye to his mother and climbed into his grandparents' limousine. He always enjoyed the opportunity to stay at their house, and this time he had the added pleasure of spending time with Bethany and John. At the house they had a snack and Michael was allowed to play a board game with them for a little while before his grandmother said, "Bedtime." He started to protest, but after a look from his grandfather, he obediently said, "Yes, ma'am," and began putting away the playing pieces. After bidding them all goodnight, he went upstairs, prepared for bed, and then called when he was ready for prayer. John and Bethany joined the Davenports as they prayed with Michael before he settled down for the night.

John paused at the door after the others had gone out and said, "We'll see you bright and early in the morning, Michael. We have a very busy day planned. So sleep well."

"Really? Mom only said I was going out to dinner with you."

"Well, since we made a decision on the trailer yesterday, we don't have anything else we have to do tomorrow. So we will spend the whole day with you."

"Wow! That's great!"

"Do you have a basketball here? I want to find a park where we can shoot some baskets."

"Cool. Yes, Grandmother has given me some things that I keep here."

"Good night, then."

"Good night, Brother Holman. And thanks."

In the morning after breakfast, they left the house in casual clothes. Michael thought it a great treat just to ride in the pickup. They spent time at a park and then had lunch at Michael's favorite fast-food restaurant. After enjoying eighteen holes at a miniature golf course, they returned to the Davenports' house to freshen up and relax until dinnertime. Michael took out his art paper and did some drawing, which they admired. Then Bethany left to change out of her culottes, giving John some time alone with Michael.

John managed to steer the conversation around to the fact that his mother had been in contact with Michael's father. "How do you feel about that, Michael?"

"I don't like it. Mom and I were doing just great on our own. Now she is always telling me what he said when they talk and that he says to tell me hi, and all that junk."

John could hear anger in Michael's tone. "I don't want to upset you, Michael, but maybe you need someone to talk to about your feelings."

"I bet my mom put you up to it, didn't she?"

"Yes, she did ask me to try to get you to talk about the situation."

"Why? So they can get back together?"

"Would that be so horrible?"

"Yes! Did you know he is an ex-con?"

"Michael, it hurts your mother when you use that name for him. Who taught you that word?"

"A kid at school."

"And what else did that kid have to say?"

"He said people would make fun of me if they found out. And he was right." Michael's voice broke, and he rubbed at his eyes to get rid of his unwanted tears.

"Kids at school have made fun of you?"

"Yes. I hate going to school now."

"Did you tell them about your dad?"

"No. Just that one guy."

"So how do you suppose they found out?"

"I don't know. Maybe my mom talked to somebody's mom."

"Is it possible your so-called friend told them?"

Michael's eyes got big and round. "Do you think he did?"

"It's possible. Anyway, the worst has happened. People know. I know it bothers you a lot when they tease and laugh at you. Children can be very cruel to others, can't they?"

"Yeah."

"I am sorry that happened, buddy, but can we talk a little about your dad?"

"I guess so."

"First, I want to show you some things in the Bible about King David. I am sure you have heard stories about how he killed Goliath, and that he was the greatest king Israel had."

John picked up his Bible, turned to Acts 13:22, and read the verse to Michael. "See, God called David *'a man after mine own heart.'* "

"Yes."

"Now let's look at 2 Samuel. I'll read some verses from chapters 11, 12, and 13." John read aloud, and then explained, "David already had several wives, but he thought Bathsheba was beautiful and he wanted her too, so he made sure her husband Uriah would be killed. That is the same as if he had killed him himself!"

"Wow! That's really bad!"

"Yes, and God sent Nathan the prophet to tell David that God would punish him. Bathsheba had a baby, which died. David and Bathsheba were very sad. Later David had other problems in his family. Sometime soon you should read Psalm 51. It is about David asking God for forgiveness for his sin. God did forgive David, but He still punished him. But God loved David, and later Bathsheba had another baby who became the famous King Solomon. Now, I read this to you to show that even though he sinned and was punished, God still called David *'a man after mine own heart.'* But thousands of years later, we are still reading about David's sin. The Bible says, *'Be sure your sin will find you out.'* Your dad, you, and your mom cannot hide what happened. Your dad got punished for what he did, but he also got saved and forgiven by God. Now God wants us to forgive him too. We aren't perfect, and God forgave us. And when He taught his followers how to pray, Jesus said, *'Forgive us our debts, as we forgive our debtors.'* I know it is hard—and more so since you've been embarrassed at school."

"Yeah. Because of my so-called friend."

"We don't know for sure that he is the one who told. Even if he is, you have to…"

"Forgive him." Michael said it along with John and grinned. He added, "Sometimes being a Christian is hard."

"Yes, it is. But it is worth it; God is with us when we go through hard times like this, and some day we get to go to Heaven. Can I pray for you now, Michael?"

"Yes, please."

They both closed their eyes and John prayed, "Father God, we come humbly before You to ask for Your help with a hard thing. Michael is Your child, and so is his dad. Help Michael to truly forgive his dad. We ask it in Jesus' name. Amen."

John glanched up and added, "Do you want to pray now, Michael?"

"Okay."

After a sincere prayer asking for help, Michael hugged John and said, "Thank you."

"You are very welcome. Now let's see if Bethany is ready to go for dinner, shall we?"

"Yes. I'm starving!"

After a lighthearted time over dinner, they took Michael home. When they reached the apartment, Elaine invited them in, and they settled in the living room with steaming cups of hot chocolate. Stirring the marshmallows in his cup, Michael looked up at his mom and said, "Hey, Mom, Brother Holman talked to me about Dad like you asked him to." Seeing his mom flinch and glance at John, he went on, "Oh, I guessed, so he admitted it. It's okay; I know I have been a brat lately. I am sorry, Mom. It's just been real hard for me. It seems like everything happened, and then the kids at school…"

"Oh! What have the kids at school done?"

"Making fun of me for having a 'jailbird' and an 'ex-con' for a father."

"You're kidding! How would they know that? I haven't talked to anyone…"

"It's my own fault Mom, I opened my big mouth to Jeremy, and I think he passed it on. He also made me feel like I didn't ever want to meet…him…my dad. But it's not only Jeremy, I am not sure if I want to. We are doing okay. Why do you want to change things? Aren't I enough? I know I haven't been acting right lately, and I am really sorry, but we were getting along great, before…you know, you started talking to him."

"Michael, I love you very much, and yes, we were doing great. You have learned to mind me most of the time, and I enjoy your company. But I get lonely for…how do I say it? God made us to want to be with… a man and a woman together."

Bethany spoke up, "Like Brother Holman and me, Michael. We fell in love and got married. Right now it is hard for you to understand, but when you get older, you will get interested in girls; and you will eventually meet the special one God has planned for you."

Michael's face showed his disgust at that idea. John laughed. "When I was your age, I felt like that too. But now," he reached for Bethany's hand, "I don't know what I'd do without Bethany."

"So, Mom, are you and…my dad," Michael still could not say it easily, "going to get back together?"

"I honestly don't know, Michael. If we ever do, it won't be for a while. But like I said, he would like to come for a visit. Your grandparents have said he could stay with them, which is very kind of them. They used to be very mad at him."

"Why?"

"Because they thought our divorce was all his fault. But I know now, that it was just as much my fault. And now that we are all saved, we can forgive each other with God's help."

"Yeah. I am going to need a lot of help. I feel kind of mad at him because I haven't ever had a dad around like most of the kids."

"I know, Michael. Both your dad and I feel badly about that. I hope you can also forgive me."

"I'll try. I already prayed with Brother Holman for God to help me. But that was just for him; I didn't think about forgiving you too."

John suggested, "Just talking to your mom about it is a first step. Anytime you have questions or are upset, be honest with her. Talk it out. All right?"

"Okay," Michael agreed.

Then they all rose, and Bethany helped Elaine carry their empty cups to the kitchen. Michael eagerly started telling his mom about everything they had done that day and what they had to eat while he was with the Holmans.

"It sounds like you had a very busy day. Thank you so much, Bethany and Brother Holman."

"Yeah! Thanks a lot!" added Michael.

"You are very welcome, buddy. We enjoyed it too. Now we better be getting back to your grandparents. We don't want them waiting up for us."

"Yeah. They are getting old and go to bed real early."

The adults laughed and then said their goodbyes.

John and Bethany spent Tuesday practicing with the church piano, and meeting with Pastor Butler to get the names and phone numbers of the other pastors who had agreed to have them. In the evening they received a phone call from Elaine. She reported that she could already see a difference in Michael's attitude. He had bravely gone to school without a fuss and reported to her when she picked him up from the sitter that he had told the children who had been harassing him that his dad had gotten saved and had changed. He had reminded them about King David and how he had been forgiven of his sin. After that they had dropped the subject and had treated Michael as they had before. Elaine was ecstatic and very grateful.

The service on Wednesday night went very well. At the end, Pastor Butler asked the Holmans to leave the auditorium. While they waited in the foyer, the church took a vote on whether or not to support them. When they were called in and informed of the decision, John assured the congregation of their joy and gratitude.

After the service, they found a few minutes to visit with their elderly friend, Mrs. Carpenter. She had been like an adopted grandmother to both John and Bethany. Mrs. Carpenter had helped John find ways to spend time with Bethany by having them at her home for meals and fellowship long before Bethany knew John's true feelings for her. Mrs. Carpenter had provided food, fellowship, advice, and entertainment in the form of working on jigsaw puzzles together.

John told her about their plans to go back to Indiana to conclude all of their affairs there and that they would be returning on Tuesday. She asked if he and Bethany could join her for dinner the Thursday night after their return. John assured her they would love to spend some time with her. When they returned to the Davenports' home later that evening, John informed them so that their cook would know not to prepare for two extras that night.

On Thursday they drove back to Indiana. John had already contacted the young man who was going to take over their apartment. He was happy about the timing, as it would give him just enough time to move his things into the apartment before leaving for his wedding. Thursday afternoon, Friday and Saturday Bethany and John paid off their utility bills, arranged for permanent replacements for their ministry positions at the church, and started packing their clothes, kitchenware, linens, and miscellaneous items into boxes and luggage. They made sure to keep their laptops, camera, and music with their personal belongings where they could find them easily. They packed carefully, keeping things as compact as possible so they could fit everything into the truck. Their friends, the Agnews and the Norbergs, took turns having them to their homes for dinner, and Saturday evening they all met at an inexpensive restaurant.

Sunday was an exciting, memory-building day filled with blessings for John and Bethany. During the invitation following the morning service, they went forward along with some other couples who were departing for their new ministries. Their names were read, and one of the assistant pastors laid his hands on the husbands' heads during a special prayer of blessing on their work for the Lord. Bethany had finished up her nursery duty that morning during the Sunday school hour and was already emotional. Now she could no longer hold back the tears and put a dainty handkerchief to good use.

After the service, a wife of one of the assistant pastors spoke to Bethany, inviting them to their home for dinner. After checking with John, Bethany happily accepted. They enjoyed the food and fellowship and then went back to the apartment for a much-needed nap before the evening service. Before leaving for church, Bethany dug out a clean handkerchief and put it in her purse, anticipating that the ordination service would also be very moving.

She indeed had to use the handkerchief that evening as she watched John kneel with other candidates at the altar. The deacons laid hands on each man as the pastor prayed. Then all of the candidates and their wives stood at the front of the church together, as the pastor and congregation prayed for the Lord's blessing on their ministries. Bethany had deep feelings of love and trust in the Lord as well as excited anticipation for their future.

Monday the Holmans finished packing and cleaned the apartment. Tuesday morning John and Bethany rose early and bought breakfast at a fast-food restaurant. They returned to the apartment and packed their things into the pickup. They were relieved when everything fit. They turned in the key to the manager, and he returned to the apartment with them for an inspection. They were happy and relieved when he returned their cleaning deposit. Then they headed out of town and toward the Davenports' home in Detroit.

During the drive they sang, joked, and talked about their expectations mingled with apprehension. They were getting very close to launching their evangelistic ministry.

When they finally arrived, Mrs. Davenport told them that her husband had emptied some storage shelves in their large garage for everything except their personal items. They unloaded the truck and finished putting the things into the garage just in time to freshen up for dinner.

Wednesday night, their friends at Faith Baptist Church warmly greeted them again. After the service, the music director asked them how long they would be in the area. When John informed him of their plans, he asked if they would do a duet for the following Sunday morning service. John looked at Bethany questioningly, and after she had nodded in assent, he answered that they would be happy to sing.

Since the day they had spent with Michael, John had thought much about his conversation with Michael. He and Bethany prayed about the situation and for Michael's struggle with his feelings and his Christian responsibility to forgive his parents. John had a thought he felt impressed to share with Michael. Thursday afternoon he had Bethany call Elaine and ask if they could spend Sunday afternoon with Michael. When Elaine asked Michael, he enthusiastically accepted the invitation.

Thursday evening was spent like so many others they had enjoyed with Mrs. Carpenter. After a delicious dinner and cleanup, they joined Mrs. Carpenter in working the usual jigsaw puzzle in progress.

Friday John worked on sermons and contacted Evangelist Gibson. They made arrangements to meet during the first week of August where Bro. Gibson would be preaching at a youth camp. He asked John to be prepared with songs that he could lead. He suggested that perhaps it would be easiest for all concerned if Bethany played for that part of the services. The regular camp pianist would do openings, offertories, and invitations. He also mentioned that they could join him in eating in the dining hall with the young people.

After the Sunday morning service, they took Michael to a popular family-style restaurant and then went back to the Davenports' home. They played some board games, and then Bethany excused herself. John asked Michael, "How are things going?"

"Lots better at school…and with Mom. The other day I asked her why she and…" he paused, "my dad made me grow up without a father. And she said that they were pretty selfish, only thinking about themselves. Now they are both really sorry. She said that's one reason he wants to talk to me. To tell me he is sorry."

"Are you going to give him that chance?"

"I suppose so. Sometime."

"Michael, I have been thinking about something you said before and again just now."

"What?"

"About not having a dad. I know that has been hard, but have you thought about the chance you have now to change that?"

"Me change it?"

"Yes. Doesn't it depend on you to let your dad talk to you? And maybe after a while, let him see you?"

"I guess so."

"What are you waiting for?"

"I don't know—I guess, I guess…I'm," he changed to a whisper, "just scared."

"Of what?"

After thinking for a few minutes, Michael said, "That then he'll want to come back, marry my mom again, and live with us. Change everything."

"I can understand that."

"You can?"

"Sure. Changes are always a little scary. Remember how you weren't too sure about you and your mother moving to an apartment? That was a big change."

"Yeah."

"And it has turned out okay, hasn't it?"

"Yes."

"How are you doing in the forgiveness department?"

"I'm trying. I pray about it. I guess I have a harder time with my dad."

"Because he is the one who left and hasn't seen you? Or because he was in jail?"

"Both, I guess."

"I can understand that too. It will take time. I wonder if it would help if you did talk to him, and maybe let him come for a visit? Finding out what he is like now might help."

"Maybe."

"I'll let you think about that, okay?"

"Sure. Thanks, Brother Holman."

"Anytime, Michael. Here is my cell phone number. You can call me whenever you want to talk."

"Do you mean it?"

"Of course. If I can't talk right then, I'll call you back."
"Wow! Thanks."
"You're welcome. Now we better get ready for the evening service."

The next week while John worked on sermons and chose songs for the youth camp, Bethany reorganized some of their belongings in the garage so that it would be easier when they did get the travel trailer. She found her scrapbooking supplies and some pictures and took them back into the house with her. Now would be a good time to work on that project. They also spent a few hours at the church using the piano to get ready for the singing program at the camp.

On Wednesday night John preached at a nearby church. Afterward the pastor said he would be getting in touch with them about possible support. The offering that night was very generous. The next morning Bethany wrote a note expressing their gratitude to the congregation, something she always did no matter the amount.

The following week, the pastor of another church told them he was confident they would be approved for support, but it would be a few weeks before the next church business meeting. Then he handed John a check covering the special offering. After getting in the truck, they praised God for another generous offering.

John was constantly working on lining up other churches to visit after they finished working with Evangelist Gibson. He knew that not every church would end up supporting them, but if they received a love offering, it would help.

One Friday they received word that the fifth-wheel trailer had arrived at the dealership. They were excited at this news. John had lined up a space in a park that allowed temporary stays. They made arrangements to pick up the trailer on Saturday and take it to the park. John explained to the Davenports that they would move into the trailer sometime the next week after they were able to get things organized and put away. "We can get used to living in it before we have the added stress of the ministry," he concluded.

— CHAPTER TEN —

Starting Life in Their RV Home

"So Abram departed, as the LORD had spoken unto him…."
(Genesis 12:4)

*O*n Monday John and Bethany started moving their belongings to the fifth wheel. While Bethany considered how to best organize them in the compartments and put them away, John read the owner's manual to become familiar with the workings of the various indoor features. He had figured out the major things on Saturday when they had set up in the RV park. They finished removing their belongings from the Davenports' garage on Tuesday, July 1, and found places for everything. Only the clothes and personal items they had been using remained in the guest room. On Wednesday they packed those into suitcases and left the Davenports right after lunch. They went to the RV park, finished unpacking, and stowed the suitcases in a built-in storage bin. Then they drove to a store to stock up on food.

That night Bethany cooked her first meal in the trailer. Since it was Wednesday and she wasn't used to the new kitchen, she made a quick meal of macaroni and cheese and a salad. She managed to make it a special celebration meal by setting the table with a candle and pretty placemats.

At the table Bethany asked John, "Could we have Elaine and Michael over for lunch on July 4? She will have the day off, and the Davenports have invited them and us over for the evening. I'm sorry; I forgot until this minute that I had not told you about that! I hope it is okay with you. I told Mrs. Davenport I was sure you would enjoy having a barbecue and staying for some fireworks. She said we would be able to see some professional fireworks the city puts on in a park close to their home. Of course, Brother Davenport will have bought some things for Michael too. I told her I would bring some dessert. I had to insist! I know they will let the cook have the day off, so it is a chance for me to do something to help them out for a change."

John answered, "Both things sound great. Elaine was so interested in our trailer purchase, I am sure she will enjoy seeing how you have fixed it up in here. By the way, it looks very homey. I like that picture your grandmother made. I had forgotten about it."

John took a bite of his salad and then asked, "What are you going to make for a dessert?"

"I am going to make a cake and try to draw a flag on top with frosting."

"Sounds good. It will be chocolate, won't it?"

Bethany laughed. "Okay, I'll make the cake chocolate, but it has to have white frosting."

"And red and blue."

"Yes, dear, and red and blue, which I will make from the white."

"You sure aren't wasting time about entertaining in our little home on wheels."

"I enjoy it, and I don't know how much of a chance I'll have to do it when we start traveling. I'll call Elaine tonight. If she says they will come, I'll call Mrs. Davenport and find out what she is having for dinner, so I don't duplicate."

"Are you sure you will have time to do all this?"

"Yes. I will keep the meal simple. I'll make the cake tomorrow."

"Okay. Let me know if you need any help."

"I'll remember that offer, and I may take you up on it!"

Elaine and Michael did come for lunch on Friday. Bethany had prepared a simple lunch of hot dogs, gelatin salad, a relish tray, and cookies. Afterward, John and Michael went for a walk while Bethany and Elaine cleaned up.

This time, Michael brought up the subject of his father. "I told Mom the next time my dad calls, I want to talk to him. I want to hear his voice and find out what he is like. Of course, we'll have to get together sometime for me to really know that. I guess I'm ready. I want to hear it from him that he wants to get to know me, that he is sorry, and all that. I want to know what happened. I think I can forgive him and my mom."

"That's good, Michael. I am really glad to hear it. Let me know how things go, will you?"

"Sure. Thanks for caring, Brother Holman."

John smiled and asked, "Are you excited about tonight?"

"You bet! Grandfather has lots of fireworks. Course, some of it I can't mess with, but he got me sparklers. And they are going to barbecue hamburgers and have pop and chips—all the things Mom won't let me have very often."

"Sounds good to me too!"

John and Michael turned around and headed back. As they approached the trailer, Bethany and Elaine came out and joined them. "We want to go for a walk. Do you two want to go with us?"

"Okay by me. How about you, Michael?"

"Sure."

Michael soon became impatient with the adults' pace and ran ahead and then back to them repeatedly. Finally, he challenged John to a race. When they returned, John was breathing hard. "Wow, buddy. I am going to have to get in better shape. Even with my longer legs, I barely beat you. You are fast!"

Michael beamed with pleasure. "You better rest up. I want to shoot baskets tonight at Grandfather's."

"Then let's go in and play a board game for a while."

Bethany said, "Elaine and I are going to sit out here and visit for a while. We want to enjoy this beautiful weather."

"I'll bring out the folding chairs. I'm glad we bought them."

Michael helped John bring out the chairs while Bethany poured cool drinks for all of them. After the ladies had settled down with their drinks under the awning that came with the trailer, the guys went back in to use the table to play a game. When Elaine suggested they should probably leave, Bethany assured her they had nothing to do but relax all day, so she and Michael might as well stay until time to go to the Davenports.

Later in the afternoon they all took another walk, and then the four of them played a game before leaving for the Davenports. When Bethany brought out the cake, Elaine complimented her on how it looked, and Michael smacked his lips, proclaiming, "It looks good for eating!" Then they headed for the vehicles. John suggested that Michael ride with him in the pickup and Bethany ride with Elaine. Michael thought that was a great idea, and the ladies agreed.

At the Davenports, the men shot baskets with Michael until dinner was ready. After they ate barbecued hamburgers, they visited and played board games until it became dark. George rebuilt the fire in the outdoor grill to roast marshmallows for s'mores. When Michael had his fill, he started playing with the sparklers his grandfather had purchased for him. The adults enjoyed watching him and the display from the nearby park. By the time the display was over and John and Bethany had driven to their new trailer-home, it was midnight. Bethany commented, "I'm glad tomorrow is Saturday so we can sleep in."

"Me too. It's been a busy week. A happy, memorable one, but busy."

"Most definitely," agreed Bethany.

Sunday at church, Mrs. Carpenter asked John how long they would be in the area. When he explained they would be leaving at the end of the month, she asked if he and Bethany would spend the next three Sunday afternoons with her. When he expressed concern that it would be too much of a strain on her, she assured him that it would not be. "I want to do it while I have the opportunity. There might not be very many more chances."

John told her they would love to keep company with her for the next three Sundays. When he told Bethany about the commitment he had made, she responded, "Oh, John, I hadn't even thought about it until now, but we should have her over here some evening. I'm sure she would be delighted to see our little home. And I do really love being with her; she is just like another grandmother."

"That is a really great idea! I'll talk to her tonight. When do you want to have her?"

"How about next Thursday?"

"Okay."

When John invited Mrs. Carpenter, she enthusiastically accepted their invitation.

That Wednesday Bethany made sure everything was spotless. The next day she prepared an especially nice dinner, including a lemon meringue pie. It was the first time she had tried to make one by herself, but she had helped her mother. She was happy that the pie turned out well. After the meal that evening John commented with his teasing grin, "We should have company more often! That was delicious. Why haven't you made that before?"

Mrs. Carpenter answered for Bethany, "It's a lot of work and very time-consuming. I am quite impressed with your cooking expertise, Bethany."

"Thank you."

"You have yourself a multi-talented little wife, John. Do you know how lucky you are?"

"I most certainly do! I'll prove it by cleaning up all by myself—while you two ladies rest and visit."

Bethany was glad for the opportunity to rest; it had been a busy day. As she and Mrs. Carpenter sat on the couch, Bethany pointed to the recliner, "Do you see the pillow on the chair? It is the one you made for me before I started Bible college. I treasure it. We continued using it once we were married. I kept it on the couch in our apartment in Indiana."

When John finished and sat down with them, Mrs. Carpenter reached for the rather large bag she had carried as a purse and pulled out a framed cross-stitched piece. Vines curled around the words in the center: "II Timothy 4:6c, *Do the work of an evangelist.*"

John was noticeably moved by the gift, and Bethany's eyes filled with tears. "How very special!" exclaimed Bethany, as she held it and examined the workmanship. "We will cherish and enjoy this gift. It will look nice with the one my grandmother made for us. I know needlework takes time as well as skill. Thank you so much," she added as she gave Mrs. Carpenter a warm hug.

John added, "It is very special—not only because it is beautiful, but because you made it."

"I was worried you wouldn't have room, so I didn't make it real big."

"There's room, see right here," Bethany pointed out a spot on the wall. Bethany immediately went to a drawer and found a stick-on picture hanger, which she used to hang it while Mrs. Carpenter was there.

Finally the time came to take her back to her home. When John had escorted her to the door, she reminded him about coming over on

Sunday. He reassured her, "Don't worry. We would never forget a chance to spend time with you."

"Well, it is very kind of you two young people. It must be boring for you with an old lady for company."

"A very special young lady at heart, and you are never boring. Bethany has fallen in love with you, just like I did many years ago. Goodnight. We'll see you Sunday."

The rest of the month of July flew by. The Davenports and the pastor and his wife had them over for dinner. Their days were busy with practicing songs and John preparing sermons while Bethany continued working on the photo scrapbook. One other church had them for a Wednesday night service. As planned, on Sunday afternoons they had dinner with Mrs. Carpenter. Afterward they would divide their time before evening service between working on a jigsaw puzzle and strolling around her beautiful yard. It brought back wonderful memories of other times spent together before Bethany left Detroit to go to Bible college, and her visits during her college breaks.

Housework did not take very long, so one day Bethany called Mrs. Carpenter. "Would you go with me to a fabric store and help me find an embroidery or cross-stitch project that wouldn't be too hard for a beginner? I have our photo scrapbook caught up, and I can't read all of the time. I want to find something I would enjoy and also be productive."

"I would be glad to go with you. I like to get out, but it gets difficult since I don't drive any more. The fabric store is one of my favorite places to go!"

At the fabric store they found some starter kits. Bethany did not want to invest in a lot of supplies until she discovered what type of crafts she enjoyed the most. Mrs. Carpenter suggested she might want to try crocheting. "When you start your family, it would be nice to be able to make things for your babies. You could come over several times in the next few weeks, and I could give you lessons." Bethany agreed with that idea, so they bought a few crochet hooks and some yarn. Mrs. Carpenter suggested, "I have some scraps of yarn you can start on to practice before you start on a project with your new yarn."

There was also an important project for John and Bethany to work on together. They had set up a budget shortly after their marriage, but now they had to make some adjustments. They were trying to be as organized and prepared as possible before joining Evangelist Gibson. The two of them were excited and enthusiastic about starting the evangelistic ministry. When they discussed their food budget, John told Bethany that Brother Gibson had said they could eat in the dining hall while at the camps.

"Oh, that will be a big blessing. The Lord is so good!"

On Monday, July 28, John surprised Bethany at the breakfast table. "Today, my love, would you like to go shopping for your piano keyboard? With what you saved from giving piano lessons, we might have enough in your special account to buy one now. If not, we have some extra in our regular account due to those generous love offerings.

"I know you have been researching them online, and I've been doing some shopping and price comparisons. At one store the owner is a Christian, and when he found out we're going into evangelistic work, he said he would give us a discount. So I'd like to show you the ones he has at his store today."

"John! That is fantastic! Thank you, thank you." Bethany jumped up from the table and ran around to where he was sitting. She planted a kiss on his cheek and threw her arms around his neck. Then she ran back to her place. "Oh, let's hurry and get done."

John laughed. "You are the one wasting time running around the table."

Bethany teased back, "It is never a waste of time to kiss my knight."

"Well, I'll have to agree with that. Do you want to give me some more?"

"When we get back," she said. "But does this store have many to choose from?"

"He has several that look to me like what you've been wanting." He grinned, admitting, "Not that I know much about pianos. I hardly know if you want a digital or a hybrid or a portable grand. But the way you play, I at least know you'll need a full-size keyboard with no missing octaves!"

At the store Bethany tried out numerous keyboards and listened to the owner's explanation about the different features. Ultimately, she and John chose a quality instrument with its own stand, a complete keyboard with full size keys and other aspects that Bethany wanted, plus a rich sound. When they got home Bethany hugged John and gave him the promised kisses before settling down to try out her new instrument.

On July 30 at the midweek service they said goodbye to all of their friends at Faith Baptist Church. A surprise reception was held for them after the service. Many people slipped them cash as they said their farewells. Bethany enjoyed the surprise but also found it hard. Her eyes shimmered with unshed tears, while at the same time she managed to continue smiling.

Elaine and Michael hung around until the end. "Michael wants to speak to you briefly, Brother Holman, if that is okay?" asked Elaine.

"Of course."

Elaine and Bethany talked while Michael told John about talking to his dad on the phone for the first time. Elaine told Bethany that the conversation had gone well, and Michael's attitude toward his dad was softening. Bethany rejoiced with her. When Michael was ready to say goodbye, the two young women hugged and agreed they would be praying for each other. John reminded Elaine and Michael that either one was welcome to call him or Bethany at any time. "We want to keep in touch," he assured them.

Bethany found it hard to sleep that night; she was feeling too many conflicting emotions. The next day they would be hooking up their "home on wheels" and heading to rendezvous with Evangelist Gibson.

— CHAPTER ELEVEN —

Beginning As an Evangelist

"Preach the word…reprove, rebuke, exhort…"
(II Timothy 4:2)

The couple traveled two days to reach the camp where Brother Gibson was preaching. He greeted them warmly and enthusiastically. "I am so happy to have the opportunity to help another evangelist get started. I am sure you and your wife will be a great asset."

"Believe me, the pleasure is ours, sir. We are really looking forward to learning from you and helping in whatever way we can."

"You can park your camper next to mine—over there next to the dining hall." He pointed it out to them. "You should have time to get it set up before dinner at 6:00 o'clock. See you then."

"Thank you, Brother Gibson."

John drove to the spot he had indicated and soon had the camper hooked up. Then they both freshened up before walking the short distance to the building. The young people were starting to gather also, and they felt many curious glances cast in their direction. After everyone was assembled, Brother Gibson rose to ask the blessing. But first he introduced John and Bethany and told the young people a little about them. "You will get a taste of their musical talent tonight, and one of these days soon we'll have Brother John preach. They'll be joining us for all of our activities from here on out. I'm sure you are going to love them, and I shouldn't have to remind you that you are to respect them. Let's pray."

They sat at a separate table with Brother Gibson. At one point he quietly asked them, in a low voice, to split up and sit among the young people to help with crowd control during the chapel service, which would start right after dinner. "Tomorrow, we will meet while the camp counselors are taking the young people on a hike, and I'll fill you in on the things I'd like you to help with. We can meet in here right after breakfast, which starts at 7:00 a.m. Are you prepared to start doing the music for us tonight?"

John assured him that they were.

After dinner John whispered to Bethany, "Let's go back to the camper briefly before heading for the chapel." When they reached it, John said, "I thought we should pray together one last time. This is a little different situation for us—with only young people in the congregation. We may find it a little intimidating at first."

"My thoughts exactly. They stared at us with such curiosity, and I spotted some that I think have 'attitudes'— if you know what I mean."

"Yes. I am sure we will be in for some testing." John prayed for the Lord's help and power and calmness of spirit for them. Then they walked hand-in-hand to the chapel. Brother Gibson met them and told them that for this first time, he would introduce them again and call them up to the platform when he was ready for them. Then they separated, John going to sit on the boys' side and Bethany heading for a seat among the girls.

After the opening prayer and a few announcements, Brother Gibson played his trumpet during the offering. Then he introduced the couple again and asked the teens to warmly welcome them as they came to the platform. While Bethany headed to the piano, John thanked Brother Gibson and the young people and then nodded to Bethany. She knew what he wanted to begin with and immediately started playing "Let's Talk About Jesus." They kept it fast-paced, singing it over several times and getting faster each time. Then they sang "I Have Decided to Follow Jesus," "Every Day With Jesus," "New Look," and ended with "Follow On" to help attain a quieter spirit. Lastly, John sang a solo, "Love Lifted Me." The couple left the platform, and Brother Gibson preached. John's hearty "Amens" also helped the spirit, and soon many of the teen boys joined him. Several of the young people came forward to pray during the altar call.

Bethany had her hands full trying to keep an unruly girl quiet during the preaching and the altar call. She sneered at statements the preacher said and tried to get the other girls to follow her example. Unfortunately, she succeeded with some. Her hair was obviously dyed black, and she wore extremely long nails, which showed traces of black nail polish, which she had half-heartedly attempted to remove. Bethany made a mental note to discuss her behavior with Brother Gibson at their meeting the next day.

After the service, John and Bethany were happy to head for their camper and fall into bed. Not only had the last week been an emotional and busy time, traveling for two days to reach the campgrounds had also been tiring. Now they were both exhausted.

They both awoke much refreshed; still, Bethany was glad someone else was preparing breakfast for them. In the dining hall, they discreetly observed the young people as they ate. Bethany found herself praying for them—even though she knew none of their names yet. The unruly girl had a cluster of girls at her table who were hanging on her every word. She would look at girls at other tables who were ignoring her, then say something to those around her. They would look at the one she had pointed out, and all of them burst out giggling at her remarks. Bethany felt annoyed and concerned about this behavior.

The young people left for the hike—in spite of protests from the gang of rude girls who proclaimed they did not want to go for a "stupid walk." Brother Gibson sighed with relief as he joined them at the table. "I knew that girl was going to be trouble. You should have seen her when she first arrived yesterday morning. She was loaded with metal jewelry and heavy black eye makeup, black lipstick, and black fingernail polish. Her church youth leader came to me and said he knew it wasn't acceptable and wanted me to help him talk to her. She had it all in her bag and applied it after she got on the bus. He told me her mother had recently joined the church after moving to their area following a divorce. She is very concerned about her daughter who has become rebellious and wants to go 'Gothic.' The mother doesn't allow that look, but the girl waits until she is out of her sight and then adds all the trappings. The mother can't afford to put her in the Christian school, so she's picking up this stuff at the public school.

"We made her take off the jewelry and the makeup and polish, and she wasn't happy about it. Now we have to try to reach her to get her to take off the attitude. The youth director said her mother told him the girl was saved when she was ten, but then the father left; and she changed. According to her mother, Rebecca was very close to her father; but he didn't visit them after he left the home. The mother moved them closer to her parents and the church where she grew up. Rebecca was not at all happy about the move."

Bethany commented, "I've noticed she is influencing the other girls to be rude, hurtful, and rebellious. I've already been praying for her. She gave me a lot of trouble last night."

"Maybe the Lord will give you an opportunity to talk to her, but be cautious in your approach, Mrs. Holman," Brother Gibson warned. He turned to her husband. "John, are you prepared to do some preaching?"

"Yes, sir, I have several sermons ready. Actually, several of them speak to this type of problem."

"I would like you to preach Wednesday night and again Friday morning as I have to attend to some business in town that day. Is that acceptable with you?"

"Definitely."

"I also would like to have both of you help out as altar workers, if you don't mind."

"We are willing to do anything you need."

"One other thing…we will have a bonfire Friday night. I would like you to lead the singing after I bring a short message. After the singing, we will have the last altar call for this week's camp, so please lead in 'Just As I Am' for that.

"Let's pray for Rebecca and that the Lord will give you guidance and wisdom as you deal with her, Mrs. Holman."

Later that day Bethany saw Rebecca sitting by herself while most of the young people were playing a volleyball game. She sat down beside her and started a conversation, all the while praying silently for guidance and help. "Are you enjoying camp, Rebecca?"

"Not especially. I only came because my mom made me. I wish I could just go home, but I can't call her to tell her to come and get me because she very conveniently had to go out of town for her job training," Rebecca answered sarcastically.

Bethany ignored the disrespectful tone and the fact that Rebecca thought she could tell her mom rather than ask her to take her home. Instead she asked, "What don't you like?"

"You really want to know?"

"Yes."

"When I got here I had to take off my nail polish, makeup, and jewelry."

"So you would wear the makeup and jewelry along with these black clothes if you could get away with it?"

"Yes. Why not?"

"Because I think it is satanic."

"What? I don't worship Satan."

"Then why do you want to dress like this?"

"Because my new friends do."

"The Bible says to avoid the appearance of evil in I Thessalonians 5:22."

"Do you think it appears evil?"

"I do. That's why I said what I did about it being satanic."

"Well, like I said, I don't worship Satan. I don't see anything wrong with it," she answered and then walked away.

Bethany thought, "She needs to get her heart right with God and surrender every aspect of her life to Him. I guess all I can do now is pray for her. She certainly doesn't want to listen."

On Wednesday night John preached that any sacrifices we make in our clothing or giving up certain activities or friends is nothing in comparison to what Jesus did for us. He gave a graphic description of all that Jesus went through physically.

Friday morning John continued with the same theme. This time he emphasized the mental and spiritual anguish Jesus suffered as the Father broke the fellowship that Father and Son had always shared.

Again he asked the young people if any of their sacrifices came near to comparing to those of Jesus.

"He tells us we are to be a peculiar people—to look and act different than the other people in the world who don't believe and aren't saved. Many temptations surround us in this world. You will have a happier life down the road if you don't give in to youthful, fleshly desires. Drugs, alcohol, and illicit sexual desires are tools the Devil uses. He does not want you to serve God now or in the future. He wants to get you off track while you are young.

"I know young people get impatient to be grown up and engage in adult behavior. But don't rush things. Enjoy your time as a teenager. Along with adulthood comes responsibilities. Trying to speed up the process will bring nothing but heartache, sorrow, trouble, and complications in your life. Wrong behavior will also hurt your parents, your testimony will be soiled, and the cause of Christ will be hindered. You may not realize that if you claim to be a follower of Christ, you have an impact on the work of God. Your wrong behavior will give Christianity a bad name.

"God wants you to show you love Him by obeying Him, your parents and others like the pastor and youth director who have the rule over you.

"Isn't that a small thing in contrast to Christ's sacrifice? If you are truly saved, God's Spirit is working in you. Don't grieve Him or keep quenching and ignoring Him."

All of the workers had been praying especially hard for Rebecca all week. During the rest of the day, Bethany kept an eye out for her and her little group of followers. But Rebecca was not hanging around with them, talking and laughing loudly and rudely to the other young people as she had all week. She was by herself, looking pensive.

That evening Brother Gibson preached a short, but powerful, message using the parable of the prodigal son from Luke 15:11-23.

He pointed out that the youngest son was rebellious. He did not want to stay in the family home, work in the family fields, and follow the family rules. "Many young people through the ages and in our time have the same feelings and do the same thing. They think life will be easier or more enjoyable without their parents ruling over them. Maybe their parents don't approve of the friends they have chosen. Those can be friends inside the church or Christian school or outside, in the 'world.'

"The young man in the parable must have had friends with him when *'he wasted his substance with riotous living.'* Young people, you need to realize that your parents know you are what your friends are or soon will be. Are you running with the wrong friends? Ask yourself, 'Will these friends help me lead the right kind of life? Will they help me grow closer to the Lord or go further away from Him?'

"Are you spending time with people who want to be successful, good citizens? Will they go to college and seek training for good jobs? Do they care about or want to help others? Or will they perhaps end up in trouble with the law? Do they talk about good things or about rebelling and breaking the rules or laws?

"Look at verse 17: *'When he came to himself...'* he arrived at a new perspective of himself, and he did not like what he saw. He wasn't getting very far in life. In fact, he was starving. He made up his mind to go back home, apologize, and admit he was a sinner. This example of true repentance is what some of you might need to do with your own parents. Of course, Jesus told the story to teach us about our relationship with God the Father. Maybe you have other problems tonight or other matters in your life that are pulling you down in your spiritual life. Why not make a decision tonight to change or to rededicate yourself? Perhaps someone needs to get saved if there is anyone here who has not made that first step."

Brother Gibson signaled to John, and he began softly singing "Just As I Am." Bethany joined in until she felt a touch on her shoulder. She turned around to see Rebecca in tears. Bethany took her hand, led her away from the group, and found a log they could sit on. Bethany held her in her arms while she sobbed out her anguish and pain over the divorce of her parents. Being a daddy's girl, she had blamed her mother, but in truth, she confessed to knowing no details of why they had separated. Deep down in her heart, she wanted to hurt her mother, but she had never admitted that truth to herself. John and Brother Gibson had made her see that she was going in the wrong direction with the wrong kind of friends, and it wasn't doing anything to help the situation. She was only making it harder on herself and her mother—when they needed each other.

Bethany led her to see that she had also been the wrong kind of friend to some of the other girls at camp and had helped to lead them astray. That realization brought on a fresh bout of weeping. When she regained control, Bethany helped her pray for forgiveness and ask for help with her feelings and actions. She agreed to apologize to Brother Gibson and to the camp counselors, the other girls, and her mother. Rebecca did not wait until she returned home; she immediately used her cell phone to call her mother and tearfully apologized.

Bethany also suggested that she get rid of her heavy makeup and jewelry, which she did that night. The next morning she gathered the group of girls around her and told them she had been wrong. Several of the girls broke down and likewise repented. Rebecca and those girls went to Brother Gibson, John and Bethany, and all of the camp counselors to apologize. The week of camp ended with a feeling of revival in the air.

When the young people had departed after lunch on Saturday, John and Bethany went to their camper. They rejoiced and praised the Lord together and agreed that it was a great beginning for their ministry. They were excited about the prospects for the next three weeks, which they would spend working with Brother Gibson at this camp.

On Sunday they went to a nearby church for the morning service. Then they went to a restaurant for a special dinner to celebrate their wedding anniversary. Back at their camper, they exchanged cards and gifts. They received phone calls from both sets of parents, congratulating them on their first anniversary. They enjoyed sharing the experiences and exciting events of their first week of working in the camp.

A new group of young people came to camp each week. Many of the teenagers made decisions about various struggles in their spiritual lives, and some rededicated themselves. They even saw a few get saved. But none of them were quite as dramatic as Rebecca's situation.

When the camp season was officially over, they now entered into a new phase of their training time with Brother Gibson. They traveled together to churches, usually arriving on Saturday and setting up their campers. Brother Gibson would preach for services on Sunday, and then in the evenings Monday through Wednesday. Then they would have two days to drive to the next church and start over. He had meetings set up for nearly every week until the week of Thanksgiving.

They were going to end up not too far from Detroit. The Davenports had stayed in contact and when they learned this, they invited John and Bethany to come to their home for the holiday. The young couple was delighted with this invitation. A few days after Mrs. Davenport called, Bethany received a phone call from Betsy, who was now a freshman at Crossroads Baptist Bible College. "Guess what! Mrs. Davenport invited Carrie and me to have Thanksgiving with them. She said you and John would be there also."

"Oh, Betsy, that is wonderful! I have been lonely for you."

"I know. You told me how seeing the girls at camp made you think of me. I wish you were here, but I have made friends, and I like my classes. Carrie has been really sweet and helpful. She has told me some about her past and showed me her scars from cutting. I never would have believed it from the way she is now. By the way, I think Doug is just about ready to ask Carrie to marry him. Isn't that great? It is so romantic."

"That is great! You are probably right, since they are both seniors this year. They have both grown so much, and I think they are perfect for each other. Oh, I can't wait for Thanksgiving. I am anxious to see her too."

The last week before Thanksgiving, Mrs. Gibson arrived to meet her husband. They were going to travel together in the camper to visit family in the area for Thanksgiving. Bethany was glad to meet her and have the opportunity to ask her some questions about the life of an evangelist's wife. She learned that Mrs. Gibson had started out like Bethany, traveling with her husband. She had homeschooled their children for a while, but then they had decided the children needed a more settled life for their high school years. They decided to enroll them in a Christian school where they would have the opportunity to be on sports teams. When the last one graduated, she would begin traveling with her husband again on a part-time basis. They had purchased a home, so she could not be with him all of the time. They also wanted a place for the young people to be able to go for college breaks.

Elaine called and told Bethany that Michael was very excited when he heard that she and John would be joining them for Thanksgiving. Elaine added that Mark would also be coming for his first face-to-face visit with Michael. "Michael feels it will be easier with John there."

"Wow, your mother is going to have a houseful."

"Well, Mark decided to stay at a hotel. He thought that would be better for this first visit. He will join us for Thanksgiving."

"He is probably right. It seems like he is a very thoughtful person."

"I think so. The more I talk to him, the more impressed I am, and the more I…"

"Love him?" Bethany finished for her.

Elaine laughed in response.

"John and I will be glad to see Mark again, and we will be praying about this first visit between him and Michael."

"One other thing, Bethany…Mark asked me to find out if you and John would be willing to go out with us one night as chaperones. He has been saving up money for this trip and wants to pay for your dinners too. He has a nice place picked out, though I'm not sure which one. He said it's a surprise. This will be a very special occasion for us. It's almost like a first date. That probably seems strange to other people, since we were married once. But a lot has happened since then. We were thinking about Friday night—if you two will still be in town."

"I'll check with John, but I think it will work out fine. We don't have to leave until Monday morning. But I don't think John will like the idea of Mark's paying for our meal."

"Bethany, he was quite positive about that. He knows you two are still trying to line up enough support and things are probably a little tight for you right now. The place he wants to go is a little extravagant. Just consider it a blessing from the Lord. Like I said, he has been saving up. Please explain that to John."

"Okay, Elaine. I'll talk to him and get back to you."

A few days later Bethany called Elaine. "John agreed to our going out with you two. He reluctantly agreed to the part about Mark's paying for our dinner."

"That's great, Bethany. Mark will be so relieved. We are really looking forward to this time."

The day before Thanksgiving, Bethany and John drove to Detroit. They stopped at Faith Baptist Church and unhitched their trailer. They were parking it there, but would not be using the hookup facilities or staying in their trailer. They arrived at the Davenports' home around noon. Betsy and Carrie had arrived a little earlier after being picked up at the train station by the chauffeur. After a joyful reunion, Mrs. Davenport showed the Holmans to one of the guest rooms, where they unpacked and freshened up. Shortly after they had gone downstairs to visit with Mrs. Davenport and the two college girls, Mark arrived. He was carrying a beautiful bouquet of flowers as a hostess gift for Mrs. Davenport. He stayed for a short visit and then left to return to his hotel. Mrs. Davenport invited him to come early the next morning so he would have plenty of time to visit with Elaine and Michael. She explained that they would have snacks out rather than having a sit-down lunch and serve dinner about 3:00. Elaine and Michael would be arriving about 10:00.

"Thank you, Mrs. Davenport. I will plan to arrive about 10:30 if that sounds okay."

"That would be perfect."

After dinner Bethany, John, and the two girls rode to church with the Davenports in the limousine. They enjoyed seeing old friends at Faith Baptist Church. Bethany was excited about introducing Betsy to everyone.

Michael enthusiastically greeted them. After the service Pastor Butler asked John how long they would be in town. When John said they were leaving on Monday, the pastor asked if they would do a special for the Sunday evening service. John answered, "We would be happy to, sir."

The next morning Bethany, Betsy, and Carrie helped Martha Davenport set the dining room table. It looked beautiful and festive with the bouquet of flowers from Mark as the centerpiece. As they worked, they enjoyed the aroma of roasting turkey.

At 10:00 sharp, the doorbell rang. As she entered Elaine exclaimed, "I could hardly make Michael wait until 10:00. I think he is a little excited."

"I am! It's great when Brother Holman and Bethany are here. But I am a little scared too."

"About meeting your dad?" asked Bethany who had gone with Martha to greet the new arrivals.

"Yes."

"Well, I promise you, he is a very nice man. I bet he is a little nervous too. Why don't you work on making him feel comfortable? I believe it will help you!"

"That is very wise advice," agreed George Davenport.

"Okay. I'll try. Can we play a game or something, Brother Holman, while we wait for him to get here?"

"Sure. I see you brought your checkerboard. Think you can beat me today?"

"You bet!"

Bethany turned to Elaine. "How are you doing?"

"I have a little of the same disease," she laughed. "I do so want things to go well between Michael and Mark."

"I'm sure they will. We have all poured an abundance of prayer into this meeting. Let's go visit until he gets here."

Carrie and Betsy, who had been working on a word game, rose from the couch to greet Elaine. Betsy had met her in Tacoma at the time of Bethany's wedding and had renewed the acquaintance the previous evening at church.

Promptly at 10:30 Mark arrived. He had brought dominoes with him. George commented, "I see you came prepared."

"Yes, sir. I figure there will be a lot of hours to fill—I'm not real used to talking with kids."

Michael and John joined them in the entrance hall. George said, "Michael, here is your father, Mark Briscoe. You two have talked on the phone, but you haven't met in person."

"Hello, sir. I am glad to see you. May I take your coat?"

"Why, yes, Michael. Thank you."

The ladies all came to the entrance hall where Carrie and Betsy were introduced to Mark. When Bethany, Betsy, and Carrie had gone back to the living room, Mark turned to Michael and said, "I brought dominoes. We can play some games, if you want to. Maybe John and your granddad will join us."

Michael took a deep breath and forced himself to answer bravely, "Sure. But first, could you, Mom, and I have some time to talk?"

"I think that would be great."

Michael turned to his grandfather. "Which room do you want us to use?"

"How about the library?"

"Okay." Turning to Mark, he asked, "Sir, do you mind if Brother Holman joins us?"

"Not at all, Michael. I want to do whatever makes you the most comfortable."

"Okay. Do you mind, Brother Holman?"

"Of course not, Michael."

As they headed for the library, Mrs. Davenport spoke up. "Don't forget, everybody. Snacks are in the morning room for anyone who wants them at anytime. We will eat dinner about 3:00."

Everyone acknowledged her announcement with "Thank you," and Michael and Elaine led Mark and John to the library and shut the door. Bethany and Martha joined the girls in the living room, and George went to the family room to watch football.

Once they were in the library, Michael waited until the adults were seated, and then he chose a seat next to John on a loveseat. Mark hesitantly began the conversation. "I know that your mom told you I was in prison. I am sorry you were teased about that at school. I know it had to be embarrassing for you. I am pretty embarrassed, ashamed, and sorry about it myself."

"That was kind of my own fault, sir. I told somebody because I thought I could trust him."

"Well, I guess we have both learned some lessons the hard way, haven't we? At least one good thing came from my being in prison—I heard about Jesus and asked Him to be my Saviour."

Michael looked surprised. "I didn't think there could be anything good about your being in prison."

"Are you saying that because of what happened at school?"

"Yeah, I mean, yes, sir. The kids were teasing me because my dad was an ex-con."

Mark winced. "That does sound pretty awful. I am really sorry, Michael. You should never have had to go through that. The Bible says, '*…and be sure your sin will find you out.*'"

John added, "Galatians 6:7 says, '*Be not deceived; God is not mocked: for whatsoever a man soweth, that shall he also reap.*'"

Michael turned to John. "What does that mean exactly?"

"Jesus is comparing it to sowing or planting seeds in a garden. What you plant is what will come up. If you 'plant' evil, you know, do bad things, you will 'reap' or get bad things—like punishment. Maybe God will let you get caught and punished, like your dad."

"Or like me when I don't obey?" asked Michael.

"Right. Or God might punish you Himself by letting you get sick or lose your job, or something like that."

Mark continued. "The bad part is that when we sin, it usually affects other people too, like your being embarrassed because of the wrong I did. I really hope you can forgive me. I know it will be very hard."

Elaine spoke up. "But remember, Michael, we are all sinners. I have done bad things, and so have you. You have changed a lot since you got saved. Do you remember how naughty you used to be?"

"Kind of…a little."

"Your grandmother told me that when Bethany first came you would scream when she tried to dress you, and you even threw toys at her. Once you were so upset, you pushed the table, and your juice went all over the wall."

"I remember that! Grandmother made me clean it up."

John chuckled. "You were reaping what you sowed. That happened to me a lot when I was a kid."

"You got in trouble?"

"Of course, I was a sinner who also had to get saved. I got lots of spankings."

Elaine added, "And I did bad things too, Michael. I used to drink alcohol, and the Bible says we aren't supposed to. Sometimes, some things grownups do are so bad, they are against the law. If they are caught, they end up in prison. That's what happened to your dad."

"Yes, and it was a horrible place," said Mark. "I hope you never end up like that. That's why I'm so glad you were saved while you were still young. But like I said, I was saved while I was there. God forgave me just like He forgave you."

"I know I need to forgive you too. I'm trying."

"Thanks, Michael. That's all I can ask."

"Don't forget, Michael," Elaine said. "When we got divorced, it wasn't all Mark's fault. I was young and spoiled, and I wasn't a very good wife or mother. I need your forgiveness too."

"I know. I've been kind of mad at you because I never had a dad around like other kids. I've been praying and asking God to help me. It is working. I don't feel so mad anymore."

"I can tell," commented Elaine.

"I'm glad to hear it," added Mark. "Michael, would it be okay with you if I take your mom out for a date tomorrow night?"

"A date? Why do you have to date each other? You have already been married. You know each other and everything."

"We have been apart for a long time, and we have both changed a lot. We need to start over. I would like to take her out to dinner. Is that okay?"

Michael looked from one to the other and finally answered, "Sure. I already know Mom still likes you a lot. I can tell by the way she acts when you call her."

"Now, Michael, you aren't supposed to tell my little secrets," said Elaine, and then she laughed and blushed with embarrassment. "I'll see if you can go to a friend's house, or if she is available you can stay home with Mrs. Williams."

"I'd rather go to Jimmy's house, if I could."

"I'll check with his mom."

"Can I go get some snacks now? I want some chips and dip."

"How about some veggies too?" suggested Elaine.

"Yes, ma'am."

John asked, "Can we pray together before we break up?"

Everyone murmured agreement, and John prayed for Michael and his parents and that they would all be able to forgive the events of the past and move forward toward positive relationships.

Mark joined Michael in the morning room. While they filled their plates with snack items, they compared notes on foods they liked and disliked. Michael found himself laughing at his father's descriptions of experiences he had with food during his childhood. He explained that he was expected to eat some of everything offered. More than once, he got into trouble because he tried to slip food he did not like to his dog. The dog did not care for it either and spit it out. When his mother found it on the floor under the table, she figured out what had happened.

"Another trick I used with food I didn't like, was to hold my breath and swallow it as fast as possible, so I wouldn't taste it."

Michael thought that idea sounded good. "I think I'll try that the next time Mom has spinach. I don't care how much Popeye liked it—I don't!"

They were both laughing when they came out of the morning room. Elaine asked, "What is so funny?"

Mark answered, "Oh, it's just…"

"Our little secret is just a guy thing. Right, Dad?" Michael startled himself, which caused him to look at Mark. The surprised look on his face at hearing Michael address him as Dad made Michael grin, and then they both burst out laughing again. Mark playfully slugged Michael on the shoulder, "That's right, our little secret. Let's go play dominoes while we eat."

"Sounds good to me."

John had gone to the living room to sit with Bethany. During a pause in the conversation, he asked her if she was ready for some snacks.

"Yes, I ate a light breakfast to save room for some chips and dip. But I'm not having much—I want to save room for the turkey dinner. Are you ready, Mrs. Davenport?"

"Yes, I'll join you."

After filling their plates they wandered into the family room to see how the dominoes game was going, and John wanted to check the score of the football game. Bethany said, "Why don't you watch for a while? I'll sit here by you."

"Are you sure you don't mind?" asked John.

Bethany answered, "Of course not. I'm used to it! My father always watches the games. When I get tired of it, I'll watch the domino players."

Later, Martha, Bethany, Elaine and the two college girls played a board game. Michael and Mark joined George and John in front of the television.

After the delicious turkey dinner, Michael suggested that they all play dominoes together. Everyone enjoyed a good game. Afterward they had their dessert with several kinds of pie from which to choose.

Then Mark excused himself, telling John that he would meet up with them at Elaine's apartment the following evening for their dinner out. "I hope things work out for you to go to Jimmy's house, Michael."

"Thanks. Will I see you again before you have to leave town?"

"I would like to, Michael."

Michael turned to Elaine. "Could he come over Saturday?"

Elaine answered, "I have to work, Michael."

"Oh, rats. Why?"

"One of the others ladies is out of town, and I have to cover for her."

Mark asked, "What if Michael and I spent the day together? Then the three of us could do something in the evening."

"How does that sound, Michael?" asked Elaine.

"Great!"

"What time should I pick up Michael?"

"About 8:30 a.m. That will give me time to get to work by 9:00."

"What time do you get off?"

"We close a little early on Saturdays, at 4:00. By the time we close up and I get home, it will be about 4:45 p.m. Should I put something in the slow cooker for dinner?"

Michael suggested, "How about we get a pizza and take it home. Then we can play games or watch a DVD or something."

"That's a good idea," agreed Mark. He turned to Elaine, "Then you won't have to rush in the morning or have cleanup to do after working all day. We can all relax in the evening. Michael and I will pick up the pizza and meet you at the apartment about 4:45."

Friday morning Bethany, Betsy, and Carrie rose very early and went shopping. Bethany shopped for Christmas gifts for her family, buying small items that she could send home with Betsy. Martha had arranged to meet them for lunch and treated them at a nice restaurant. After lunch she took them to a dress shop and bought each of them an outfit. Then they went back to the Davenports' home for naps.

Friday evening on the way to Elaine's apartment to meet Elaine and Mark, Bethany suggested, "John, why don't we sit at a different table at the restaurant? It will seem more like a date for Mark and Elaine and for us too. That's what my parents did when they were chaperoning Bob and me during the summer after my first year of college."

"That idea sounds good to me. I will ask Mark privately if he likes the idea. Thanks for suggesting it."

When they arrived at Elaine's apartment building, they found Mark waiting in the lobby. John shared Bethany's suggestion with him. "That is very kind of you two. Are you sure you don't mind?"

"Not at all. My wife and I need a date night too. We'll wait here while you go up and get Elaine."

"Okay. Then we will all ride together in my car, right?"

"Yes."

When Mark and Elaine joined them in the lobby, Bethany noticed that Elaine had obviously spent extra time on her hair and makeup. On the way to Mark's car, she managed a whispered conversation with her. "You look especially nice tonight, Elaine. How did you manage it? Didn't you have to work today?"

"I had my hair done at a shop during my lunch hour, and my boss let me off an hour early."

"Oh, that was nice of him."

"Yes, I am very lucky. He is very understanding. He has two teenage daughters, so that helps," she added, laughing.

At the restaurant they arranged for separate tables as planned. Throughout the evening Bethany could not help taking a few glances in their direction to see how the night was progressing. Mostly, she concentrated on enjoying a date with her own husband. The restaurant was a nice one with a romantic atmosphere and good food, and she and John thoroughly enjoyed the experience. She noticed that Elaine and Mark also seemed to be having a good time together.

When they took Elaine home, they waited while Mark escorted her up to her apartment. When they were taking their leave of him, he thanked them for taking the time to act as chaperones. John protested, "We want to thank you. It was a nice restaurant and the food was delicious. We had a great time. How about you and Elaine?"

"I think she enjoyed herself. I know I did."

John shook hands with him and said, "We will continue to pray that the three of you can reunite as a family in the not-too-distant future."

"Thanks, John. I am feeling fairly positive about that happening. At first I really had my doubts that it could work out. But I felt the visit yesterday went quite well. I am looking forward to spending the day with Michael tomorrow."

"Will we see you at Faith Baptist Sunday?"

"Yes, I will be there for the morning service, but I'll have to head for home right after the service."

"See you then. Goodnight."

On Sunday morning when the Davenports arrived for Sunday school, Michael sought out Bethany before heading for his class. "Hi, Bethany. May I talk to you for a few minutes before class?"

"Sure. How did yesterday go?"

"It was great. My dad is a lot of fun. Sometimes he acts crazy, like imitating the monkeys at the zoo. We also went to an indoor miniature golf course. He's really good."

"It sounds like you had a great day."

"Yes, and then we took pizza home and met Mom. Dad helped Mom make the salad and helped with the clean up. He's a pretty neat guy."

"I am so glad that things are working out for your family, Michael."

Michael glanced around. When he saw no one was nearby, he quickly hugged Bethany and said, "Thanks, Bethany. I am too. I'll see you after Sunday school; Mom said I could sit with them in big church today since Dad has to leave right after the service."

"Oh, that's nice. I'll see you later then."

During the morning service, Bethany and John sat with the Davenports. Elaine, Mark, and Michael were on the other side of the Davenports. Betsy and Carrie had left on Saturday to return to college.

After the service Michael and Elaine walked with Mark to his car. After they had said their goodbyes and joined the others at the limousine, Elaine's eyes shimmered suspiciously. Michael was excited. "My dad said he is going to ask his boss for a transfer to the Detroit office. That will be great! Don't you think so, too, Mom?"

"Yes, Michael, I do. We need to pray really hard that the transfer will work out."

"Will you and Brother Holman pray about it too, Bethany?"

"Of course we will, buddy," answered John.

"I hope it will work out really soon, Michael," said Bethany.

Bethany and John were surprised and grateful when they learned that Mrs. Davenport had invited their friend, Mrs. Carpenter, to have dinner and spend the afternoon at their home. As usual, they both enjoyed visiting with the elderly woman until time to return to the church for the evening service. During the service, Bethany played and sang with John, which the congregation appreciated. The pastor also asked John to give a short account of their ministry so far. At the end of the service the pastor took up a special offering for them, knowing they were still trying to raise more support.

The next morning they gave the Davenports a scented candle as a hostess gift and then said their goodbyes. Elaine and Michael had come for breakfast in order to see them off. Bethany asked Elaine, "Will you keep in touch and inform us how things progress?"

"Of course, thanks for your interest."

Michael reminded them, "Don't forget to pray about my dad's getting a transfer to Detroit."

"We won't. We have it written down in our prayer journals."

Bethany hugged Martha and said, "Thanks again for your generous hospitality. We had a wonderful Thanksgiving."

"You are so welcome! We love having you, but I do hope next year you can work it out to be with one of your families. If not, you have a standing invitation here anytime you are in the area."

"We do so appreciate that," said Bethany as she got into the truck. As they drove away, Bethany looked back and saw that Michael kept waving until they were out of sight. They went back to the church to hitch up the trailer and then started driving to the next church on Brother Gibson's schedule. On the way they would be stopping at a church for a Wednesday night service to present their work in hopes of raising some more support.

Sometimes as they drove, Bethany would call her friends to keep in touch. When Sarah Norberg found out that they would be in her area around Christmas, she invited them to spend the day with them. Donna and Peter Agnew would also be there for dinner. Bethany was happy to accept the invitation, as she had been thinking they would have a lonely Christmas in their trailer—even starting to feel sorry for herself. She thought, "The Lord is so good!" She chided herself for not trusting Him more for even the small things in life. She had not even thought to pray about the matter.

During the next few weeks, they received other encouraging news. Elaine called to tell them Mark was going to be transferred in January to the Detroit office. Several churches called to set up meetings or inform the Holmans they would take them on for support beginning in January.

Christmas Day started out with phone calls to each of their families. Then Bethany and John exchanged gifts with each other and had breakfast before heading for the Norbergs in mid-morning. The day was made more festive when Cindy called from Georgia to say that she and Randy had set a date in August for their wedding. They wanted the three couples to be in the wedding party. Since Peter and Paul were still finishing their schooling for master's degrees and John was just starting out in evangelism, Cindy's parents were going to provide the plane tickets for all of them.

Cindy asked if Bethany would be in the area long enough to shop at a certain bridal store to try on a bridesmaid dress that she had seen online. As it turned out, the Holmans would be, so the three young ladies agreed to get together to shop. Teasingly, the three men rolled their eyes and made comments to their wives about their excitement. The women simply ignored them and continued on with their happy, animated chatter.

They finally settled down enough to exchange gifts. Bethany and John also had gifts from family members who had been happy to find out their plans in time to send their gifts to the Norbergs' address.

Bethany and John both enjoyed holding Donna and Peter's little girl during the day. Before the day ended, Sarah made a big announcement to her friends. "Paul and I are expecting a baby in June!"

When Bethany and John returned to their trailer, which was parked on the grounds of the Crossroads Baptist Church, they had a hard time settling down to sleep. John mentioned that they would have to be careful with their plans for camps and church meetings to work around the wedding. Bethany was looking forward to the day of shopping with her friends and musing about the progressions and changes in everyone's lives. Then her phone rang, and she heard Carrie's voice, "Doug presented me with a ring today!" she excitedly announced.

Bethany exclaimed, "Oh, Carrie! That is wonderful. Just a sec. John, Carrie and Doug are engaged!"

In a booming voice, John answered, "That's great! Give them my congratulations."

"Carrie…"

Carrie laughed, "I heard him."

"Now tell me all about it."

"Well, I'm spending the Christmas break with Mom and Dad Briggs. They invited Doug to come over for the afternoon. He came in with a big box, all wrapped up very pretty. He wanted me to open it right away, but I made him open his gift from me first. He was acting so excited and nervous that I was suspicious; so I was teasing him a little, making him wait. I figured it must be something really special, but to be truthful, I was a little disappointed because the box was so big. He quickly tore open his gift, thanked me and then urged me to open his." She laughed. "I was so mean. I carefully took off the bow and the paper while he sat and fidgeted. When I finally got the box open, it had another, smaller box inside. It was also all wrapped up pretty. Now he was laughing. I opened that one a little faster. Guess what I found inside?"

"The ring?"

"No. Another wrapped box! I found out later that some of the girls at college helped him. They had wrapped a total of five boxes! The last one was quite small, and it contained a piece of paper with writing: 'Go look under your pillow.' So I did. Of course I found the ring box there. Everyone had followed me in there, and he went down on his knee and said, 'Carrie, I love you. I want to spend my life with you. Will you marry me?' "

Carrie continued tenderly, "I managed to say 'yes,' even though I was crying by then. He is used to my doing that when I am happy, so he just stood there and grinned."

"Carrie, that is so sweet and special. He went to a lot of work. How did he get the ring in your room under the pillow?"

"Mom Briggs sneaked it in there right after he arrived. He had come over the day before and given it to her. She kept the secret really well."

"When are you getting married?"

"In September, and you have to be a bridesmaid."

Bethany assured her she would try to work that out. "I will get back to you after I talk it over with John."

John knew Carrie's history and what a friend and mentor Bethany had been to her, so he readily agreed. They would simply have to do some careful planning.

Bethany called Carrie back the next morning to give her the good news. A little later Donna and Sarah picked her up, and they went to the dress shop. They all liked the dress Cindy had picked out and made arrangements for ordering them. Bethany asked that they ship hers to Donna. Back in the car they put Donna's phone on speakerphone and called Cindy. She was amazed and happy to hear it was all accomplished already.

After Christmas John and Bethany joined Brother Gibson again and traveled to churches with him through the end of January. Their first church revival meeting independent of Brother Gibson was scheduled for the second week of February. Both of them were excited and a little nervous when their six months with Brother Gibson were completed, and they were to start out on their own. Nonetheless, they trusted that the Lord had worked and guided them this far, and He would continue to do so.

John and Bethany were grateful to Brother Gibson for the opportunity to learn from him. In addition, Brother Gibson had recommended the Holmans to other churches and helped John to get started in scheduling further meetings. His help and training had been a wonderful blessing, and they praised the Lord for putting them under his tutelage.

— CHAPTER TWELVE —

On Their Own

"…teaching and preaching the word of the Lord…"
(Acts 15:35)

Bethany and John found that they enjoyed holding meetings on their own. John had prepared sermons ahead and continually worked on more. Bethany practiced on her piano keyboard at every opportunity, as well as on church pianos when she could. She and John had sung together for several years, beginning when they had first met while she was working as a nanny for the Davenports. Now they had grown accustomed to singing together while she played.

Many of the churches, which had their own Christian school, gave John the opportunity to preach for the school's chapel services. Sometimes they had split sessions with just the high school students, so that Bethany could address the young ladies while John preached to the young men. Bethany would teach about modest apparel, and she also warned them about hazards to young women including cutting and eating disorders, wrong friends, and attitudes. She and John would both discuss the need to date with chaperones and encourage the young people to save their first touch and kiss for the marriage altar.

One topic about which they felt a definite need to teach was phone etiquette. Young people were getting their own cell phones at younger ages, but often they were not thoughtful about others around them when they were using them. John and Bethany pointed out the need to turn off their phones, not only in church and school, but also in social settings.

"If you are a guest in someone's home, don't exchange calls or text messages with your friends," they instructed. "Give your undivided attention to your hosts. Unless it is an emergency call from your parents, other matters can wait. The same rule should be followed when you are having a meal with someone in a restaurant, especially if that person is treating you.

"When you are at home with your parents, be courteous to them also. You only have a few more years to be in their home. Use that time wisely. Show them you love them and that they are important to you. You spend a big part of your day with your friends at school; you probably don't usually need to talk to your friends in the evenings."

During the next few months, they visited churches in the Midwest. A few times John flew alone to churches that were farther away. He would leave the fifth wheel parked in a church lot or an RV camp, as long as he felt it was a safe place for Bethany to be alone. Bethany had her crochet materials with her. While John was gone on these trips, she made great progress on baby blankets, which she was making for gifts. "Possibly," she thought, "I will have a use for them myself in the not-too-distant future."

Bethany would telephone her friends, being careful to call Donna and Sarah when she knew their husbands would be away from home. They enjoyed long chats that really helped her lonely times to pass quickly. During one call to Cindy, she was happy to hear that Cindy had landed a job as a temporary teacher at the Crossroads Baptist Church School. One of the regular teachers was taking maternity leave. Cindy would teach for one year, starting in the fall after her marriage. This temporary position would work out very well, as Randy would be finishing up Bible college. Frequent conversations with her parents and John's family also helped the time pass.

When the school year was over, John and Bethany began to minister at summer youth camps. Bethany especially enjoyed this break, and found that the class she had taken on Adolescent Behavior was a great help. During one week, she happened to notice a group of girls who hung out together, and none of them were eating much. They did not show up for some meals, and when they did, they only picked at their food, leaving most of it on their plates. Danger signals went off in Bethany's mind. She alerted their youth pastor and his wife, who asked Bethany to help her confront the girls. During the meeting, the girls denied that there was anything unusual going on. Bethany still felt the need to outline the signs and dangers of anorexia.

"It is possible that you girls are becoming overly concerned about staying slim. By the way, none of you look like you have any problem in that area. You all look attractive and of normal weight right now. But if you have made an agreement or a pact together about skipping meals, or if any of you have thought about or actually started making yourselves throw up," Bethany said, pausing as she saw two of the girls exchange secretive glances, "then you are headed for a dangerous problem. Please take this issue seriously because you can do real damage to your physical and emotional health. This is a spiritual matter, also." She noticed startled expressions on their faces. Bethany continued, "It is spiritual because we are the temple of the Holy Spirit, and God cares about every aspect of our life. If any of you want to talk to either myself or your youth pastor's wife, we are both available to you at any time."

After the girls were dismissed, Bethany pointed out the two who had responded to her remark about forced vomiting. She encouraged the other woman to watch them carefully and alert their parents.

Remembering the young man that he had helped in Yellowstone National Park, John often preached to the young people about avoiding cheap thrills. "I've heard of young people dying from attempting to get a thrill from partially strangling themselves. They ended up killing themselves accidentally. If you aren't frightened enough for yourself, think about your parents. Can you imagine their finding you dead, and how they would feel? You may think they don't care or they don't understand you. You may be having problems getting along. But I promise you, they care and such a loss would cause them terrible grief.

"Others have had permanent brain damage from smoking cigarettes or cigars dipped in formaldehyde! I met a young man who was gasping for breath and probably would have died if I had not discovered him and gotten him help. Maybe you are tempted to try marijuana or some other drug. If you take part in any of these so-called avenues of pleasure, you are messing with the temple of God's Holy Spirit. If you are saved, you are grieving and quenching the Holy Spirit.

"If you want a high, then get involved at church. It can be exciting to learn to lead singing on a bus and making the ride to church fun for the kids so they will want to come back. Or what's more thrilling than leading someone to Christ? Some of you can have fun and thrills by being involved with sports in your Christian school. I beg of you, run with the right crowd and stay away from these harmful activities."

At the youth camps, Bethany began additionally teaching about avoiding piercing and tattoos, though first she always taught the girls about modest clothing. "I know low-cut tops and short skirts are popular and the latest fashion. But the Bible tells us in I Timothy 2:9, *'In like manner also, that women adorn themselves in modest apparel…'* I can assure you the Lord does not think low-cut blouses that show your cleavage and short skirts that show off your thighs fit the definition of modest apparel.

"God equates bare thighs with nakedness. In Isaiah 47:2 He says, *'Take the millstones, and grind meal; uncover thy locks, make bare the leg, uncover the thigh, pass over the rivers.'* Then in verse 3 He says, *'Thy nakedness shall be uncovered, yea, thy shame shall be seen…'* The thigh is that part of your leg above the knee. So your skirts should cover your knees. Most women's knees are not that attractive anyway. My grandmother told me she once read a quote by a woman who dressed the Hollywood stars. Even though I am sure she did not concern herself with modesty, she felt their knees should be covered simply because they are not good-looking. You also need to remember that even if your skirt covers your knees when you are standing, it may not when you are sitting. And girls, please remember to be ladylike and keep your knees together when you are sitting so people cannot see up your skirt.

"Another very popular trend these days that Christian young people should avoid is tattoos. In Leviticus 19:28 the people are commanded, *Ye shall not make any cuttings in your flesh for the dead, nor print any marks upon you: I am the* Lord.' That verse plainly states to avoid tattoos, don't you think? Also, some people cut themselves for attention or to punish themselves. This is usually because they don't feel loved, or they have emotional problems. Cutting can cause infections, not to mention permanent scars you will be sorry about later. If you do this or are tempted, please speak to me or some other counselor. We can get you help. God loves you, and we love you."

The couple also warned the young people about wrong types of music, television programs, the Internet and other modern electronic devices that could tempt them to do wrong.

At one camp a woman counselor approached Bethany to discuss her concern about one girl in her group. She told Bethany that the girl always wore long-sleeved tops and was a loner. She knew the girl had recently been removed from an abusive home and was living in a foster home. "After your talk I asked her if she might be having a problem like you discussed, but she denied it and is avoiding me. Do you have any suggestions?"

Bethany answered, "When you get back from camp, get in touch with the foster mother. Suggest she take the girl in for a routine physical before school starts. She won't be able to hide it at the doctor's office."

"Thank you. That does sound like a good idea."

Bethany asked for the girl's name so she could add her to her prayer list.

June and July passed quickly for Bethany. August arrived, and soon it was time for them to fly to Georgia for Cindy's wedding. Bethany was eagerly anticipating seeing their friends from college, especially Sarah, who had notified them in mid-June that she and Paul were the proud parents of a baby boy named James.

The Holmans parked the fifth wheel at the church in Detroit on Tuesday and then headed for the Davenports' home. Margaret had invited them for dinner when she found out they would be there for a few days. She invited Elaine, Michael and Mark also. As soon as he arrived, Michael joyfully informed them that his parents were getting remarried in September. "We all want you to come. Mom told me to invite you."

After inquiring about the exact date, John assured them they could make it. It was scheduled for two weeks after Carrie's wedding. After dinner Bethany and Elaine had time for a private conversation. Elaine confided to Bethany that she and Mark had recently come to an agreement that she would quit her job and be a stay-at-home wife and mother. They were hoping to have more children, and Mark felt strongly about the need for Michael and any future children to have her undivided attention. Elaine explained that she had gone through quite a struggle and spiritual battle before getting the matter settled.

"To be honest, my struggle was tied up with the submission issue. I have been rearing Michael on my own, supporting us, advancing in my career. It was hard to give up, but at the same time, I really love Mark. I was really at a crossroads in my life. I finally went to Pastor Butler, and he was very helpful. He pointed out that my friends at work and the world's point of view were influencing my thinking. The women's movement and the entertainment industry all glamorize careers and make a woman feel worthless if all she does is stay home. Pastor Butler reminded me that, in God's eyes, nothing is more important.

"He kindly pointed out that my pride was getting in the way because of my success. I need to give thanks and glory to God for that success, but I need to be willing to give it up. He suggested I could maybe do a little home decorating for friends or use my talents at church. He said he is wanting to redecorate the restrooms and some classrooms, and I could do that."

"That would be great, Elaine."

"I know. I am looking forward to it once I quit, which will be soon—and after we have had some time to adjust to married life. I also told Pastor about my struggles with submission. I wanted to know I could do that before I got married. I remember we used to have fights whenever Mark tried to tell me what to do or made a decision I didn't like," Elaine said. She paused and then added, "I don't suppose you can understand; you are such a good Christian."

Bethany laughed. "Oh, if you only knew! I think every woman struggles with submission issues, Elaine. I've had my share of problems with it."

"Really? You and John always look so happy and loving."

"We are, but I pray constantly for the Lord to give me victory in that area. What helps me is knowing the Lord commanded it. So if I don't agree or I get angry and upset, I remember that when I submit, it is out of love for my Saviour—not just John. I heard a speaker once say that we can't have the proper fear of God without respecting and reverencing our husbands."

"I'll remember that. Pastor also told me I have to learn to trust Mark. I waited a few months after our talk. I prayed a lot, and I watched Mark. He keeps growing in his faith, getting more and more involved in the church. He has become a good soul winner. He is also doing well on his job. Father was able to do a little detective work and found out his firm is happy with his work. It is also a matter of our trusting God, Who has already answered so many prayers and worked in our lives. I have come to realize I can also trust Him in this relationship."

Bethany hugged Elaine. "It is so exciting to see how you are growing in your faith too, Elaine."

"Do you really think so?"

"Oh, yes. It is very evident."

"That means a lot to me, Bethany—especially coming from you. Thanks."

"I'm just a sinner saved by grace too, Elaine."

They flew to Georgia on Thursday for Cindy and Randy's wedding. Bethany enjoyed the reunion with her friends from college days. It was a joy to hold Sarah's baby boy and to see how much Donna's little Elizabeth had grown. Besides being in the wedding party, Bethany and John sang two songs during the ceremony. Cindy wore a beautiful gown with a long train and looked radiant. The ceremony went smoothly except for one rather amusing incident. The little flower girl entertained herself by counting the satin-covered buttons running down the back of the bride's gown. What she was doing became very obvious to the audience when she pointed with her finger as her eyes moved down the back of the bride's gown.

The reception that followed was a gala affair, which was held in a beautifully decorated rented hall. Uniformed waitresses served a delicious roast beef catered dinner to all of the guests. Then the bride and groom cut the large beautifully decorated cake. Of course, the irrepressible Cindy smashed the piece she was feeding to Randy in his face. Randy, who was not at all surprised that she would do that, took it in good humor.

At the rehearsal on Friday night, Cindy's pastor had heard John and Bethany sing and had made a point of talking with John during the rehearsal dinner. When he had learned about their ministry, he invited John to preach and to share about his work on Sunday night. He also wanted them to sing, as they usually did when John was holding meetings. John was happy to oblige, and the couple received a generous offering. The pastor also set up a future meeting and said he would spread the word to other pastors in the area. "Maybe you can set up additional meetings around the same time, when you are in the area." John thanked him for the help.

Monday during the plane trip back to Detroit, Bethany exclaimed, "What a great, unexpected blessing! The Lord is so good."

"Yes, He surely is," agreed John.

They had meetings set up in the Detroit area during the weeks before Carrie's wedding. They were able to leave the fifth wheel set up at the Faith Baptist Church and drive to the other churches from there. The Davenports had them to dinner one Thursday night, as did Mrs. Carpenter the following week. John had some meetings Monday through Wednesday, and others were from Friday through Sunday. They were keeping busy; and between support they received from churches and love offerings, they were managing fairly well financially.

Carrie's wedding, held at the Crossroads Baptist Church, was simple, but beautiful. She and her foster parents, the Briggs, had grown very close. Carrie now called them Mom and Dad and had come to an appreciation of what they had done for her by taking her into their home—in spite of all her problems. They did what they could to help make the day special, but they simply did not have the finances for an elaborate wedding like Cindy's had been. But Carrie was content and appreciative. Looking back over her life, she could hardly believe it was really happening. She told Bethany it was like a fairy tale come true. She was a radiant bride.

Bethany and John were almost as excited as Carrie. Doug was a proud groom as he watched Carrie come down the aisle. No one but Bethany and the Briggs knew that her lovely gown was purchased at a second-hand consignment shop. With the kind of work they were planning to do, Carrie's thriftiness would be an important asset. Bethany was so proud of her!

Shortly before Elaine's wedding, Bethany began to suspect she might be expecting. She bought a home pregnancy test, which confirmed her suspicions. Before announcing it to friends and family, they decided to have her see a doctor for further assurance. They were both having a hard time containing and hiding their excitement until they could find out for sure. She had to wait two weeks before an appointment was available. The Briscoes' ceremony was being held on a Saturday afternoon, and John had a week-long meeting scheduled beginning the following Monday. Bethany's appointment was not until Friday. They decided that John would take the fifth wheel, and they would ask the Davenports if Bethany could stay with them. They told George and Martha that Bethany had a doctor's appointment. Both of the Davenports were happy to have her stay with them.

Bethany and John stood up with the Briscoes. They had a simple ceremony for which Elaine wore a pastel lavender dress and a simple headpiece. Elaine had told Bethany to wear one of her formal dresses that would fit in with the colors of the flowers in the decorations. Elaine did not want the Holmans to have the expense of buying another. Bethany had given many of them away, but the one from Cindy's recent wedding was a pastel green, and the dress was a similar style as Elaine's, so it worked well. She and John were again asked to sing a duet.

During the week at the Davenports' home, Bethany began experiencing morning sickness. She excused herself from breakfast and looked pale when she finally came downstairs. By lunchtime she usually felt better and was able to eat lunch with Martha and Michael, who was staying with his grandparents while his parents went on a short honeymoon. Michael asked questions, but Martha, who was beginning to suspect the truth, ran interference to save Bethany embarrassment. Bethany tried to spend some time each afternoon going for walks with Michael or tossing a ball with him. She enjoyed the fresh air, but she was already experiencing unusual fatigue, so she kept the walks short. Michael was perplexed and impatient with her lack of energy and enthusiasm.

The doctor confirmed her suspicions, which she joyfully reported to John when he called her Friday evening after the service. "That's great, honey. I am so happy. How are you feeling?"

"Rotten in the mornings. Thankfully, it doesn't last all day."

"I am so sorry. I was hoping you wouldn't have morning sickness."

"Me, too. It usually doesn't last too long."

"I hope not. Do you think you will be able to travel with me?"

"I don't honestly know. I tire so easily too. I am taking naps every day. Michael doesn't understand, of course, and he has been pretty disappointed. Luckily, he is used to not having other kids around and entertains himself. Mrs. Davenport hasn't said anything, but I think she suspects."

"What makes you think so?"

"She changes the direction of the conversation whenever Michael starts asking what's wrong with me. He wonders why I don't eat breakfast, why I nibble on crackers, and why I get tired and have to take naps."

John laughed. "I can see why he is wondering. That is unusual behavior for you. You are usually so energetic." His tone of voice changed. "I have really missed you this week, sweetheart."

"I promise you, the feeling is mutual. I can't wait for you to get back."

"Me either, but I am concerned because we have a busy schedule lined up, and it will entail some traveling. Remember, we are traveling south and then going west. I have it planned so we can be with my folks in California for Thanksgiving. Then we will travel north and end up in Tacoma at your home church around Christmas."

"I know, and I was really looking forward to it. We will simply have to see how it goes."

"Are you ready for us to tell our families and friends about the baby?"

"Oh, yes. I am bursting with the news! But I'll wait until you are here, and we can call people together."

"I will leave here bright and early Monday morning. I should be there around 6:00 p.m."

"Okay, honey. See you then. I love you soooooo much!"

"Goodbye, love."

Saturday morning Mrs. Davenport knocked on Bethany's bedroom door. After Bethany asked who it was and she heard Mrs. Davenport's familiar voice, she told Martha to come in. Mrs. Davenport had some fresh crackers and a cup of peppermint tea. "I think these will help with what ails you. I hate to be nosy, but if I suspect correctly I would like to take you shopping for some 'special' clothes this afternoon. It would be my only chance."

"Oh, Mrs. Davenport, you are right, of course. I am expecting. We were going to tell you right after we called our parents. You have already done so much for us, I hate…"

Martha interrupted her, "Now Bethany, we have gone over that before. Just let me do this for you so you will be prepared with some outfits to wear when things start getting too tight. I am so excited—you would think it was *my* grandchild!"

Bethany hugged her. "You are just so sweet, and you and your husband are so generous. That would be a load of fun!"

"Good! We will leave after lunch. I will have the cook make an extra nourishing lunch since you can't seem to manage breakfasts these days."

"You are so very thoughtful. By the way, I was fairly sure you knew. Thanks for running interference for me with Michael. I am so sorry I can't do as much with him as usual."

"He'll have to get used to this type of thing when his mom goes this route—which I hope is very soon!" she said, laughing.

They had a wonderful time shopping. Mrs. Davenport took her to a specialty motherhood shop and bought her a casual denim skirt and two tops to wear with it and a nice outfit for church.

Bethany commented, "This is really special. I thought I would have to get everything from thrift stores—which I don't mind, of course. I must admit that new things are a real treat."

Monday evening the Davenports had dinner later than usual, so that John could join them. Afterward, the Holmans excused themselves, explaining they needed to phone their parents. By now Martha Davenport had shared their news with her husband, but they had not told Michael as of yet.

As they expected, both sets of parents were thrilled with the news that they were going to be grandparents for the first time. It took close to an hour to make the two calls. Then they went downstairs to rejoin their hosts. Michael had already gone to bed, so Martha commented, "I am sure your parents are ecstatic. I myself am so excited! Do you want us to keep it a secret?"

"No. We are going to call our close friends tomorrow to tell them, including Elaine and Mark."

"You won't have to call them. They plan to be here around noon tomorrow."

"Great! We will tell them in person."

The next morning they called their close friends. Everyone responded with enthusiasm and happiness. Elaine and Mark arrived in time for lunch. Afterward, John and Mark took Michael out to shoot baskets while Bethany told Elaine. She would pass on the news to her husband and son later. She hugged Bethany and whispered, "Maybe it won't be too long until I have such an announcement. Mark doesn't want to wait real long."

"Oh, I hope so, Elaine."

The next morning Mark, Elaine, and Michael returned to the apartment. Mark had the rest of the week off before going back to work. They had some special things planned to do with Michael.

Bethany and John also had to leave. They had a meeting scheduled to begin that night.

— CHAPTER THIRTEEN —

Growing Through Trials

"Blessed be God…Who comforteth us in all our tribulation…."
(II Corinthians 1:3, 4)

*K*nowing how sick she felt every morning, Bethany took the precaution of keeping a small wastebasket lined with a plastic bag in the cab of the truck. When she felt ill, John tried to pull over, but he wasn't always able to because of the fifth wheel. Besides feeling sympathetic, John discovered that the sounds and the smell of her sickness made him start feeling ill. They had to stop several times for both of them to get fresh air. They did not make it to their destination as early as John had hoped. Because of the motion of the truck and not being able to lie down, Bethany did not recover as quickly as usual. She finally stopped vomiting, but still felt queasy, looked pale, and had no appetite for lunch.

By dinnertime, she was able to eat a little. Her lack of appetite concerned John. They were also both disappointed that by the time for the service she still did not feel well enough to play and sing with him. She barely felt well enough to sit with the pastor's wife during the service. When the pastor offered to take them out for coffee and dessert after the service, John politely explained the situation and reluctantly declined the invitation. An exhausted Bethany fell into bed as soon as they returned to the trailer.

This pattern continued for a few days. It soon became obvious to John that their traveling together was not going to work. He had a heart-to-heart talk with Bethany to present a plan he felt they had to implement. He tried to do this as they drove toward their next planned stop where he was to hold revival meetings for a whole week. He told her he felt she needed to fly to his parents' and wait for him until Thanksgiving. Then they would see how she was doing physically.

Bethany started crying uncontrollably. John was glad they were close to a rest stop. He pulled in, and they both got out of the truck and went to the trailer where he held her in his arms until she quieted. "I am so sorry, honey. I hate it when we are apart. But this just isn't working. I'm sure you know this down in your heart." Bethany nodded in agreement, but she could not speak. John continued, "I'm not simply concerned about arriving late at meetings. I'm even more concerned about you and the baby. You aren't eating enough to keep a bird alive."

"I'm sorry, John. I try, but I can't."

"I know that, my sweet. I'm not criticizing you." He hugged her tighter to back up his words. "Our next meeting is a week long, so I will work on getting you a ticket while we are there. Okay?"

"Okay," she whispered reluctantly and started weeping again. It took about ten minutes before she could get control of her emotions. Then they both used the public restrooms, where she splashed water on her face. They took a short walk in the fresh air before getting back on the road.

As they drove toward their destination, Bethany mulled over all that John had said. She had to admit that it would be a blessing not to have to endure the motion of the truck, which made her nausea even worse. She would enjoy the time with her in-laws, even though she would miss John terribly.

John did not wait to start his preparations until they had reached their next destination. That evening after dinner he called his parents, who were sympathetic about Bethany's sickness and readily agreed to her staying with them. Then he called the next few churches on their agenda to let them know he would be alone; therefore, he would need an accompanist if he sang. Bethany tried to keep busy so she would not sit around crying. She knew it really did not help or change anything and was upsetting to John. Instead, she made a list of items she needed to take with her, which included craft items and more crochet yarn that she had already bought. Now she was really inspired to try making baby sweaters as well as blankets. Some of the items were in the storage bins. By now it was dark, so John said he would get them, along with suitcases for her to use, at their next stop.

When they reached their destination, John quickly began checking about plane tickets. Bethany began packing her clothes and other items. After being at their destination for two days, Bethany began feeling better. She could eat more and was able to play and sing by the third night. They had a few pleasant days together before she had to leave. John drove her to the airport on Saturday. Bethany tried to be brave, but when it was time to go through security and she finally had to say goodbye, she was tearful. She could not keep from thinking about two whole months away from John. This would be their longest separation since getting married. As soon as Bethany was through security, she found a restroom, where she washed her face and repaired her makeup, all the while preaching to herself.

When she arrived at the waiting area for her flight, she pulled out a book to keep her mind occupied. She had purposely brought a Christian fiction novel that she had wanted to read, knowing it would grab her attention. Since they had wisely chosen a late afternoon flight, she managed not to be sick, although she did feel a little queasy during the takeoff and landing. She was relieved when she was able to get off the plane and calm her stomach before meeting John's parents at the luggage claim. Fortunately, their home was not far from the airport, and the short ride did not bring on the sickness. Mrs. Holman had homemade chicken soup cooking in a slow cooker, which settled well on Bethany's stomach. She was very grateful for her mother-in-law's thoughtfulness.

Mrs. Holman had prepared the guest room, and Bethany noted that she had made a few changes in the decorations. On the bed was a beautifully decorated basket full of bath and body products, as well as saltine crackers and other snacks that might help to settle a sick tummy. She gave Mrs. Holman a grateful hug and said, "I feel very pampered. Thank you so much."

"You know we love you, Bethany, and we are looking forward to having you with us. We can have so much fun shopping and making things for the baby."

"That will help with my loneliness for John. I am hoping your mother can help me with my crocheting. I want to learn some more advanced stitches and try to make a baby sweater."

"Oh, she will be thrilled if you ask her for help. She has already started making things. She is very excited about her first great-grandchild."

Bethany and the Holman family soon developed a workable routine. They did not expect to see her until late morning. She was grateful that the downstairs guest room was close to a bathroom, which she had to herself most of the day. The family room was also downstairs, and everyone gathered there in the evenings to play games or watch DVDs.

Bethany was able to eat lunch and help with cleanup afterward as well as preparation and cleanup for the dinner meal. On the day of the week that Mrs. Holman cleaned, Bethany helped by doing the downstairs rooms. Mrs. Holman also designated one day for Bethany to use the laundry facilities. They found several times to shop as well as working on projects for the baby. Mrs. Holman was not as advanced in sewing skills as Bethany's mother, but she had a machine and knew the basics. She was working on a crib blanket.

Bethany often talked to John and her family on the phone. Both of her siblings were now attending Bible college in Indiana. Betsy always had exciting stories to report about college life. She was enjoying the opportunity to date young men, but she had not settled on anyone special as of yet. College was all still very new for Brian, but he seemed to be doing well and enjoying the experience.

Bethany also kept in touch with the friends she had made at college, as well as the Briscoes and the Davenports. She kept busy, and the time passed quickly. Nights when she went to bed alone were the hardest times. John reported that he was experiencing the same melancholy. They agreed to pray for each other and not dwell on their lonely feelings. Bethany usually awoke in the morning and realized she had fallen asleep praying, which was much better than crying herself to sleep.

John's grandmother was indeed happy to help Bethany with learning more advanced crocheting skills. Bethany was making good progress on a baby sweater. She had also started decorating scrapbook pages, leaving places to add photos. Occasionally, she was asked to help with the music ministry at the Holmans' church. Thankfully, she did not have time to sit and feel sorry for herself, which was the way she wanted it.

John was pleased and proud of her. Her contentment made it easier on him so he could concentrate on preaching. He continually thanked God for giving him a wife who was truly his help meet.

When he arrived home the Monday before Thanksgiving, they had a joyful reunion. Bethany was excited to show him her little tummy. "Don't you think I am starting to look a little bit pregnant?"

John laughed. "I wonder if you will be as excited about it by your ninth month? Yes, I can see a difference. You look pregnant to me, at least, my little mother-to-be."

"Oh, John, I am just so thrilled about it!"

"Even in the mornings, love?"

"Well…"

John laughed and pulled her into an embrace. "I so hope that part will be over soon."

She sighed. "Me too."

"Do you see any improvement?"

"I'm afraid not, John."

"Then I'll get you a plane ticket to fly to Tacoma. I'll be there for Christmas."

"Can we afford that?"

"We'll just have to trust the Lord to meet our needs. I have enough extra right now to get the ticket. I'll do that tomorrow. Hopefully, I can get you a flight for a week from today."

"I am so sorry, John."

He put his fingers to her lips. "None of that, love. There is nothing to be sorry about. Now show me the things you have been working on."

Bethany was grateful that John remembered and showed an interest. She knew he was trying to redirect her thinking, and she loved him for it. His genuine interest showed as he attentively looked at the items she was making and listened to her explanations. Bethany mused later that it continually surprised and pleased her that this big, tough ex-football player husband could be so tender.

They enjoyed Thanksgiving with his family. John's three siblings were all in Bible college now. James was a freshman, Naomi a sophomore, and Ruth was a senior. The Holmans had planned ahead to save up enough for them to all fly home for Thanksgiving. Mr. and Mrs. Holman were planning to fly to Chicago at Christmastime. They would do some sightseeing for a few days with the young people and then use a rental car to drive to Mrs. Holman's sister's home in southern Indiana.

The three young people came in on Wednesday morning, so Bethany did not go to the airport with John and his parents to pick them up. When they arrived at the house, Ruth rushed down the stairs to greet Bethany. After they hugged, she exclaimed, "Oh, Bethany! You are going to make me an aunt! I am so excited. Can I feel your tummy?"

Bethany laughed. "Of course, but there isn't much to feel yet!"

Next came Naomi. She was a little more reserved as she had not spent as much one-on-one time with Bethany. Laughingly Bethany asked, "Do you want to feel the baby too?"

"Oh, yes, may I?"

"Of course, but I hope you're not disappointed. The baby isn't very big yet."

"This is just great. I can't believe I'm going to be an auntie!"

James came downstairs to greet Bethany with a handshake and a grin. "I am real happy for you and John. I am looking forward to being an uncle."

"Thank you, James. How do you like college?"

"It's fantastic!"

Mrs. Holman came downstairs and shooed the three young people upstairs. "Bethany doesn't feel too well in the mornings. You can visit more this afternoon. Let her rest now."

"Thank you, Mom," Bethany gratefully whispered as she headed for the bed. Mrs. Holman had come just in time. Bethany knew she needed to lie down to settle the queasy feeling. She felt so lazy, but she had learned the hard way that she did better if she didn't push herself in the mornings.

Bethany was grateful that the sickness did not last all day. Mrs. Holman had planned the next day's Thanksgiving meal for the usual dinnertime this year to allow time for Bethany to feel well enough to enjoy it. Her plan worked. They were all glad to see that Bethany was able to eat a decent amount of food.

Ruth and Naomi spent part of their time both Friday and Saturday mornings sitting by Bethany's bed, visiting with her and being careful not to stay too long. John used the time to work on sermons. Since his arrival on Monday, he had tried to spend as much time as possible with Bethany, knowing that they would be separated again for a month. But he did have meetings planned for those weeks and had to do some preparation.

Bethany's flight was scheduled for Tuesday afternoon. John would leave right after taking her to the airport for a meeting scheduled about two hours away. Then he would travel to Oregon and work his way up to the Tacoma, Washington, area by Christmas.

In the meantime, John and Bethany appreciated every moment they had together and with his family. John's brother and sisters left Saturday afternoon to return to college. Sunday afternoon Mrs. Holman told John and Bethany that she and her husband were going to spend Monday afternoon and evening together shopping for after-Thanksgiving specials and going out to eat. Bethany and John were grateful to have the time alone. Bethany told John, "I suspect your mom did it for us as much as for them. She is so sweet and thoughtful."

They enjoyed being alone together, forbidding themselves to think about the coming month-long separation. Without planning it together, they were each praying that Bethany's morning sickness would end so she could travel with John again. Bethany was also praying that she could say goodbye at the airport without crying—at least not until she was alone. She kept reminding herself that she had counted the cost before agreeing to be John's wife. She had known they would face these times of separation.

On Tuesday she did manage to part from John without tears. His last words to her confirmed how important it was as he whispered, "Thank you for being so brave about this, sweetheart." She gave him a weak smile and hurried into the boarding line. Tears stung her eyes, but she managed to hold them back until she was through security. She found a restroom and went into a stall, where she cried quietly for a few minutes. Then she wiped her eyes, blew her nose, and emerged looking calm and confident. Again she had a book to read, as well as a crocheting project to occupy her while she waited to board and on the plane.

She and her mother had a happy reunion. While driving to the house, Mrs. Prescott commented, "I am sorry you are having these problems. But looking on the bright side, we will have more time together. Hopefully you will soon feel better."

"We will have a nice long visit. John has several churches lined up after Christmas, so we will be around for several more weeks; that is, if you can put up with us that long."

"Don't worry about that! We never get too much time with our girl. Daddy is so excited. He wanted to come with me today, but he couldn't get the day off."

"It was sweet of him to try. I am also anxious to see Betsy and Brian, but I know it is going to be a houseful for you as well as being a very busy time. I hope it isn't too much."

"I have planned ahead. Most of my shopping is done, my packages for those out-of-town are wrapped and ready to be mailed; and I have planned my menus for the time everyone is here."

"Wow! I am impressed," answered Bethany, laughing.

"I am pretty impressed with myself," replied Margaret, tittering.

The rest of the trip mother and daughter talked about the latest they had heard from Brian and Betsy, and Margaret shared some of the happenings at their home church. Bethany was trying to keep her mind off her stomach. She was glad when the hour-long drive was over, and she had somehow managed not to get sick. She walked around in the fresh air for a while, and finally felt up to going in and helping her mother with the final touches to the dinner.

When her dad arrived home, she was happy to be encased in his loving arms for a big hug. "Oh, it is so good to have my little girl home for a while." He held her at arm's length. "Do I detect a little tummy starting?" He hugged her again. "I am so excited for you…and us. We are looking forward to being grandparents!"

"I am sure you are not half as excited as John and me."

Margaret added, "We were so happy to hear the news. Your grandparents are also thrilled."

James asked, "How are you feeling?"

"About the same as I have been. By the time we arrived here today after both the plane and car rides, I wasn't feeling too great. But it cleared up when I walked around in the fresh air. I don't usually get sick in the afternoon or evening—only in the morning."

"No improvement yet?"

"No, I am sorry to say."

"Well, you take it easy while you are here and let us pamper you."

"I don't have much choice in the mornings. I feel so lazy. But in the afternoon I feel pretty well and have more energy."

"I'll keep that in mind when I plan our shopping trips," replied Margaret.

Her husband teasingly questioned, "I thought you had all your Christmas shopping done?"

"I do. But there is a baby to shop for, you know."

He chuckled and answered, "I know, I know."

"I also want to look for patterns and material for maternity outfits. I want to make some for Bethany"

"Oh, that is so sweet, Mom. Which reminds me, I want to show you what Mrs. Davenport insisted on buying me at one of those nice maternity specialty shops."

"I'm not surprised—that sounds like Martha."

"She is almost as excited as you, like it was her own grandchild."

Changing the subject, Margaret said, "I better get dinner on the table. James, could you bring in Bethany's luggage while I do that? By the time we got back from the airport, I had to start dinner."

"I'll be happy to."

"I'll help you, Mom," interjected Bethany.

After the emotional parting from John and the flight, Bethany was ready to retire early. When she got upstairs, she was happy and grateful to discover that her parents had purchased a double bed and put it in Brian's bedroom for her and John. Brian would "camp out" in the family room when he arrived home for Christmas break.

"How considerate of you two!" exclaimed Bethany when they showed her to the room. "Thank you so much. But what about Brian?"

"We talked to him before we did it. He doesn't mind sleeping in the family room when someone needs his room, and his bedroom was large enough for the double bed. We figured we might as well do something permanent for you and other out-of-town guests who might visit."

"That's kind of Brian to be so cooperative."

"He is becoming a very mature, considerate young man. Physically, he has shot up too. You will be surprised when you see him."

She and her mother managed to go shopping twice during the next two weeks. Once they went to the fabric store where they purchased the fabric and pattern for a maternity outfit she could wear to church. The second time they shopped for some baby body suits and sleepers that would be appropriate for either a girl or a boy.

Bethany gradually began to feel better. The sickness was not as bad and did not last as long. Some mornings she only felt a little queasiness. She finally improved enough to be able to eat a piece of toast. She was so happy to tell John one morning, "I think the sickness might be pretty much behind me."

But early one Thursday morning, she began having other frightening symptoms. When she shared them with her mother, Mrs. Prescott was immediately alarmed. She tried to stay calm and hide her true feelings from Bethany. Since they planned to have Bethany come back to her parents' shortly before her due date and give birth in Tacoma, she had already started her care with a local obstetrician. Mrs. Prescott advised her to call the office.

The receptionist told Bethany, "Come in immediately." As Bethany hung up the phone, tears started. "I'm having a miscarriage, aren't I?"

Her mom gave her a quick hug and then took charge. "Put on your coat and grab your purse. Let's get going." Bethany obeyed with tears running down her face.

In the car Mrs. Prescott tried to reassure her. "Don't assume the worst until we know for sure what's going on. Do you want to call John? He could be praying, and he should have a chance to be prepared in case there is something wrong."

Bethany nodded her head, tried to get control, and punched in the number. When she heard John's cheerful voice on the other end, she broke down again. Mrs. Prescott could hear his voice on the other end. "Bethany, what's wrong? Honey, tell me."

Mrs. Prescott pulled the car over and stopped on the shoulder of the road, took the phone, and briefly explained the situation. She told him they would call back as soon as they knew anything.

With a choked voice, he answered that he would be praying.

At the doctor's office, after an ultrasound was performed, the doctor gently and kindly confirmed Bethany's suspicions. "Yes, you have miscarried this baby." Bethany began weeping; tears ran down her face, but she held back the sobs. She kept thinking about being a good testimony in spite of her great disappointment. The doctor continued, "There should be no reason you can't get pregnant again and carry a baby successfully. I would advise you to wait a few months to heal physically and emotionally. I am so sorry. I know this loss is hard. It is something that simply happens sometimes."

Once they were in the car and ready to head home, Bethany could not hold back the sobs any longer. Mrs. Prescott held her for a few minutes and then gently released her. "Let's get you home. I'll call John and let him know as soon as we get you settled."

This statement brought on a fresh torrent of tears and sobs. Bethany managed to whisper, "He's going to be very disappointed. He was so excited."

"I know, honey. But you can try again soon. This will only be a temporary setback. This happened to your Aunt Melanie and later she had four children—Jessica and her three brothers."

Bethany appreciated her mother's efforts to comfort her. Yes, she wanted others, but she had also wanted this child. Through her pain, Bethany managed to answer mournfully, "That's encouraging. Though losing a child at any age—before or after birth—is very painful. It will be a long wait before we see this little one in Heaven."

Her mother placed a tender kiss on Bethany's forehead. "Indeed, you are right," she acknowledged sorrowfully, before starting the car and heading for the house.

John was just arriving at a church when he had received the first call. He sat and prayed for a few minutes before steeling his emotions and climbing out of the truck to seek out the pastor. Usually John left his phone on vibrate and turned off the text message signal when he was fellowshipping with a host pastor. Now he was so anxious about Bethany and the baby that he explained the situation and asked if the pastor would mind if he left his phone on.

Pastor Green was kindly concerned and agreeable. When he suggested they get something to eat, John thanked him but said he could not possibly swallow anything at the moment. The other man understood and remarked that they should get John's trailer set up as quickly as possible while they waited for news.

John agreed and numbly followed the man from his office. He barely took in the information as to where to park and hook up. The pastor disappeared for a while as John struggled to concentrate on the task at hand. His mind was racing with questions and silent prayers. "How can I stay here and preach as scheduled when I long to be with Bethany? If she indeed loses our baby, I desperately want to be able to hold her, comfort her, and grieve with her."

The pastor had seen and heard the grief and worry in John's face and voice. He returned to his office and checked the financial books to see what was available in the discretionary benevolence fund, then called as many of his deacons as he could contact at that hour of a weekday. He returned to John and found he had finished hooking up the trailer. He invited him back to his office, where he handed him a cup of coffee, which John drank, barely noticing what he was doing. Kindly and gently the pastor mentioned that his own wife had experienced a miscarriage in her third pregnancy.

John asked, "Did she have any problems with your first two children?"

"No, and after the miscarriage, we had another child without any special problems. It's very hard to go through, but I can promise you there is hope for the future."

"Thank you, sir. I appreciate your sharing that."

"You are welcome. I see you finished your coffee. Would you like to go to your trailer to wait for the news? I imagine you would like to be alone. Please let me know as soon as you can when you hear something. I plan to be in my office all day."

"Thank you, sir, for your understanding."

Remembrance was starting to affect the other man. He realized he also needed some time alone. He rose and managed to say in a choked voice, "I'll be praying."

John said, "Thank you," and hurried out.

A few minutes later, after the pastor had regained his composure, he called his wife and explained the situation. Through the instant tears that came from the memories of her own sad experience, she whispered, "I'll pray."

The time dragged by for John. He tried to work on a sermon. He tried to read his Bible; but in the end, all he could do was cry out to God in prayer. Finally the phone rang, and he heard his mother-in-law's strained voice. He knew before she could finish getting out the words. When John was able, he headed for the pastor's office with his news. On the way, he met the older man who was on his way to John's trailer to check on him. He responded to John's news by giving him a firm hug. "I'm sorry, son. Is your wife okay?"

"Physically, yes. I haven't talked to her yet. She couldn't…"

"I understand. You desperately want to hear her voice, but she can't manage to talk yet. I know you also ache to hold and comfort her. So I have made arrangements for you to fly out in about two hours. You need to pack a few things as quickly as possible, and I will drive you to the airport. We need to leave within fifteen minutes for you to get through security and make your flight on time."

"Oh, but sir, the meetings…"

The pastor interrupted, "We will work all that out later. Now you and your wife need each other. You probably couldn't preach tonight anyway."

"But the cost…"

"Don't worry about it. We have a benevolence fund for exactly this kind of need. Now we must hurry."

John grabbed the pastor's hand and squeezed so hard the older man could barely keep from wincing. "Words cannot express my gratitude." Turning quickly to hide the tears springing to his eyes, John headed for the trailer to throw a few things in a bag.

Pastor Green quickly called his wife, asked her to contact another pastor in the area to see if he could preach at the scheduled meeting for that evening, and then went to his car.

On the way to the airport, the pastor kept his phone on and used his Bluetooth so his wife could call him. She reported back that the other pastor was happy to help out when she explained the situation to him.

During the ride to the airport, John called Mrs. Prescott to let her know he was coming in that evening. She was surprised and happy to hear of this development and assured him someone would be at the airport to pick him up. Then John called his father to share the sad news. Mr. Holman prayed with his son and then called his wife. As gently as possible, he shared the disappointing news.

When Bethany had gotten home and into bed, she cried herself to sleep. When she awoke in about an hour, she lay quietly for a time to think and pray. She realized she was at another crossroads in her life—she could be bitter and angry or trust God and His Word that promises, "...*all things work together for good to them that love God*..." She could not see the good right now, but she decided she would trust God—even if He never showed her the purpose for this hurtful happening in her life. She went downstairs and sought her mother.

Mrs. Prescott gave her a quick hug, held her at arm's length, and searched her face. She smiled. "I can see the Lord has given you peace and comfort."

Bethany whispered, "God is always good."

"I have some good news for you, sweetheart. John is on his way here. He will arrive at Sea-Tac about 5:00. Your dad will leave work early to pick him up."

"How did that...?"

"The pastor of the church where he was going to preach this week paid to send him home. I don't know how long he'll stay."

Tears came to Bethany's eyes. "How sweet of that pastor! God is so good. It will be so comforting to have John here with me."

The time dragged for Bethany as she waited for John to arrive. Her mother tried to distract her. "Bethany, could you make a salad for dinner? Do you feel up to it? You could sit at the table while you prepare it."

"Of course, Mom. That will help the time go by."

Finally, they heard the car as it approached the house. Bethany went to the back door to greet John, knowing he and her dad would come through the garage. John swept her into his arms and whispered against her hair, "Bethany, Bethany, my sweet, I am so sorry."

Bethany pushed away from his embrace so she could see his face. With tears streaming down her face, she answered, "I know, John. It is so good to have you here. That pastor was so kind."

With tears swimming in his own eyes, John answered, "Yes, he was. I am so grateful. Are you doing okay? Shouldn't you be in bed?"

"The doctor only said to take it easy. I don't have to be bedridden."

"Just don't overdo."

"I'm not. But unless I'm asleep, simply lying in bed is not helpful." She paused, as she fought for control, then whispered, "It does no good to dwell on it."

John hugged her again and then passed her to her dad's eager arms. "I am so sorry, sweetie, but I am proud of how you are handling this disappointment."

"Thanks, Daddy."

～

"I'll give you fifteen minutes to get washed up for dinner," said Mrs. Prescott, knowing they all needed a break from their emotions. "Bethany, show John to the room you are using, please. John, how long can you stay?"

"I honestly don't know. Tomorrow, I'll call Pastor Green and see what we can work out. Maybe by then I'll be able to think straight."

"You know you are welcome for as long as you want."

"Thanks, Mom."

Knowing they both had to get control so they could at least eat a little, John was all business when they went upstairs. He refrained from holding Bethany again, put down his suitcase in the bedroom and headed for the bathroom to wash up. Then Bethany took her turn, sponging her red eyes again and washing her hands for dinner. They went down the stairs hand-in-hand, each putting on a brave front for the other's benefit.

Mr. and Mrs. Prescott were doing the same. Everyone managed to eat a little, and then Margaret suggested that Bethany and John go upstairs for some much-needed time alone. In the bedroom, John drew her into his arms and began sobbing. Finally, with being able to hold her in a private place, he could no longer hold back his emotions. Now Bethany was comforting him. She had done her crying earlier.

"Maybe I should give up evangelism, settle down and pastor a church. This kind of thing is so hard for you—for both of us."

For an instant, Bethany felt delight, but then steeled herself not to show it on her countenance or by her words or actions. Instead she asked calmly, "Is that what God wants? Has He shown you that?"

John hesitated. "I don't know. I am so confused."

"There's no need for you to be confused. Weren't we taught to continue doing what He calls us to do—until He shows us differently?"

"I know, Bethany, but…"

She put her fingers on his lips. "There are no 'buts.' You know in your heart and so do I that you…we…are exactly in the center of His will. That doesn't mean we won't have struggles and heartaches. Let's allow this loss to make us stronger. Now we can relate to others who have lost a child and to military wives who go through heartaches when their husbands are gone. You know my home church, as well as several of the churches we travel to, minister to military families."

John was calmed by her words. He knew everything she had said, but it was good to be reminded by Bethany. Wiping away his tears, he softly quoted 2 Corinthians 1:3 and 4, *"'Blessed be God, even the Father of our Lord Jesus Christ, the Father of mercies, and the God of all comfort; Who comforteth us in all our tribulation, that we may be able to comfort them which are in any trouble, by the comfort wherewith we ourselves are comforted of God.'"*

Bethany hugged him. John asked, "Are you ready to go down? Your folks probably need to know we are okay. Maybe we can now comfort them."

"Yes."

The next morning John called Pastor Green and was happy to learn that the other pastor was going to take that evening's meeting. John told Pastor Green that he could get a flight back to their city Saturday morning, so he could handle the Saturday night and Sunday meetings. The pastor asked, "Are you sure you can leave Mrs. Holman?"

"Yes, sir. She insists she will be okay and that she does not want to interfere any longer with my work. Last night she was comforting and encouraging me! I am so proud of her."

"She sounds like a wonderful young lady. I hope to meet her sometime. She is staying there, I presume?"

"Yes, we agreed that would be best. She can get her strength back faster that way, I think."

"That sounds like a wise decision to me. Tell me the time of your arrival, and I will be there to pick you up."

After working out the details, John hung up and went to find Bethany. She was in the kitchen helping to clean up after breakfast. John sat down at the table and told her and Margaret, "The arrangements are all made for my return flight tomorrow morning. Pastor Green will pick me up at the airport."

"He certainly seems like a very kind and considerate man," commented Margaret.

"Yes. He shared with me that he and his wife experienced this after their first two children. They went on to have another child after…" His voice trailed off. He couldn't finish the sentence. He regained his composure and asked, "So what have you two been up to these last two weeks?"

"Now what would you expect?" answered Margaret. "We did some shopping. Bethany finished buying Christmas gifts, and we did some baby…" She too left the sentence unfinished.

Bethany took a deep breath. "We bought some basics—things we can use whether we have a girl or boy…" she paused before finishing, "next time."

John asked, "Have you been doing more crocheting?"

"Oh, yes. I'll show you as soon as we are finished here."

Margaret told her daughter, "You go on now. You have done enough. Go put your feet up and rest a while, while you show him the progress you have made."

Upstairs in their room Bethany pulled out the items on which she had been working. John asked, "Are you sure you can handle this?"

"Yes, I want you to see everything. And I am going to continue working on things. The doctor says there should be no reason I can't have a normal pregnancy. I need to keep busy. I have to concentrate a lot on the crocheting since I am still a beginner. It will be therapeutic. Look, I have a sweater almost done. I am going to try to make a matching bonnet. I used green so it can be used for either a boy or girl."

John took the tiny garment and examined it. "Wow! I am impressed. This looks really nice. What else have you done?"

"I finished the album. It is all ready to add pictures," she said as she found it and gave it to him to examine.

"This is really cute. I like it. You are getting real crafty," he said with a grin.

"Real funny," responded Bethany.

"I hope we can have a little girl who looks just like her mommy," John managed to whisper before choking up, as he reached to embrace Bethany.

She answered, "I definitely would like a girl, but I also want a boy who will be like his daddy. A boy first would be nice. I know I always wished I had a big brother."

"We will be happy and very grateful with whatever God gives us," whispered John.

"Probably more so now," she said, pushing back from his arms enough to look into his face. Both had tears shimmering in their eyes, and both were bravely holding them back. She continued, "I am just glad I didn't carry the baby for eight or nine months and then lose it. That would really be hard."

John said, "Honey, I am so proud of how you are responding to this. Let's pray together." They knelt together next to the bed while John asked the Lord to continue to help them both during this time of sorrow. He thanked him for the little one who had brightened their lives for a short time—even though they did not understand the why of their loss. He ended by entrusting their little one into God's care until such time that they would be reunited.

When they rose from their knees, John said, "Why don't you lie down for a while? I'll sit here by you and tell you about things I've seen driving and about my meetings."

"I'd like that. And then maybe you can read to me from the Bible."

One of the passages John chose to read was Psalm 73:26: *"My flesh and my heart faileth; but God is the strength of my heart, and my portion for ever."* John prayed again, asking God to help them keep their eyes on Him and to draw their strength from Him to face difficult times.

Later they played board games, and Bethany played the piano while they sang a few uplifting hymns together. In the afternoon, they took a nap. Mrs. Prescott assured them she did not need or want Bethany's help with meal preparations. "I want you to use your limited time together to enjoy each other's company."

Saturday morning came all too soon. John and Bethany both kept up a brave front for each other's benefit. Knowing they only had two weeks of separation ahead of them helped. They said goodbye at the house, and then Mr. Prescott drove John to the airport.

A few days later, Elaine called Bethany. After the greeting, Elaine exclaimed, "Oh, Bethany, I just received the most wonderful news!"

"What was it?"

"I'm pregnant! We are so excited. Michael is beside himself. He wanted me to call you and let you know that our babies will only be a few months apart. Won't it be fun whenever you come through Detroit, and we can get together?"

Bethany managed to choke out, "I'm happy for you," before breaking down. Since she was in the living room with her mother, she handed her the phone and then hurried upstairs to the bedroom, where she collapsed on the bed and gave way to tears and sobs.

Margaret explained the situation to Elaine, who responded, "Oh, Mrs. Prescott, I am so sorry. I had no idea, and I said all the wrong things." She started crying and barely managed to say, "I'll let you go," before hanging up.

A few days later Bethany called Elaine. "I'm so sorry, Elaine."

"There's nothing for you to be sorry about. I'm the one who feels badly."

"Please don't. You didn't know. How are you feeling?"

"A little tired, but otherwise, just fine."

"No morning sickness?"

"No. I am happily surprised because I had it for three months with Michael. A friend told me she had it with her two boys, but when she had a girl, she didn't. Who knows, maybe that is an indication I'll have a girl this time. I would like that, but Michael would like a brother."

"I am glad for you. I was so sick…" Bethany's voice trailed off, and Elaine could hear her sniffle.

Elaine quickly changed the subject, relieving a grateful Bethany. "You should hear Michael on the piano. I told you he started lessons. His teacher is very pleased with his progress. She says he is catching on very quickly and has natural talent. He is very excited about it. He makes himself practice an hour a day. He is doing well in school, also. So far he is keeping up with both."

"I am so glad, Elaine. Tell him I am proud of him."

"I will. What are you and John doing for Christmas?"

"He will be here by then. I am looking forward to seeing Betsy and Brian too. We will be here for a few weeks into the New Year, as he has scheduled some meetings nearby. After that, I'll be traveling with him as we start heading east again.

"How about you and Mark and Michael? Are you spending Christmas with your folks?"

"Yes. Part of the day Mark will spend with his parents. They still don't want anything to do with me."

"Oh, I am so sorry. Their indifference toward you has to hurt."

"Yes, but Mark is going to tell them about the new baby, and he will try to help them see it is time for them to get over their hard feelings. He wants to try to convince them it wasn't entirely my fault. He will tell them as kindly as possible that if they want to see their grandchildren, they will have to accept being around me. I told him he didn't have to do that, but he says he doesn't want the children around them if they are going to hang on to bitterness. We are praying for their salvation; that is the real problem."

"We are still praying with you for that."

"Thanks. Listen, I need to go now to pick up Michael from school. My parents send their love and asked me to tell you they are praying for you. They were sorry to hear the news."

"Please tell them I appreciate their thoughts and prayers, Elaine. Goodbye."

"Goodbye. Talk to you again soon."

When Bethany finished the conversation, she sought out her mother.

Margaret could see the tears shimmering in Bethany's eyes. She put her arms around her, drawing her close for a hug. "How did it go, dear?"

"I managed to get through it, but it was hard. I really need to let my other friends know, but…"

"I'll be happy to call them for you, Bethany."

"Are you sure you don't mind, Mom? Do you have time?"

"I am sure, and yes, I can fit it in. It won't take that long. In fact, right now would be a perfect time."

Wiping at her eyes, Bethany asked, "What can I be doing that will be helpful while you do that for me?"

"How about making a batch of cookies?"

"Okay. How about if I make some cut-out sugar cookies and decorate them?"

"Well, I was hoping we could work on that together—like old times. Could you make another kind?"

"Sure. That's a great idea. I'll enjoy making the decorated ones with you. Can we do those tomorrow?"

"Yes, right after lunch. Okay?"

"Perfect." Bethany went to the kitchen and concentrated on her baking so she could block out thinking about the conversations she knew her mother was having.

After about forty-five minutes, her mother came into the kitchen. When Bethany turned to look at her, her mother's eyes gave evidence of crying. Bethany's eyes instantly filled with tears, and she went to Margaret and hugged her. "I am sorry, Mom. That task was probably as hard for you as it would have been for me. I shouldn't have asked you to do it."

"It's okay, Bethany. All your friends said to give you a hug and to tell you they would be praying for you. They all expressed their sorrow…" She took a deep breath, pushed back from Bethany's embrace, and asked, "How is the baking coming along?"

Bethany wiped at her tears and answered, "Come and help me fill this last baking sheet. I am almost done. How is everyone?"

"They are all doing well. No big changes or news to share."

Shortly after taking the last cookies out of the oven, Bethany's cell phone rang. "It's John. I'll go up and rest on the bed while I talk."

"Yes, enjoy the visit. I can manage finishing the cleanup here."

Time flew by as Bethany helped her mother wrap gifts, decorate the house, and do more baking. Brian and Betsy arrived one day before John. Bethany went with her mom to pick them up at the airport. When Betsy hugged her, she whispered, "I am so sorry, Sis."

"I know," answered Bethany as the two sisters both struggled to hold back their tears.

Brian gave his big sister an awkward hug and patted her on the back. Bethany helped him out. "I'm okay, Brian. It's so good to see you both." She looked up at him and interjected a light note. "Would you please stop growing?" Brian laughed gratefully.

Bethany was very happy to be held in John's loving arms the next evening when he arrived. They had an hour to spend together before joining the family for dinner.

The two weeks with Brian and Betsy helped Bethany and John not to dwell on their loss. John enjoyed the three-week break from his evangelistic work, and Bethany loved having him around. After Brian and Betsy left to go back to college, John had a few more days before another meeting. One night he took Bethany out to a nice restaurant for a romantic dinner, which they both enjoyed.

When John started back to work, Bethany went with him to churches in the nearby areas. They were able to return to her parents' home each evening. Their trailer was parked on the property of Bethany's home church. Even though the trailer was comfortable, it was a nice change to be in a roomy house for a few weeks. Bethany was feeling almost back to normal physically and was strong enough to play and sing with John. She was happy to be at his side, helping with his ministry again.

After a few weeks, the time came for them to move on. On a Saturday morning John brought the trailer from the church to her parents' home and picked up Bethany. They loaded their suitcases and Christmas gifts into the trailer; then Bethany kissed her parents goodbye and climbed into the truck. John had made allowances for winter weather in his planning and had not scheduled meetings too closely together, so they would have plenty of time to travel slowly and carefully. Bethany found that being away from her parents' home, where her painful loss had occurred, actually improved her emotional state.

In March John started hinting about trying again, before too long, to have a child. He felt another pregnancy would be therapeutic. Bethany was not sure she had the courage yet. One day she had some time alone when she could make a phone call to her mother. She expressed her concern.

"I know John is getting anxious for us to try again, but I'm just not ready yet and I feel badly."

"Don't beat yourself up, Bethany. Give yourself time to heal emotionally. Everyone is different. You'll get over this, and you will know when you are ready to try again."

"What if I never get up the courage?"

"I'm not worried about that. You have always wanted children."

"But the loss was so hard and emotionally painful. I don't know if I could get through it again. I've heard of people who have had one miscarriage after another. How do they do that?"

"By God's grace. But those situations are very rare. Don't forget that God is not the author of fear. Where does that come from? Maybe it would help to memorize II Timothy 1:7: *'For God hath not given us the spirit of fear; but of power, and of love, and of a sound mind.'* "

"I am trying to trust the Lord."

"I know you are, sweetheart. I'm not being critical. I haven't walked in your shoes."

"I keep reminding myself of Proverbs 3:5: *'Trust in the LORD with all thine heart and lean not unto thine own understanding.'* "

"I like that verse, also. You are trying, Bethany. That is all anyone can expect from you. That is all you can expect of yourself. You just need a little more time."

"Thanks, Mommy. And thank you for being such a comfort when I lost the baby and for making Christmas as close to normal as it could be this year."

"You are welcome. But your dad and I were talking recently about how some people would have ruined it for everyone, but you didn't mope around feeling sorry for yourself. We really appreciated your attitude."

"Thanks. I have to run now. Love you."

"I love you, too. Give our love to John."

"I will."

"You two are constantly in our prayers."

"Thanks, Mom; we need that."

A few weeks after this conversation, John and Bethany started a weeklong revival meeting at Bible Baptist Church in Idaho. Sunday night after the service, Bethany saw a group of ladies gathered around a young mother holding her newborn. Suddenly it was as if the Lord was whispering in her heart, "Go over there." Bethany obeyed the urging and was soon gazing at the sweet little boy with longing, not realizing she was showing her feelings. As some of the ladies moved away, the young mother spoke to Bethany. "You look like you would like to hold him. I don't mind."

Bethany put out her arms and said, "Thank you." Tears filled her eyes, so she put her head down and snuggled her face against his blanket. When she raised her head and handed him back, she gave the mother a brave smile and said, "He is so sweet and so cute. Congratulations."

The mother smiled back and said, "Thank you," but looked concerned because of the tears still shimmering in Bethany's eyes.

Bethany moved away and quickly made her way to the restroom and entered a stall for privacy, where more tears flowed. When she finished weeping, she dried her eyes and repaired her makeup. Then she returned to the auditorium and joined John.

He had seen her holding the baby and watched her swift departure afterward, so he whispered, "Are you okay, love?"

Without hesitation Bethany reassured him she was doing fine. She amazed herself when she realized it was true! Holding the baby had been a healing experience, and she felt the Lord was reassuring her about trying again.

When they were alone in their trailer, she shared this assurance with John.

"You're sure?"

"Yes."

"I am very proud of you, Bethany."

"It wasn't me. The Lord worked it all out." She went on to explain the urging she had sensed in her heart.

The next night after the service, Bethany again approached the young mother.

Remembering the tears she had seen in Bethany's eyes the night before, she hesitantly asked, "Would you like to hold him again?"

"Oh, yes, if you don't mind."

"Not at all." As she took the baby into her arms, Bethany asked the infant's name.

"This is little Peter, and I am Susan Lundberg. Your name is Bethany, right?"

"Yes."

Bethany held baby Peter for about ten minutes while she and Susan got acquainted. They discussed how he was doing with sleeping and eating. John wandered over, and Bethany introduced him. Then Susan's husband joined them.

Susan said, "This is my husband, Steven." Turning to her husband she said, "Steven, this is John and Bethany Holman."

"I am glad to meet both of you. I have been hoping for a chance to get acquainted. I am just a little curious about your life on the road."

While the men discussed traveling, Susan and Bethany continued their visit. Before they parted, the Lundbergs invited John and Bethany to go home with them the following evening for dessert. Before accepting the invitation, John looked questioningly at Bethany, who nodded in agreement.

At the couple's home the following night, John and Bethany took turns holding the small infant before Susan tucked him in for the night. Then the two couples played a board game while enjoying cake and ice cream. After that they visited for several hours, sharing their testimonies and courtship stories. Finally, John said they had to leave or he would not be able to get up in time to preach at the Christian school chapel at 10:00 a.m., and he felt badly because Steven had to be at work by 8:00 a.m. Steven assured him he would be fine and that he had enjoyed every minute of their visit. He told them that if they came to their church again, he definitely wanted them to get together. They exchanged addresses and phone numbers and promised to keep in touch and to pray for one another.

— CHAPTER FOURTEEN —

Joy Comes in the Morning

"...weeping may endure for a night, but joy cometh in the morning." (Psalm 30:5)

O*ne day in* early June when John and Bethany were holding a meeting at a church in Colorado, the pastor invited them to have breakfast with him and his wife the next morning. John was happy to accept the invitation. However, in the morning Bethany asked to be excused, telling John that her stomach felt a little queasy. "I hope I'm not coming down with a stomach bug. I'll stay here, and if I feel better later, I'll make myself some toast. Please apologize to the pastor and his wife. I'm sorry I can't go."

"I am too, honey. I can call and cancel if you want me to stay with you."

"Oh, no, John. That's not necessary. I'm not that sick. We don't want to be rude."

"Okay, if you are sure. I'll try to keep breakfast as short as possible."

Bethany followed him to the door. Fearing he might catch something, John kissed her on the cheek instead of her lips, before going out the door.

As soon as John had left to walk across the parking lot to the church building, Bethany went into the bathroom, opened the medicine cabinet, and pulled out a home pregnancy test she had purchased some time back "just in case." She used it and was overjoyed to see that the result was positive. She still felt queasy, but didn't care! She went back to bed for a while but was too excited to fall asleep. She propped herself up and opened her Bible to the Psalms and found some of her favorite praise verses, including Psalm 3:4, *"I cried unto the* LORD *with my voice, and he heard me out of his holy hill. Selah,"* and Psalm 9:1, *"I will praise thee, O* LORD, *with my whole heart; I will shew forth all thy marvelous works."* Also Psalm 19:1, which says, *"The heavens declare the glory of God; and the firmament sheweth his handywork."*

She then turned to the chapter where she had left off in her regular reading schedule and tried to concentrate. How the time was dragging by! She wanted to share her good news with John. She knew he would be ecstatic. Finally she gave up on reading and began praying. "Thank You for this new little life, Lord. I pray I will be able to carry it to full-term, but Your will be done. If I am able to give birth to this little one, please help me be the right kind of godly mother. Give me wisdom, patience, love, and the courage to discipline when necessary. Help John and me to agree always or, at least, not discuss any difference of opinion in front of this child and any others You may see fit to give us. Oh, Father, I am so happy. I give You all the praise and glory, and thank You that I haven't thrown up!"

Bethany continued her prayer time by following her prayer list. When she had finished, she realized she felt hungry, and the sick feeling had gone away. She fixed herself a piece of toast and some tea and was seated at the table, enjoying her snack when John returned.

"I'm back, honey. How are you feeling?"

"Better. I'm having some toast."

John went to her and gave her another kiss on the cheek. He still kept up the tradition he had started at the beginning of their marriage—kissing her when he left and when he returned.

Bethany rose from the table and said, "Come with me. I want to show you something."

"Where are you going? Your toast and tea will get cold."

"This will only take a sec. Come on."

He followed her into the bathroom, where she showed him the test results. He stood speechless for a few seconds and then exclaimed, "Bethany! Are you telling me…?"

"Yes! We are expecting! Are you happy?"

"Happy? What do you think?" He picked her up and danced her out of the bathroom and into the living room. Then he stopped. "Oh, sorry. Am I making you sick?"

"No, don't worry. I don't feel nearly as bad as before. I hope that continues."

"Me too! You better go back and finish your food. You and our little one need nourishment."

Bethany laughed happily. "Okay. Then put me down."

Instead, John carried her to the kitchen area and deposited her at the table. "Let me warm up your tea in the microwave. When did you start suspecting? I can't believe you didn't tell me anything; and I am so dense I didn't even think this morning when you said you didn't feel well. Come to think of it, you haven't been eating much for several mornings. I feel so stupid. I am sorry. How soon shall we tell our folks? Do you think you will be able to keep traveling? Maybe I should send you back to your folks? What do you think? We better get you to a doctor soon. We'll see what she thinks. Okay? When do you think the baby will come?"

"John." He didn't even hear her. She said it louder. "JOHN!"

"What?"

"Which of your seven questions do you want me to answer first?" asked Bethany, as she laughed so hard she could hardly speak.

"What?"

"You only asked me seven questions, nonstop."

"Oh. You counted?"

Bethany laughed. "Yes."

"I can't even remember what I asked you! Can you? I am sorry. I think I am a little excited."

"Maybe just a little," said Bethany with a grin.

"Now don't make fun of me, you little imp," answered John as he swept her up in his arms again.

"I thought you wanted me to eat," laughed Bethany. "The microwave dinged."

"Oh, yes. Sit down and finish. Here, I'll get your cup. Oh, I know we should wait for a while to tell people, but I am going to burst trying to keep the news to ourselves."

"I'm sorry, John. I know it will be hard, and I have thought the same. But I don't want to go through…"

"I know, I know, my sweet. I will have to be patient and keep my mouth shut."

When Bethany had finished her toast and tea, she said, "Now I will try to answer your questions. Let's see, I have only suspected for a couple of days, but I didn't want to get your hopes up until I could do the test. I think we should wait at least a month to tell our folks and wait longer to tell anyone else. I want to keep traveling with you if I can. We will have to wait and see whether or not it works. We leave here in two days, and then we should know within a few days if I can handle it. Okay?"

"All right, that is if you are sure you want to try."

"I am. I think the baby will be due in the middle of January. We have been to the next church on our itinerary before, correct?"

"Yes, and several others in that area. We will be in that vicinity for two weeks."

"So I have at least met the pastor's wife. I will call her and ask her to recommend a good obstetrician in her area and to give me the phone number. I will ask her to keep it in strictest confidence. I can then call to make an appointment during the time we are there. Hopefully I can get in within those two weeks. We will tell the doctor what happened before and see what she thinks. By then we will know how I am doing with the traveling. There, I think I answered all of your questions."

"Oh, Bethany, I love you so much. Thank you for being willing to try again."

"I want a child too, John. Just pray that all will go well."

"I have been praying for that constantly, my love."

Bethany discovered that her morning sickness this time was not nearly as severe. A few crackers in the morning helped her, and she could even ride in the truck. By mid-morning she was ready to stop and have breakfast. She had a healthy appetite and was able to catnap in the truck as they traveled. The doctor told her she thought it would be okay for her to travel with John, but she warned Bethany that if she started having any cramping to immediately stop and find a doctor.

Bethany and John were both very happy about how this pregnancy was progressing. However, they did not want to take any chances. John felt she should go to visit with his parents in October and November and then go to stay with her parents until the baby was born.

In July Bethany called her mother with the happy news. Mrs. Prescott rejoiced with her, and then added, "I have some news I feel I can share with you now. I have known for a while that Elaine is not only expecting a baby, she is expecting twins!"

"Oh, my goodness! They must all be so excited. Are they identical?"

"No, they are fraternal, and she said the doctor is fairly sure she is having one of each."

"Then everyone will be happy. She wanted a girl, and Michael wanted a brother. I will have to call her. But I'm keeping my news to myself for a while, so please don't pass it on yet."

"How are you doing…" Mrs. Prescott paused, considering how to word her question, "emotionally, sweetheart?"

"I have my moments of worry and fear, but I confess it and start quoting trust verses."

"That's good. You are in our prayers."

"Thanks, Mommy."

"Tell me where you are going to be in a few weeks so I can send you the maternity clothes. Remember you helped me cut them out? I finished them."

Bethany checked their schedule and gave her mother a church's address.

"Good. I'll get them in the mail tomorrow."

"Thanks so much, Mommy. They will be a big help."

John called his mother. She was overjoyed at their news. John explained that they had decided to wait even longer this time to announce their news to any others and asked that she not yet spread the word except to his dad and siblings.

Bethany also called Sarah in July to find out how things were going for her. Sarah shared that they had a healthy baby boy named David. Bethany enthusiastically congratulated her but felt she needed to keep her own news to herself for the time being.

In August Elaine Briscoe called Mrs. Prescott to share the good news that she had given birth to a boy and a girl. Elaine was happy to report that Michael was thrilled with the babies and was being a good helper. She asked Margaret if Bethany would want to hear her news. Margaret assured her that Bethany would want her to call.

Elaine allowed Michael to call with his happy news. When Bethany answered the phone, Michael exclaimed, "Bethany! I have a brother and a sister. They are so cute. Guess what we call the girl?"

"Now let me think. Maybe Martha after your grandmother?"

"No. We named her Bethany—after you."

"Oh, Michael, that is very nice. That makes me feel real good. What did you name the boy?"

"Benjamin."

"Both start with 'B'. That's cute," Bethany said. "Guess what? I have news too."

"What?"

"I am going to have a baby in January."

"That's great, Bethany!"

Bethany could hear him telling Elaine. "My mom wants to talk to you, Bethany."

"Okay, Michael. Thanks for calling me with the good news. Whose idea was it for your baby sister's name?"

"Mine."

"Thanks, Michael."

Elaine came on the line. "Bethany, I am so happy for you."

"Congratulations to you, Elaine. Can you send me some pictures on my phone?"

"Sure, I would love to."

"That was really sweet of you guys to name your baby girl Bethany."

"It is a beautiful name, and she will always remind us of a beautiful woman who had a great influence on our lives."

"Well, thanks for those kind words."

"How are you feeling? Are you still traveling with John?"

"Yes, praise the Lord. I never had bad morning sickness this time, and it is pretty much cleared up.

"What are your babies' full names? How much did they weigh?"

"Bethany Elaine and Benjamin Enoch."

"What great names! I like that they have the same initials. That's clever."

"They each weighed a little over five pounds. Praise the Lord! They are strong and healthy, and there were no complications."

"I'll be looking forward to getting the pictures and sharing the news with John. Keep in touch."

"Is it okay for me to tell my folks about your pregnancy?"

"Yes, and please let Mrs. Carpenter know too. I'll be calling my college friends in a few weeks if everything is still progressing well."

"We will be praying that it will be."

"Thanks. Talk to you later."

While they traveled between churches, Bethany and John spent a lot of time thinking about names. One day John teased her by suggesting some of the most unusual ones he could find from the Bible—Adonibezek, Nahamani, or Telharesha. He had spent a few minutes the night before finding these so he would have them ready to suggest. Then he became serious and suggested *Dawn* for a girl and *Michael* for a boy. "Dawn makes me think of a new day with new opportunities for serving the Lord and living a joy-filled life with my beautiful wife and a beautiful daughter, since she will probably look like her mother."

"Thank you, Sir Knight."

John added, "I would like *Michael* because it is a special Bible name—one of the archangels. His name means, 'Who is like unto God.' Also, that name would mean so much to our little friend. After all, the Lord used him to introduce us."

They both laughed at the memory of how they had met. Michael had run away from Bethany on an icy morning, and John had come to Bethany's rescue by catching him.

"Let's settle on both of those. I like them. We will eventually need to come up with middle names to go with them," Bethany added.

"Let's buy a book of names with their meanings."

"Good idea."

John had arranged meetings for October in California around the area where his parents lived. He had lined up meetings in nearby cities and would return to enjoy Thanksgiving with Bethany and his family.

When John had left and Bethany had more time to herself at his parents' home, she contacted their friends from college. She also called her newest friend, Susan, in Idaho. The young woman was thrilled to hear the news. They tarried on the phone, catching up on events in each other's life. Bethany was happy to hear that little Peter was growing and thriving.

She told Susan that John had managed to plan their meetings so they would be in the Northwest around the time the baby was due and for several months afterward.

"That will be good. Will we get to see you?"

"Yes! I am excited about that. We have a meeting scheduled at your church in April."

"Oh, I am so glad! Let us know when you find out whether it's a girl or a boy."

"Okay. I will be having an ultrasound next week. I can hardly wait to find out who this little one will be. Then I'll contact you again. I enjoy keeping in touch. We had so much fun getting to know you two and little Peter."

"I feel the same. I should think that getting acquainted with people all across the country must be one of the great blessings about being in evangelism."

"You are right. I like that part about traveling very much."

The following week Bethany's mother-in-law drove her to the doctor's office for the ultrasound. Afterward, Bethany shared with her that everything looked good, and she was carrying a girl.

Mrs. Holman exclaimed, "That will be so much fun! Let's make a little dress. We can work together."

"I would like that, but you must know that I'm not the world's greatest seamstress."

"Neither am I, but my mother will help us if we need it."

Bethany could not wait to tell John. She called him during the ride back to the house. "Well, we are expecting a little girl."

"Oh, good! I'll have a daddy's little girl to spoil."

"I am really surprised at you—I thought you would want a boy to play football with and wrestle and things like that."

"I do—I want several of both."

"Me too."

"Are you happy we're expecting a girl?"

"Yes, I am looking forward to dressing her up. But I want some boys too."

"I remember you said it would be nice to have a boy first."

"I know, but mostly I want a healthy baby; I am glad for whatever the Lord gives us. Hold on, honey. We just arrived at the house."

While her mother-in-law went on into the house, Bethany lingered outside to talk privately. "I miss you, John. I want to feel your arms around me."

"The feeling is mutual, sweetheart. This two-month separation is hard. I am sorry."

"You have nothing to be sorry about, John. Remember, I counted the cost before I entered into this union."

"I really appreciate your attitude. I love you, Bethany."

"I love you too, honey. Are you taking care of yourself? Eating properly?"

"I am trying, but I do miss your cooking."

"Good."

"Good?"

"Yes, that way you will appreciate me more."

"I couldn't."

"How sweet!"

"I have to go, sweetheart. Talk to you again tomorrow. Thanks for letting me know the results. A girl. Yes!!!"

Bethany hung up the phone, laughing—a welcome change. She usually had a few tears after hearing John's voice. Before lying down for a much-needed nap, she made several more calls to her mother and some friends.

During her stay with her in-laws, Bethany had a few more crochet lessons with John's grandmother. One day when Bethany was at her home, she brought out a beautiful baby dress that she had crocheted. She had made the loosely stitched pattern of fine pink yarn. She had also made a white slip to go under it.

Bethany exclaimed, "This is beautiful! But how did you get it done so quickly?"

"I had it almost done before you arrived. I made something for either gender. I'll hold onto the other one until a boy comes along in the family."

Bethany and Mrs. Holman did work together on a little dress. One cut out and pinned, the other used the machine to sew the seams. They finished it shortly before Bethany was scheduled to leave for Tacoma.

At her parents' home, Bethany and John would be using Brian's room again. When she walked into the room, Bethany saw that her mother had also been busy sewing. On the bed were several beautiful baby dresses. Bethany was surprised and thrilled with the different sizes of beautiful handmade garments. She had always loved and proudly worn the garments her mother had made for her. She was almost overcome with emotion when she realized one dainty little dress was made from scraps left over from the dress her mother had made for her high school graduation. The fabric was a print with little blue flowers on a white background. It was even trimmed with the same narrow lace. She picked up the dress from among the group on the bed and took it with her. "Oh, Mommy. This is so special. What a wonderful surprise! I didn't know you had scraps from my graduation dress."

"I am glad you like it. I enjoyed making that one so much. It brought back happy memories. You know me—I save everything. But many times I do end up using the things I save. Come with me to the sewing room, and I will show you another example." Once there, Margaret showed Bethany a baby-sized patchwork quilt made from many scraps of fabric that Bethany recognized.

"Mommy, these are scraps from dresses you have made for me through the years. Oh, look, this is another piece from my graduation dress, and this was an Easter dress. But there are some I don't recognize."

"That is because I made them when you were a baby, so you obviously wouldn't remember them."

"This is so sweet. What a keepsake!"

"But I do want you to use it for the baby, not just save it. I was so excited when I heard you were expecting a girl, as I have been planning this for many years. I got the idea from a friend who did something like this. You can either use it in the portable play yard you will be using as a crib or put it over her in the baby carrier or stroller."

"I will probably use it with the stroller and carrier, so I can show it off to people in nurseries all across the country. You will be famous."

"I don't know about that," answered Margaret, laughing. "But I will have my initials on it. A square on one corner will be embroidered with the words, 'To (whatever name you pick) from Grandma M. P.' By the way, now that you know the baby is a girl, have you decided on a name?"

"We are fairly sure we have, but John wants us to wait to tell people until after she is born in case we change our minds or something."

"Okay, I'll have to cool my curiosity," agreed Margaret, laughing.

Bethany said, "I am sorry. I am having a hard time keeping quiet too."

"It's all right, sweetheart. Lots of people do that."

"Actually, we haven't picked out a middle name yet. John bought a book of baby names, and we are going to go through it when he gets here."

The month before John was going to join her in Tacoma was a busy time. Wherever she was, Bethany always tried to get involved in church activities; so she rejoined the choir, which her father still led, and went out soul winning with the group of ladies with whom her mother went. At home she practiced on the piano and her crocheting; several times a day she found a quiet place and prayed for John—for his safety and for God's power on his preaching and singing. How she missed being at the meetings—playing and singing with him.

Several times, deliveries arrived from one of her friends, who had been waiting to hear the gender of the baby. The gift packages contained beautiful little dresses, pink bodysuits, and booties. Mrs. Davenport sent a beautiful coordinated set, which included a crib-size blanket, receiving blankets, changing pads, a sweater, and other matching accessories. She wrote that she had purchased the items in a small shop carrying handmade items.

The day that package arrived, Bethany was so excited that she called John to tell him about it. She tried to keep up with his schedule and figured he would be on the road traveling between California and Oregon. When he answered, Bethany was instantly alerted—his voice sounded strained.

"Bethany, I can't talk right now. I'll have to call you back."

"John, what's wrong? You sound upset."

"I'll call you back as soon as possible. The tow truck is here."

"Tow truck? What…?"

"I had a little accident."

"Accident! Are you okay?"

"Yes. I'm fine. Please don't worry. I have to go, love."

"Okay, but call me back as soon as you can."

Bethany hurried to find her mother. She was so nervous and excited that Mrs. Prescott had to tell her, "Bethany, slow down. Calm down. Did something happen to John?"

"Yes, he had some sort of an accident. He had to call a tow truck. But he said he is okay. That's the important thing."

"Oh, thank the Lord. I hope there isn't too much damage."

"Me too. The tow truck will be expensive and who knows about the repairs…? We don't have a lot of extra money on hand. He will probably have to put it on the credit card, and John hates that. He tries not to use it."

"I know, sweetheart. But for this kind of situation, he needs it."

"We will have to trust the Lord to help us pay it off. Oh, I hope he was telling me the truth, and that he really is okay."

"Well, at least he could talk and call for emergency help. He couldn't be seriously hurt. Besides, he would tell you if he had been injured."

"Yes, I guess he would. Let's pray, Mom."

After praying together, Bethany asked, "Should I call his mom or wait until I know more?"

"Let's wait a little and see if John calls soon."

They both tried to keep occupied, but neither one could concentrate. Mrs. Prescott called her husband at work so he could be praying. About forty-five minutes later, John called Bethany.

"John! What happened? Are you sure you are not hurt?"

"Please don't get excited, Bethany. I am a little bruised, and I'll probably have some sore spots tomorrow from the air bag. I was held up earlier today because of a bad accident. I was close to my destination, so I pushed myself—the pastor was expecting me tonight. I got drowsy, and I guess I fell asleep. When I opened my eyes, a deer was in the road right in front of me. I swerved to avoid it on a narrow road and the back of the fifth wheel hit a rock wall. The back end is pretty messed up. I couldn't pull it. Thankfully, no car was coming the opposite way."

"Oh, praise God! He heard my prayers and answered. The last few days I have felt impressed to pray more than usual."

"God is good!"

"What about the cost?"

"We had enough to pay for the tow truck. I will have to put some of the repair bill on the credit card. I may end up having to pay some interest. I hate that, but I won't be able to pay it off soon enough to avoid charges. But without it, I would really be stuck.

"Honey, I need to throw some clothes in a suitcase before they tow away the trailer. I am glad the church has a prophet's chamber I can use so there won't be a hotel bill on top of everything else. I'll call you again tonight. Now don't worry. It isn't good for the little one or you," he said with a chuckle.

"Okay. I'll try not to. I'll call your folks and let them know so they can be praying about the bill and everything. Okay?"

"Yes, but tell them not to be concerned about me. I really am fine."

John did call her later that night and again in the morning. He had to admit he had some aches and pains, but nothing serious. Bethany was relieved; she had been afraid that he might have a whiplash. John also reported that the repairs were going well, and the shop had assured him they would be done by the time he would be ready to leave.

The pastor and others in the congregation were inviting him to their homes for dinner, and he had gotten breakfast that morning at an inexpensive cafe nearby. He and the pastor would spend the mornings going door knocking or visiting church members.

"I am so glad you weren't in the truck!"

"You probably wouldn't have fallen asleep if I had been there! I hate not being with you."

"I know, sweetheart. I miss you terribly, but it is worth it to keep the baby safe."

Bethany sighed, but agreed with him and then asked, "What about your laptop and my piano keyboard? I have been wondering about them."

"I checked them, and they are both okay. I take the time to stow them carefully under the bed in that storage area with blankets stuffed around them every time I'm traveling."

Bethany said, "I am glad we have that hard travel case for the keyboard. By the way, I have been doing lots of practicing on the piano here."

"Knowing you, I am sure you are keeping busy. Just don't overdo."

Bethany laughed and said, "I am doing great. I feel fine, and I take a nap every afternoon."

"That's good. Goodbye for now, honey. I love and miss you."

"I love you too, John."

Life settled back to a normal routine. Bethany wrote thank-you notes to people who had sent gifts, and she made several prenatal visits to the obstetrician whom she had seen with the first pregnancy. All of the doctors she had seen for this pregnancy in other cities had sent their records to the doctor in Tacoma.

One Friday night Pastor Noble called the Prescott home and asked to speak to Bethany. He told her the lady who usually babysat at the church on Saturdays was ill. "My daughter and another teenage girl will be there, but we need an adult. Are you feeling up to helping? I thought you might like the opportunity to make a little spending money."

"Oh, yes, I have been praying about that very matter. I want to be able to buy a Christmas gift for my husband. What time do you need me to come?"

"Some of the bus workers leave their little ones while they go to the meeting and then out visiting. The meeting starts at 9:00 a.m., so we would need you there by 8:45. The two teenage girls helping you will be my daughter and one of her friends."

"I'll be there. Thank you so much for thinking about me."

After hanging up, Bethany went to find her mother. "God is so good! Pastor Noble asked me to babysit tomorrow. Now I'll have a little cash of my own to spend on a gift for John."

"Are you sure you feel up to it?"

"Yes. Pastor's daughter, Rebecca, will be there to help, and she is a good worker. Pastor said another girl would also be there. They can do all the lifting. I'll enjoy the time."

On Monday morning Mrs. Prescott took Bethany shopping at a discount department store. Bethany wanted to look at the portable play yards, which they would need to use instead of a crib. She saw one she really liked, which had a removable bassinet, a changing table, and an attached container to hold wipes and diapers. "Look at this one, Mom. It would be perfect. I need to ask John if we can afford it, as it costs a little more than some of the others. After his accident, our resources are a little strained." Bethany had tried to call him, but she didn't have good reception in the store.

Mrs. Prescott said, "Let me write down the information in my notepad, and you can talk to him later. We can come back." What Bethany did not know was that her mother's friend, Mrs. Durham, was planning a surprise baby shower, and some ladies wanted an idea for a group gift.

Bethany then found a diaper bag she liked. Margaret said, "Here, let me add it to my notepad. You can get it when you come back. It might be wise to wait a little longer. Some more of your friends may be sending gifts or gift cards."

"I guess you are right. I just really feel I need to start getting some necessities."

"We'll come back soon," her mother assured her.

"Okay, but if you have time, I'd like to look for something for John for Christmas. I want to have something to give him, and I have that money from babysitting at church."

"Sure. It would be good for you to have that out of the way before the baby is born."

They walked to the men's section, where Bethany found a belt and a tie. "That will give me two packages to put under the tree. I think for his stocking gift, I will look for a word game book. He likes working on those for relaxation in the evenings when he isn't preaching."

Her mother suggested, "Let's go to the store where everything is a dollar. I have seen some Bible word search and crossword books there."

"Oh, that would be perfect. I do hope they still have them. We could go to that one that's right on our way home. Is that where you saw them?"

"Yes. I stop in there often and find some good buys."

When they arrived at the store her mother had mentioned, Bethany was happy to find a large variety Bible puzzle book. "Look at this one,

Mom, it has word search, crosswords, cryptograms—which we really like working on together, and lots of other kinds I've never seen before. He will really enjoy this one!"

"That looks great. Go to the checkout line, and then we'll get some lunch. My treat."

"Oh, Mommy, you and Daddy have already done so much."

"Daddy wants me to take you to your favorite place. You haven't been able to go there for a long time."

"Ooh, I won't argue about that. Thanks so much! You spoil me."

Mrs. Durham was the mother of Bethany's friend, Kathleen. The next Monday she called to invite Bethany and Mrs. Prescott to come over for coffee the following Saturday. Mrs. Prescott had answered the phone, so acting innocent, she said, "Bethany, its Mrs. Durham on the phone. She would like us to come over for coffee and a visit on Saturday."

"Oh, that sounds like fun!"

With Bethany in the room listening, Margaret told Mrs. Durham they would be happy to accept her invitation. The previous Wednesday night at church Mrs. Prescott had already slipped a piece of paper to Mrs. Durham containing the information she had written down at the store.

Bethany called John to ask him about buying the play yard, not knowing that her mother had warned him about letting Bethany buy anything until after the shower. She told him about the model she wanted to buy and the price. She was disappointed when he told her they would have to wait on buying anything because of the extra expenses from the accident. Actually, he would have had to tell her that whether or not her mother had called him. On top of the unexpected expenses, some of the churches he had visited lately were small and the offerings were, of course, not as large. He knew Bethany was very disappointed, although she tried not to let him hear it in her voice. He loved her for her consideration. She never wanted him to feel like he was not adequately providing for her.

Bethany changed the subject and asked, "Are you getting enough sleep so you don't have a repeat of what happened a few weeks ago? I have been praying even harder for you. You scared me so much!"

"I am sorry about that, love. Thanks for the prayers. I am trying to be even more careful, although I thought I was before. If I start feeling drowsy, I will open the windows and pull over as soon as possible. I always try to plan it so I'm not driving too long, but like that other time, I can't predict traffic problems. I have been praying that the Lord will keep me awake."

"Did I tell you Kathleen Durham's mother called? She invited us over on Saturday for a visit and coffee. I am looking forward to it."

John was glad they weren't speaking face to face—he would have had a hard time hiding a smile. He answered, "That's nice, honey. Enjoy your visit. I am pulling into the town where my next meeting is scheduled. I better hang up so I can watch for street signs."

"I'm glad you made it there safely. I'll be praying for the meeting. Goodbye, my love."

On Saturday as they drew closer to the Durham home, Bethany noticed a lot of cars lining the street and driveway. "Mom, what's going on? Look at all these cars. That's Pastor Noble's car, and there's the Porters' car, and the Lamberts'. These are all cars belonging to people from the church. What do you know about this?"

Her mother pulled into a parking space. "Let's just go in and find out."

Mrs. Durham greeted them at the door and led them to her great room. Bethany was greeted by everyone's shouting, "SURPRISE!" As she glanced around, she saw a sheet cake on the dining table at one end of the room, and a decorated chair was in front of the fireplace. The hearth was covered with gift bags and beautifully wrapped boxes. Many ladies were seated in a semi-circle around the fireplace. Directly in front of them, a pink plastic tablecloth covered something.

Bethany gave an exclamation of delight and then turned and gave Mrs. Durham a hug. "What a surprise! I never suspected. Mom, you are very sneaky!"

Her mother laughed and gave her a hug.

Mrs. Durham directed her to the decorated chair and brought her a cup of coffee. "I told you we would have coffee," she said with a smile.

"Thank you so much, Mrs. Durham, for everything."

They played a few games, and then Mrs. Noble, the pastor's wife, gave a short devotional. She reminded Bethany and the ladies present that motherhood, next to being a wife and a help meet, is the greatest calling for a woman. She mentioned how proud they all were of Bethany for dedicating her life to be an evangelist's wife—with all the challenges that decision entailed. She also briefly touched on what an example Bethany had been of faith and trust through the hard times during the previous year. Then each lady wrote down something as encouragement or advice, and the papers were given to Bethany to keep. After the refreshments were passed around, and before Bethany began opening gifts, Mrs. Durham removed the pink tablecloth and revealed the play yard that Bethany had chosen. Inside it was a wrapped package that proved to be the diaper bag she had desired.

Bethany enthusiastically thanked all of the ladies who had had a part in those purchases and then said again, "Mom, you really were sneaky!"

Mrs. Durham then placed another large gift in front of Bethany, which proved to be a gift from the Davenports and Elaine. Bethany exclaimed, "Mrs. Davenport already sent me that beautiful blanket set. She always does so much." As she tore off the wrapping paper, she explained to the ladies who Mrs. Davenport was. Her gift was a combination stroller, car seat, and baby carrier. "Oh, my, this is something we had to have. They were so sweet. But how did it get here?"

Her mother explained that she had been talking to Mrs. Davenport about the shower, which had been planned before Bethany had even arrived. "She asked me for the address of the hostess and told me what she was sending so no one else would get one for you." As she was talking, Mrs. Durham handed another gift to Bethany. When she read the card, she discovered another special surprise—Mrs. Carpenter had sent a little dress decorated with beautiful embroidery. Bethany cried when she opened the gift.

Then she opened all of the other gifts. She received many practical items as well as more beautiful dresses and other clothing items. She was happy to receive diapers in several sizes. With tears in her eyes, she commented, "Oh, my goodness, you ladies have been so generous—I won't have to buy much of anything! Thank you all so much."

After visiting for a while, some of the ladies helped them load up the Prescotts' van with all of the gifts. Bethany was so excited that she simply had to call John and share it with him while they were driving home. He surprised her by saying, "I have been waiting for your call. I figured you would want to tell me all about it as soon as you were able."

"You mean you knew too? That isn't even fair," answered Bethany, laughing. She turned to her mother and asked, "Why did you tell him?"

"In case you called and asked him about buying that play yard."

"I did call him, and he put me off by saying we didn't have the funds to cover it right now. And of course, I believed him."

John said, "Well, that's good. After all, it was supposed to be a surprise."

"Well, they succeeded. I didn't suspect a thing. Oh, John, the ladies were so generous. It will save us so much money. The Lord is so good."

"Yes, He is, my love."

Bethany went on to tell him about some of the gifts, being sure to include the ones from the Davenports and Mrs. Carpenter.

"But didn't Mrs. Davenport already send you a gift?"

"Yes! They are so generous!"

"I am anxious to get there and see everything. I hope we can fit it all in."

"I think there is still enough room in the storage area for the stroller. We may have to put her clothes in a suitcase and shove it in the bottom of a closet or under something."

"We'll figure it out, I'm sure."

"We are pulling into the driveway, John. We have a big job ahead of us, taking all of these gifts inside. I better go for now."

"You be careful. Don't take the heavy things."

"Don't be a mother hen. I won't overdo. Love you. 'Bye."

James Prescott heard them drive up and hurried out to help. "Let me get the heavy items."

"We will. You are as bad as John," said Bethany, laughing.

"My goodness. Look at all this!" her dad exclaimed.

"Quite a few ladies were there, and they were very generous. Plus, there were two gifts from out-of-town. That big one is from the Davenports and Elaine," answered Margaret.

"I should have guessed that. They do so much for you and John, Bethany."

"That's for sure."

Bethany made two trips with light items into the house and piled them in the family room before she sank down on the couch. When her mother came in, Bethany said, "That's enough for me. Sorry."

"Don't be. You go up and rest for a while. You feel okay, don't you?" she asked with concern.

"Oh, yes. I just need a nap. It has been an eventful day! What a nice surprise!"

An hour later, Bethany awakened to the aroma of fried chicken. She suddenly felt very hungry.

She quickly touched up her hair and makeup and then hurried downstairs to see if there was anything she could do to help.

Margaret greeted her. "Oh, good. You are ready. I am just putting the food on the table."

"Can I help?"

"Yes, you can bring in the platter of…"

"Chicken!" Bethany laughed. "It smells wonderful, and I have an appetite to do it justice."

When the three of them had settled at the table, and James had prayed, he said, "We got everything in from the car, and I was thinking that maybe we should organize your gifts into two organizer bins. We could put clothing items together and other things in another box and store them in the garage. Your room really doesn't have space, and John will want to load them into the RV when he gets here."

"That sounds sensible, except for some of the smallest size of clothes and other essentials we will need to keep in our room while we are in this area. Remember, we will be here for several months, if that is still okay with you."

"Of course it is. I am so excited about having you two here that long. Are you up to starting the sorting and organizing tonight, or do you want to wait?"

"If you are in the mood to help, I am definitely up to starting tonight. How about you, Mom?"

"As soon as I get the kitchen cleaned up."

"I'll help you with that, and then we'll all work together on the organizing. We can at least get a start on it. I am kind of surprised that you want to help with that, Dad."

"To be honest, I want to see what you got. But don't tell any of my buddies."

Bethany and Margaret laughed. Bethany said, "It makes me feel good to know that you are interested."

Margaret and Bethany enjoyed taking their time looking at everything in more detail as well as showing it to James. This slowed them down, but there was no need to hurry. As they were working, Bethany had a thought. "John is arriving Monday. He is going to want to see it. Let's not seal up the boxes yet. After he looks at everything, we can seal them up and put them out in the garage until John is ready to put them away in the RV."

"Good idea," responded James. "You are looking so tired. Let's leave these boxes here until tomorrow afternoon. If it doesn't get done before John gets here, it won't matter. That way he can help sort and carry it out."

"I agree. I am ready to call it a day," said Margaret.

"Now that you mention it…" agreed Bethany.

They all laughed and headed for the stairs, wishing each other good night.

Monday morning Bethany settled in the living room near a window so she could look outside. She worked on thank-you notes for all of the baby shower gifts, but every time she heard a vehicle, she looked to see if it was John. When she finally saw him pull up in front of the house, she called to her mother and then hurried out the door. Bethany rushed into John's arms as soon as they met on the walkway. After hugging her and a quick kiss, he stepped back. "Whoa! Our little Dawn has done some growing!"

"Well, it isn't long before she will make her appearance. Believe me, I am ready for that to happen."

"You're feeling okay, aren't you?"

"Yes, yes, don't get worried. I only feel awkward, and I am getting tired of being kicked," answered Bethany, laughing.

"Well, you look as beautiful as ever, sweetheart. So she is an active one?"

"Very much so. I'll let you feel her when we get in the house."

"I am so anxious to hold her," he said.

"Me too."

Later that day James went with John to take the RV to the church property. They did not have to hook it up, as they would be staying at the Prescotts' home. During the rest of that week, Bethany showed John the gifts she had received at the shower. Then they sealed up the boxes and placed them on the storage shelves. He and James moved things around in the bedroom to make room to set up the play yard for the baby to sleep in when she arrived.

Bethany and John had a lot to catch up on from their time apart. Finally, reluctantly, he told her, "I had a really special gift planned for you for Christmas. I was saving up for it, but I had to use it for the tow bill." He choked up and couldn't go on.

"John, I don't need a gift. Your being okay is the best gift I could have."

"But I really wanted to be able to do something…"

Bethany put her hand on his lips. "Just get me a bag of my favorite candy."

"Oh, Bethany…"

"John, it's really okay. We have so much. God has been so good. At least we aren't homeless and living under a bridge somewhere. You had to do the repairs, and you have to buy gas. Those have to be our priorities. Your ministry is the priority."

John took her in his arms and hugged and kissed her. "God surely gave me the right gal! I do have a little something I had already bought."

"That will be fine."

"We didn't add tow coverage on our insurance because we couldn't afford the extra premium, so I had to pay that bill in full. Then I had to pay the deductible for the repairs. I was glad I didn't have to get a motel."

"What was their prophet chamber like?"

"Well, to be truthful, it wasn't anything fancy. Simply a bed and a stand with a lamp on it set up in a classroom they aren't currently using.

They have a big building, but they had a church split about a year ago, so all of the facilities aren't currently being used. It is such a shame. But I think this new pastor is doing a good job and will get the church rebuilt. He and his wife had me over for several meals, as did another family in the church. They were very kind and thoughtful."

"I am glad they took care of you and even happier that I can take over that job again!"

"Me too. I missed your cooking and…your kisses," he added with a grin.

Bethany kissed him tenderly. "I had better do some catching up."

"Sounds good to me."

On December 20 Brian and Betsy arrived home from college. Bethany enjoyed the reunion with her siblings. Betsy was especially excited about the upcoming birth but disappointed that it would not happen until she was back at college. Bethany considered it a special treat and blessing to share Christmas with her family again.

Pastor Noble had asked John to preach the evening service the first Sunday of January. Afterward he told the congregation about the extra expenses that they had incurred from John's accident. The couple received a generous offering for which they were very thankful. It would be a great help, especially since some of the churches they had planned to visit in the near future were very small.

James had taken vacation time for the next week, and Bethany and her parents attended the revival services where John was preaching. John was glad that he had only planned meetings for that week because Sunday afternoon Bethany began having contractions. She and her mother stayed home while James went with John for the last night of the revival meetings.

He told the pastor why Bethany was not with him, so he asked the congregation to pray for her. John had a hard time concentrating and kept praying for the Lord to keep him focused. As soon as he had left the platform, he slipped out into the foyer and called Mrs. Prescott. She assured him that it did look like Bethany was starting into labor, but her pains were still far apart. When John told the pastor about it, he quickly made arrangements about where to send the check for the love offering and then told him to go be with his wife. "I'll be praying for her. I hope all goes well with the delivery."

John answered, "Thank you," and hurried to the car. He was glad that James was with him to drive, as John was beginning to get very nervous. James tried to distract him with conversation and kept reassuring him that he was sure everything would go smoothly and normally.

As soon as the car stopped in the garage, John got out and ran for the back door. He hurried into the house and started calling Bethany's name. He followed her answering voice into the living room where she was resting on the couch. "We're here. Are you ready to go?"

"Go where?"

"To the hospital!"

Bethany giggled. "Calm down, love. We have to wait a little longer—until the contractions are closer…" she was interrupted as her breath was taken away by a strong pang.

John turned white. Mrs. Prescott was quick to assuage his fears. "It is part of the normal process, John. Don't worry. They have to get stronger and closer together before this baby can join us."

Bethany's emotions were somewhat out-of-control. She could not hold back another giggle. "You have seen guys hurt worse than this on the football field."

"They weren't my wife. I'm going to get a cup of coffee."

About an hour later, they decided it was time to go to the hospital. John was instantly relieved; but at the hospital, Bethany's contractions grew stronger and kept on for many more hours. John hated seeing Bethany in so much discomfort for so long. He was glad Bethany's mother had gone to the birthing classes with her. They took turns staying with Bethany and coaching her. Several times he had to leave the room to go out for some fresh air. He was glad for the cold Washington State winter air. Sometimes it was raining so hard that he did not go out. Then he walked the halls for a while.

Toward the end, John forced himself to stay by Bethany's side. He was irritated with himself and felt foolish because at times he felt like he would faint! He had never reacted that way to any of his own football-related injuries. He discovered that he had a problem watching someone else suffer, especially someone he loved. He had never prayed so hard or so constantly before.

Finally as the first haze of dawn lit the morning, they heard the welcome cry of the newborn. John was amazed to see Bethany rally from her exhaustion and desire to hold the baby girl soon after the birth.

After Bethany had a chance to hold her, the nurse gently took the baby and invited John to go along to measure her and give her a bath. He looked at Bethany, who nodded at him to go. When they returned to Bethany's room, John put the baby in her arms and then put his arms around them both. He prayed that they would be good parents and that this little girl would be saved at a young age. He asked for the Lord's blessing on the three of them.

Then the nurse helped Bethany start nursing the tiny infant, and afterward John and Mrs. Prescott each held the baby while the other took pictures. Mr. Prescott came in from the waiting room and took his turn.

They laid the baby down to let her sleep. The Prescotts left for a while so they could call the great-grandparents. Bethany also went to sleep, and John dozed in a recliner in the room after leaving long enough to call his parents with the news.

Then the little girl awoke, started fussing, and roused Bethany. She asked John to bring her the infant so she could make her second attempt at feeding her.

While their newborn nursed Bethany said, "We never did settle on a middle name to go with Dawn. Did you find one you like?"

"Yes. Idony."

"Idony? That's different, but it does sound pretty with Dawn. What does it mean?"

"That's one of the reasons I like it. It means 'reborn.' Is it okay with you? If not, we can look for something else."

"No. It is fine with me."

"I also have an idea for our first boy's name."

"What?"

"Daniel Reuben. They are both Hebrew names, of course. *Daniel* means 'judged of God' or 'spiritual.' And the name *Reuben* means 'behold, a son.'"

"That would be appropriate and meaningful. I like it. Do you have others picked out already?" she asked, laughing.

"Yes, as a matter of fact I do," admitted John grinning sheepishly.

"Let's hear them."

"Well, actually I only have one more. Another boy's name—*Matthew Osborne*."

"Okay—what are the meanings?"

"*Matthew* means 'God's gift,' and the name *Osborne* means 'strong-spirited.'"

"I like that one, too. You are good at this."

"Thank you," John answered with a grin.

Bethany asked, "Do you have your pocket Bible?"

"Yes. Would you like me to read to you?"

"Yes, please."

"I was reading Psalm 30 last evening. I kept thinking about verse five all night." He read the entire Psalm and then reread verse five. "'*For his anger endureth but a moment; in his favour is life: weeping may endure for a night, but joy cometh in the morning.*'"

John added, "Last night I just wanted it to be over. I hurt so much for you."

"She was worth it," answered Bethany.

"Oh, definitely. I was thinking also of all our trials, sadness, and disappointments in the past year. But this morning it was all joy, just like the verse says. '*Joy in the morning.*'"

Bethany's face lit up as she repeated, "'*Joy cometh in the morning.*' Joy! What a lovely and meaningful name that would be."

Excitedly, John said, "Hey, why don't we name her Joy? That would be appropriate, and it's a pretty name. It would be kind of a testimony. What do you think?"

"That would be great with me, but I thought you wanted Dawn?"

"We'll name our next girl Dawn, okay?"

"Yes. I think that is very pretty, too. Now, what about a middle name for our little Joy?" she asked while she tenderly kissed the little head.

John answered, "Let me run out to the car and get the name book."

When he returned he said, "I think I remember one in the 'Z's. Yes, here it is. Zerlinda."

"That's another one that's a little different. *Joy Zerlinda*. I like the sound of it. What is the meaning?"

"It is a Hebrew name, and it means…you won't believe this. It means 'dawn'."

Bethany laughed. "How perfect! We still have our Dawn, and she was born right at dawn."

At that moment her parents arrived in the room. Bethany let them each hold her again. Margaret exclaimed, "She's beautiful!"

"Isn't she! We've decided that her name is Joy."

"What a sweet name," said Margaret, looking tenderly at the infant.

John quoted the verse to them and said, "After all of the trials and testings of the last year, we think the name is appropriate."

"Very much so," agreed James. "Do you have a middle named chosen yet?"

John answered, "We picked a Hebrew name that means *dawn*. Zerlinda. Joy Zerlinda Holman."

"Very nice," agreed James.

"That's pretty. I like it, and Zerlinda's meaning 'dawn' is also appropriate since that was when she was born," commented Margaret. She added, "John, you look tired. Why don't you go to the house and rest, have something to eat, and get freshened up? We'll stay with Bethany and little Joy. You probably need to make some phone calls too."

"Yes, I need to call my parents and tell them her name. I also need to call our friends. But I think the first order of business will be a nap."

"We both had a nap and feel better for it. Help yourself to the leftovers in the refrigerator. Let me give you my house key." Margaret searched her purse and then handed John the key.

"Thanks, Mom." He went over to the bed and kissed little Joy and Bethany. "You look like you are ready for a nap too, Bethany. I'll be back in a few hours. Thank you for our little Joy."

Bethany gave him a sleepy smile and murmured, "You are welcome." As he turned to leave, she added, "John." He stopped and looked back. "I love you, honey."

Tenderly he answered, "I love you too, sweetheart."

> "All these were under the hands of their father for song
> in the house of the Lord...."
> (I Chronicles 25:6)

$\mathcal{B}$ethany was supervising her busy family as they packed all their instruments on a Sunday evening. This was the first day of a four-day meeting at Bible Baptist Church in Idaho. Her children had made a good start without her—she had been visiting with her friend, Susan Lundberg. Bethany handed some sheet music to one of her children, then turned back to Susan and invited her family to join them for dinner on Thursday night. Susan started to protest, but Bethany told her, "We have a very adequate kitchen, and I've already purchased extra food." Laughing, she added, "So now you have to come."

Susan asked, "Do you have room for five extra people?"

Bethany answered that they would sit outside under their awning; it was the first week of August, and the weather was still warm. They could borrow a few folding chairs from the church since they were parked on the church property. Through the years the Lundbergs had entertained them many times, and Bethany was determined to repay their hospitality.

Bethany added, "If it rains, we can manage inside. I don't think you had the opportunity to see inside our newest motor home when we came last year. Thanks to Brother and Mrs. Davenports' generosity again, we are blessed to have this larger one, which has two additional bedrooms, each with two bunks. The girls use these rooms. The extra bunk is handy for storing home-schooling materials. We even have a second bathroom. The couch and dinette make out to beds for the boys."

Susan answered, "Well, I'm looking forward to seeing your new home on wheels, and we'll be delighted to come on Thursday." Seeing her husband waiting, she added, "I'd better go. We'll see you at tomorrow's service."

She left then, and Bethany scanned the auditorium, looking for Joy. She and her younger sister, Dawn, had been working at a table in the back where they displayed CDs of John's sermons and the family's music. The sale of this material helped with their expenses. After they were finished Bethany had seen Joy talking with Susan's son, Peter Lundberg; but now that the Lundbergs had left, Bethany wondered where she was. She spotted her hurrying toward her.

When Joy reached Bethany, she said, "I was at the back of the auditorium, Mom. I wanted to check out that list of volunteers the pastor mentioned—the one for taking food to the lady who just had a baby. As I had thought might happen, not many had signed up. You know how people forget in their hurry to get home. Do you think we could do one meal this week? We don't get the opportunity to do things like that very often."

"That is a sweet idea, Joy, but I'm not sure. I just asked the Lundbergs over for Thursday night."

As her mother had expected, Joy's face lit up at that news. Bethany commented, "I thought that would make you happy." Joy blushed. The last time they had been at this church, Peter had approached John and asked if he could speak to him privately. He had asked for permission to write to Joy. Several months later, after again checking with John, he had begun calling her about once a week.

Joy changed the subject. "Could we sign up for a different day? Maybe Tuesday? We could make two pans of lasagna. Theirs could be smaller, since there are just the two adults—the pastor said this was their first child."

Bethany did not want to squash her daughter's enthusiasm or her desire to serve others. It would also be a good teaching opportunity for the other children. "That should work. Thank you for thinking of this, Joy. Please go back and sign us up for Tuesday."

As Joy started toward the back of the auditorium, Bethany had another thought. She called to Joy, "Wait a minute." Then she asked Daniel to stop his work and come with her. They went to where Joy was waiting. "Have your brother write our name with that scrawl he has perfected. I don't want us to get a lot of attention or praise for doing this. Put my cell phone number on the sheet, in case the person in charge wants to contact us. If they don't, we can get the address from the church secretary and use our GPS to find the house." Daniel's handwriting was the brunt of family jokes, and he had learned to exaggerate it to be funny.

Joy laughed and headed to the back with Daniel. By the time they returned, the others had already taken down the display table, and they were ready to take their instruments out to the motor home. Daniel's twin sister Danita playfully teased Joy and Daniel for getting out of the work. Daniel grabbed the two heaviest items and headed out with a grin. "Pretty smooth, don't you think?"

Monday morning at breakfast Bethany shared with the family about Joy's plan. "Our little chef wants to make lasagna…"

She was interrupted by a whoop of happiness from John and the two boys, who then all said, "Sorry."

Bethany smiled at her enthusiastic men. She had not been surprised by their reaction. "I am sure you won't mind— she is making it for the couple who just had a new baby." This announcement was met with loud groans. Joy was grinning. Bethany laughed and said, "Just kidding." As the three guys brightened, she went on. "She will make enough for both families. As there are only two of them, they can have a smaller pan. Daniel, I want you to go with your sister to the store today and then to their home tomorrow to help her deliver it." The young people would use the family van that one of the older children drove behind their motor home. Usually several siblings rode along.

Instantly Danita spoke up. "May I go too, both times?"

Everyone laughed. It was a family joke that she lived up to her name. The name *Danita* was derived from Daniel, and her middle name *Ruth* meant "loyal friend." She was more than loyal to her twin brother Daniel; everyone said they were actually Siamese twins joined at the hip. At times her parents had to insist that she give Daniel some "alone" time or let him and her younger brother Matthew do "boy things" without her. This time Bethany agreed to her helping with the shopping and going along for the delivery. But they weren't all to go in at the home unless the husband invited them. Now it was Danita's turn to groan—she loved babies.

Dawn spoke up. "May I make a dessert and go along to deliver it?" Bethany quickly gave her assent. She was happy to see this quieter, less naturally sociable young lady of sixteen making the effort. Dawn's favorite activities were baking and reading. She was quite content with her own company. Bethany had recently carefully and lovingly talked to Dawn about the need for her to come out of her shell. "Why don't you make a cake and decorate it appropriately? Did the pastor say it was a boy?"

Joy answered in the affirmative.

Bethany asked Dawn, "Do you want to go to the store and get what you need?"

"Yes."

"Okay, and then when you get back, you better make it today so the kitchen and oven will be available for Joy to use tomorrow."

Monday night after the service, Joy and Dawn were again in charge of the table display in the back of the auditorium. This job was a natural for Joy. Dawn let her older sister do as much of the talking as possible; she preferred just handling the money. Peter hung around, talking to Joy between sales.

Tuesday afternoon, when the four oldest Holman young people were ready to go deliver the food, Bethany suggested, "Why don't you stop at the store and pick up two loaves of garlic bread?" Her answer was a spontaneous cheer from all her children. She had known they would be happy about adding that to their dinner menu.

When they arrived at the home of the young couple with the new baby, Joy went to the door while the other three took the food out of the van. When the new father opened the door his face registered both surprise and delight when he recognized Joy. She said, "We have brought you some dinner. May we bring it in?"

"Of course, of course! Oh, this is a surprise. We had no idea it was your family who was bringing food. Is your whole family here?"

"Oh, no, we didn't want to overwhelm your wife while she is recovering."

"Actually, she would have been thrilled. She loves it when your family visits our church. We both think your dad is a great preacher, and your music—well, we have every one of your CDs. How many of you came?" he asked, stepping out and looking toward the van.

"Four of us."

"Could the four of you sing just one song? It would mean so much to my wife. We have a piano. One of you plays, I think?"

"Actually all of us play the piano as well as other instruments," answered Joy. "I think I can speak for the others that we would be honored to do a song—if you think your wife would enjoy it."

"I don't think, I know! Let me go tell her so she can make herself presentable."

The excited young man disappeared into the house and then called back over his shoulder, "Oh, please, come on in and take the food to the kitchen. I'll be right out."

As the other three Holman young people arrived at the porch with the food, Joy said, "Come on in. He wants us to sing for them while we are here. I hope you guys don't mind."

They took the food into the kitchen. Then they went back to the living room and sat down for a few minutes. Soon the new mother appeared followed by her husband carrying the newborn boy. He introduced himself and his wife. "We are Larry and Kathy Chapman. I think you are Joy, Dawn, Daniel and Danita. Right?"

"Yes, that's correct," answered Joy. Daniel shook hands with Larry.

Kathy said, "I can't believe you are actually in my house! I am so excited."

Joy said, "We brought some lasagna. Do you want me to put it in the oven to keep warm?"

"Oh, yes, please. That sounds wonderful!" answered Kathy moving toward the kitchen. Joy and Dawn followed her, while Danita edged closer to Mr. Chapman to get a closer look at the baby boy. When he noticed her interest, he asked, "Would you like to hold him?"

"Oh, may I? Are you sure you don't mind? I love babies."

As he handed her the baby, he said, "I don't mind at all."

"He is so sweet," she murmured. "What is his name?"

"Luke."

"I like that. Hey, Luke, maybe you will grow up to be a doctor."

Larry Chapman laughed.

In the kitchen, Mrs. Chapman was enthusiastically admiring the food, which included a tossed green salad. "Oh, my goodness, you did so much. It is a complete dinner, and it all looks delicious. Please thank your mother for all the work she went to."

Dawn spoke up. "Actually, Joy made the lasagna."

Joy added, "And Dawn made the cake."

Kathy moved over to inspect the cake. "Oh, you decorated it so cute! I will have to take a picture before we cut it. Thank you, girls, so much. What a talented family!" Embarrassed by her praise, the girls laughed off the compliment. Kathy went on, "My husband said you are willing to sing for us? I am so excited and honored. Let's go back into the living room."

When they had rejoined the others, she told her husband, "You won't believe all the food they brought. It looks delicious, and these girls did it all!"

"How nice. Now, how about that song? Do you have time?"

Glancing at the time, they assured him that they did.

After they had sung and were ready to leave, Kathy hugged the girls, thanked them again, and said, "I am planning on coming to church tomorrow night. I can't miss your dad's preaching and more of your music. Do you have any new CDs?"

"Yes, we have made a new one since we were last here," answered Joy.

"Oh, good. We will have our checkbook with us, you can be sure of that!"

Wednesday night after the service Danita kept her eyes on Mrs. Chapman, waiting for her to get baby Luke from the nursery. When she reappeared at the table where Joy and Dawn were selling CDs, Danita moved close. Mrs. Chapman had seen how carefully Danita had held the baby at the house the day before, so she turned to her and asked, "Would you mind holding little Luke while I make out my check?"

Danita was overjoyed as she answered, "I'd love to!"

Smiling, Kathy Chapman handed him to her and turned back to the table, asking Joy, "Where is the new CD?"

When she had finished her purchase, she said to Danita, "Would you mind walking with me over to my husband? I have my purse and the diaper bag…"

Danita eagerly answered before she could finish her sentence, "I wouldn't mind at all!"

Kathy let Danita continue to hold the baby until Bethany joined them and asked Danita to let her have a turn. "Daniel was wondering where you were. He and Matthew have started putting things away. I think you better go help them now."

"Yes, ma'am," answered Danita with one last loving look at the baby.

Kathy commented, "I think she will make a great mother someday."

Bethany responded, "Usually she sticks close to Daniel, but if there is a baby around I always know where to look for her!" She and Kathy laughed together. "You have such a sweet baby. He almost makes me want to have another, until I remember how bad the morning sickness was with a couple of my pregnancies and the sleepless nights for the first few months!"

"Were you traveling with your husband when they were babies?"

"Sometimes I was with my parents for a little while, but other than that, yes."

"That must have been challenging."

Bethany paused, thinking of the little one whom she would see in Heaven one day, as well as each of her other five. Smiling, she answered, "It was at times, but I loved every minute of their babyhood and all of the years since. I hope motherhood is as rewarding and fulfilling for you."

"I hope so too. And I hope my children turn out half as sweet and respectful as yours. Oh, I wish you were going to be here the rest of the week. I enjoy your family so much!"

"That is very sweet. Thank you. We will be back next year."

"I'll be looking forward to it."

"This little guy will probably be walking by then," said Bethany with a smile as she handed little Luke back to his mother.

Thursday all of the members of the Holman family were excited about an evening spent with the Lundbergs. Their two younger children, Phoebe and Jacob, were close to the same age as the Holman twins and the youngest Holman child, Matthew Osborne. As soon as dinner was over, the five of them took a basketball to an outdoor hoop set up on the church parking lot.

Joy and the Lundbergs' son Peter placed their chairs far enough apart from the adults to have a private conversation. Peter had just completed his first year at Crossroads Baptist Bible College, and Joy was eagerly absorbing everything he told her about his experiences there. She would be starting as a freshman in September.

Joy had mixed emotions about leaving for college. The Holmans were a loving, close-knit family, and she knew she would miss her parents and siblings. But on the other hand, she was eagerly anticipating this new milestone in her life.

Peter asked Joy about her family's travels during the past year. She shared that during the summer months they always worked at youth camps. "We all look forward to the change—it's a little more of a relaxed atmosphere. Even my folks enjoy dressing more casually. My dad and the boys enjoy being able to wear jeans, and we girls like our denim skirts and culottes. We still play our instruments and sing, and Dad still has sermons to prepare. We all feel like we are doing our part to help keep kids out of gangs and away from drugs and alcohol. They split up the boys and girls for part of it, and Mom teaches the girls about how to dress and do their makeup without being 'worldly,' and also about social issues like cutting and anorexia. It is amazing how much of that sort of thing goes on."

Peter shared about some of the young people who had not made it at college because of those kinds of problems.

At the motor home, Dawn was happy with listening to the adults' conversation, and freeing her mother of hostess duties by occasionally checking to see if anyone wanted more food or drink. Even when the five younger ones took a rest from basketball to start a board game and invited her to join them, she politely declined. She curled up on the couch with a crossword puzzle close to where they were using the inside table for their game. She had learned that her parents thought it antisocial if she retired to the girls' bedroom by herself.

Meanwhile, Bethany and John were sharing their plans for spending a week of vacation at a ranch in Montana, which was operated by a

Christian couple, the Schaffers. They described the wonderful experiences their family had enjoyed in past years. They had all learned to ride and enjoyed going on the trails. Everyone liked the times around a campfire at night. Daniel would get out his guitar and join Mr. Schaffer in leading a hymn-sing. They would also do camp songs that the younger ones were especially fond of. Steven Lundberg commented that maybe for their vacation the following year they would join the Holmans at the ranch.

Bethany did not miss the look of delight and hopefulness that passed between her oldest daughter and Peter Lundberg. She had mixed emotions—she liked Peter and his family and would not mind having him for a son-in-law some day; but she did not want the two young people to get serious too soon. She hoped Joy would have the opportunity to date several young men before she settled on one. Bethany was sure Joy would have no problem attracting young men. Besides her happy, upbeat and outgoing personality, she was a very attractive young lady. She was taller than her mother but had the same delicate features and long, blonde hair.

When the Lundbergs had left and the Holmans were all settled for the night, Bethany and John quietly talked in bed before going to sleep. Bethany mentioned her concern. John reassured her. "When Peter called some months ago and asked permission to phone Joy, I told him then that even when she started college, I wanted them to go slowly. She needs to date several young men to compare personalities and know what she really wants in a husband, as well as to give God a chance to lead her to the right one. He assured me he would not monopolize her time, and that he would check with me before asking her for a date. I shared with him about how I had waited for quite some time before letting you know how I felt. He is a fine young man. I think he will adhere to our wishes, and I know Steven agrees totally."

"That relieves my mind. I should have known I could trust you to have the situation under control."

"Thanks for the vote of confidence, my love."

The next morning while John and the boys got the motor home and the van ready for travel, the girls and Bethany went to a nearby self-service laundry. When they returned, they said their farewells to the pastor and headed for Montana. Everyone was excited about beginning a two-week vacation. They planned to be at the ranch by Sunday afternoon, stay a week, and then travel toward Indiana without holding any meetings during the second week. John enjoyed being able to simply sit in the congregation with his family for a change, and they all enjoyed a break from supplying the special music.

When the two weeks were over, they all felt refreshed and energized to begin the ministry again. They had about two weeks more with Joy in their midst. Bethany and Joy were busily buying things Joy would need to begin college life—a few new clothes and some items needed for living in a dorm. Joy was excited, happy, nervous, and fearful all at once. When the day came for them to leave Joy at the college, she stood outside her dorm and hugged her sisters and her mother and cried. Her brothers gave her a quick hug. John was the last to wrap his arms around his firstborn and whisper encouragement in her ear. Then the family held hands in a circle, and John prayed in a choking voice.

Bethany gave her oldest daughter one more hug, whispering, "Remember, you will get to spend Thanksgiving with the Davenports in Detroit; and we will all be there for Christmas. It's not such a long time; and I am sure you will be so busy that the time will fly by. Some of the girls you have met and stayed in contact with through the years are going to be here at the college, and you don't have a problem making friends. You are going to do fine."

"I know, Mommy. I'm just going to miss all of you."

"We will miss you, too. 'Bye, sweetheart."

Bethany forced herself to let go, turn, and walk away. She thought back to when she first left home—at least Joy wasn't going to start out with a harrowing plane trip by herself across the country. She was grateful they had been able to bring her here. She smiled as she remembered that there are always blessings to see even in difficult situations. She would need to get used to this as over the next few years all her chicks left the nest. They would all have their own crossroad decisions and choices to make. She could only pray that they would make the right ones.

About the Author

Gary and Yvonne Coats

Yvonne Coats was born during World War II in Portland, Oregon, two minutes after the birth of her identical twin sister, Dawn. When they were 14, a brother, Clark, was born. Their father served in the Marine Corps and then worked in civilian jobs. They moved to Milwaukie, Oregon, where they attended a small church; and Yvonne met her future husband at the age of seven.

She did not date Gary Coats until they were both students at Portland State College. When he had obtained his master's degree from the University of New Mexico and she had graduated from Portland State, they married in 1965. The couple moved to Tacoma, Washington, in 1968, where they reared two daughters, each of whom now has three children. Gary and Yvonne are glad to have recently celebrated their fiftieth anniversary.

Yvonne and Gary were both saved as adults while their daughters were young. They attend and serve in the ministries of Bethel Baptist Church of Spanaway, Washington, where Gary has served on the deacon board and in teaching an adult Sunday school class. Yvonne leads a ladies' Bible Study, and for years worked with children's classes.

Their youngest daughter Christine and her husband, Deren Wolfe, are also actively involved in church ministries. The Coats' eldest daughter, Debbie, is the wife of Kerry Brown, who pastors Bible Baptist Church of Marysville, California.